Three Documentary Filmmakers

THE SUNY SERIES

HORIZ O NS ⅎ CINEMA

MURRAY POMERANCE | EDITOR

Also in the series

William Rothman, editor, *Cavell on Film*

J. David Slocum, editor, *Rebel Without a Cause*

Joe McElhaney, *The Death of Classical Cinema*

Kirsten Thompson, *Apocalyptic Dread*

Francis Gateward, editor, *Seoul Searching*

Michael Atkinson, editor, *Exile Cinema*

Bert Cardullo, *Soundings on Cinema*

Paul S. Moore, *Now Playing*

Robin L. Murray and Joseph K. Heumann, editors,
Ecology and Popular Film

Three Documentary Filmmakers

Errol Morris, Ross McElwee, Jean Rouch

Edited by
William Rothman

Published by
State University of New York Press, Albany

© 2009 State University of New York

All rights reserved

Printed in the United States of America

For information, contact State University of New York Press, Albany, NY
www.sunypress.edu

Production by Marilyn P. Semerad
Marketing by Michael Campochiaro

Library of Congress Cataloging-in-Publication Data

Three documentary filmmakers : Errol Morris, Ross McElwee, Jean Rouch /
edited by William Rothman.
        p. cm. — (Suny series, horizons of cinema)
    Includes bibliographical references and index.
    ISBN 978-1-4384-2501-6 (hardcover : alk. paper)
    ISBN 978-1-4384-2502-3 (pbk. : alk. paper)
    1. Morris, Errol—Criticism and interpretation.   2. McElwee, Ross,
1947—Criticism and interpretation.   3. Rouch, Jean—Criticism and
interpretation.   4. Documentary films—History and criticism.   I. Rothman,
William.

PN1998.3.M684T47 2009
070.1'809—dc22   2008020818

10 9 8 7 6 5 4 3 2 1

Contents

Introduction

WILLIAM ROTHMAN

DESPITE THE INCLUSION OF ACCOMPLISHED documentary filmmakers in so many university film faculties, film study has tended to treat documentaries as if they were marginal to its concerns. In the past few years, of course, a number of documentaries have attained such an unprecedented degree of popularity that the field has belatedly taken notice of documentary's political, social and cultural influence. Even today, however, there remains a dearth of serious critical studies of documentary films and filmmakers.

Ten years ago, I argued in the preface to *Documentary Film Classics* (1997) that the scarcity of critical studies of documentary films was indicative of film study's more general neglect of criticism, a consequence of the revolution the field underwent when it began to accord precedence to what it called theory. As I pointed out, there was also a special animus in film study's resistance to devoting sympathetic critical attention even to the most significant works within the documentary tradition. It derived from the claim sometimes made on behalf of documentaries—less often by their makers than by their detractors—that documentaries are capable of capturing unmediated reality, or "truth."

From the standpoint of the film theories that dominated the field for many years—theories that take reality to be an illusory ideological construct—such a claim seems intolerably naive or disingenuous and in any case pernicious. Now that those theories have loosened their grip over film study, it has become clear to most scholars and students in the field that, although documentaries are not inherently more direct or truthful than other kinds of films, it does not follow that they must repudiate and subvert the traditional documentarian's aspiration of revealing reality. Of course, great documentary films—great fiction films too, for that matter—are capable of revealing truths about the world. What revelations documentaries are capable of achieving and what means are available to them for achieving their revelations are questions to be addressed by acts of criticism, not settled a priori by theoretical fiat. Therefore, what critical approaches, what terms of criticism, do documentary films call for? How are we to acknowledge what separates what we call "documentaries" from what we call "fiction films" without denying what they have in common? (What they have in common, first and foremost, is their medium: film.)

The papers in *Three Documentary Filmmakers* demonstrate, singly and collectively, that the films of Errol Morris, Ross McElwee, and Jean Rouch call for, and reward, criticism of the sort that is invited and expected by serious works in any medium. They are works in which, as the philosopher Stanley Cavell puts it, "an audience's passionate interest, or disinterest, is rewarded with an articulation of the conditions of the interest that illuminates it and expands self-awareness" (Cavell 2005, 335).

As these essays also demonstrate, documentary films pose special challenges to serious criticism. Critical methods that enable one to illuminate what makes *Citizen Kane* a great film may not be adequate for articulating what it is about, say, Morris's *The Thin Blue Line* or *The Fog of War*, McElwee's *Time Indefinite* or *Bright Leaves*, or Rouch's *Les maîtres fous* or *Funeral at Bongo: The Old Anaï (1848–1971)* that makes them—each in its own way—great films as well. It is a challenge to find terms of criticism capable of illuminating such works. The writings in *Three Documentary Filmmakers*—each, too, in its own way—aspire to rise to that challenge.

The American documentary filmmakers Morris and McElwee, although contemporaries, differ strikingly from each other in their styles and their approach to filming. And they both differ in almost every imaginable way from Rouch, a trained anthropologist whose ideas were formed in the intellectual ferment of post–World War II Paris and in West Africa. Because of the magnitude of their differences, the films of Morris, McElwee, and Rouch pose different, if related, challenges for criticism. They also have affinities so deep as to make it fruitful to devote to the three filmmakers a single volume of criticism, even though, as this volume illustrates, their films call for modes of critical writing no less different in tone, mood, and approach than are the films themselves.

I find a key to these affinities in the eloquent remark by the anthropologist Paul Stoller, who observes, in "Jean Rouch and the Power of the Between," that Rouch's greatest contribution was to have created a body of work in which "the limits of the ethnographic are the limits of the imagination. In Rouch's universe ethnographers participated fully in the lives of their others. Dreams became films; films became dreams. Feeling was fused with thought and action. Fusing poetry and science, Jean Rouch showed us the path of wise ancestors and guided us into a wondrous world where we not only encounter others, but also encounter ourselves."

Of course, Morris and McElwee are not—or are not exactly—ethnographers. In their films, it is not—or not exactly—*science* that is fused with poetry. But their films, too, meditate—in very different ways!—on the impossibility of knowing with certainty where the imagination ends and the world begins. They, too, explore the ambiguous and paradoxical relationships between fantasy and reality, self and world, fiction and documentary, dreams and films, filming and living. Their films, too, are both philosophical and deeply personal. And their films, too, are preoccupied with the lengths to which human beings go in our efforts to transcend or overcome—or simply deny—our fear of death.

Errol Morris: The Fog of Film

Errol Morris gained fame when his third film, *The Thin Blue Line* (1988), was submitted in court as evidence to secure the retrial and eventual release of the man who, the film reveals, had wrongfully been convicted of murder. Morris won the Academy Award for Documentary Feature in 2004 for *The Fog of War: Eleven Lessons from the Life of Robert S. McNamara*, his eighth film, which revolves around an extended interview, if we can call it that, with the Vietnam-era Secretary of Defense.

Breaking with the conventions of American direct cinema, Morris places interviews at the heart of his films. As he proudly avers, "No hand-held camera, no available light, no nothing of that sort. A camera planted on a tripod in front of people speaking. Breaking stylistic conventions but still pursuing truth" (Morris 2005a). From the beginning, he attempted to film interviews in such a way as to convey the illusion—if it is an illusion—that the camera's subjects are speaking to us, not to him. When they look directly into the camera, it feels as if they are making eye contact with us.

To achieve this effect, Morris invented a machine he calls the Interrotron. In Morris's words:

Teleprompters are used to project an image on a two-way mirror. Politicians and newscasters use them so that they can read text and look into the lens of the camera at the same time. What interests me is that nobody thought of using them for anything other than to display text: read a speech or read the news and look into the lens of the camera. I changed that. I put my face on the Teleprompter or, strictly speaking, my live video image. For the first time, I could be talking to someone, and they could be talking to me and at the same time looking directly into the lens of the camera. Now, there was no looking off slightly to the side. No more faux first person. This was the true first person. (Morris 2004)

The films of McElwee and Rouch are in the first person as well insofar as each narrates as well as shoots his films, with the filmmaker's distinctive voice, combined with the handheld camera, serving to make us mindful of the author behind the camera. By contrast, the Interrotron enables Morris to efface himself completely, it would seem, enabling him to become one with the camera as long as he remains silent.

But the Interrotron also enables—or compels—us to become one with the filmmaker. As Gilberto Perez shrewdly observes in "Errol Morris's Irony," because the interviewees look straight into the camera as if there were no interviewer, and because Morris gives them center stage and allows them to talk on and on, they "cease being mere interviewees and become full-fledged storytellers." And yet behind them "we sense an ironic author, an author who asks few questions and yet is felt all the while as questioning."

As the people he is filming pursue or avoid truths about the world and about themselves, at times intending to deceive their interlocutor and/or themselves, Morris must entertain the possibility that he is being deceived or deceiving himself. And we, too, must entertain that possibility about ourselves. However transparent, even laughable, we may find the deceptions or self-deceptions of these interviewees or storytellers, Morris provides us—and himself—no secure position from which to assume our own superiority to them. "Morris's storytellers may be considered unreliable narrators," Perez writes, "not because they're liars, not because they're crazy, but because we can't be sure how far to trust them, because the ground on which to credit them or discredit them has been pulled out from under us. Morris may not endorse them but neither does he disparage them. His irony is not at their expense. Rather, it's directed at us in the audience, and it leaves us unsettled, in suspension."

Carl Plantinga argues in his chapter "The Philosophy of Errol Morris: Ten Lessons" that Morris doesn't merely find and tell good human stories, "but stories that raise philosophical questions or through which Morris explores human nature." The first of the philosophical lessons Plantinga draws from Morris's films is "that objective truth exists; that truth can be known; that truth is difficult to know."

"My view is that the truth is knowable," Morris has said, "but that we often have a vested interest in not knowing, not seeing it, disregarding it, avoiding it. Consequently, my interest in truth has two parts—an interest in the pursuit of truth and an interest in examining how people manage to avoid the truth in one way or another—how we turn evidence into a form that's palatable to us, even if it means accepting untruth" (Morris 2005a). When Morris adds, "Who is the one truly self-deceived?" and answers, "You should always entertain the possibility that it is yourself," he gives us a clue to his filmmaking method.

The second of Morris's philosophical principles, as Plantinga understands them, is that "as an epistemology, philosophical realism [the view that reality exists independent of observers] is to be preferred to postmodernism." And yet what Plantinga calls "mental landscapes"—the myths and fictions human beings construct, individually and collectively, to make sense of our lives and our world—are part of the reality whose existence Morris believes in. Indeed, as becomes clear from "Errol Morris's Forms of Control," Ira Jaffe's rich and detailed analysis of Morris's innovative and controversial cinematic style, subjective reality—the reality of subjectivity—is what most fascinates Morris as a filmmaker, what drives him to film.

Ross McElwee: I Film, Therefore I Am

For almost three decades, Ross McElwee has been making quirky, highly enjoyable documentaries that, as eloquent chapters in this book demonstrate, deftly mingle the personal, the historical, the cultural, the political, and the philosophical (indeed, even the metaphysical).

McElwee's films, like Morris's, are in the first person. Unlike Morris, however, McElwee narrates as well as shoots his films. These are not impersonal "voice of God" narrations that impute omniscience, hence absolute authority, to the speaker. In his narrations, McElwee is speaking as his merely human self. The distinctiveness of his voice on the soundtrack, combined with a handheld camera that seems to be an extension of his body, makes us ever mindful of who was behind the camera when these shots were taken, the reality of the filmmaker's own subjectivity.

Unlike Morris, McElwee is a leading character—indeed, the protagonist—in his films. When McElwee is filming, he feels free to speak and be spoken to and even on occasion to step in front of the camera to let others film him. In this practice, he was influenced and inspired by Edward Pincus's monumental *Diaries: 1971–1976* (1982). McElwee received his filmmaking training in the 1980s at the MIT Film Video Section, which was presided over jointly by the already legendary Richard Leacock and his younger colleague, philosophy graduate student–turned–filmmaker

Pincus, who encouraged his students, in a countercultural spirit, to break with Leacock's strict direct-cinema discipline, which dictated that the filmmaker had to become the proverbial fly on the wall.

Influenced and inspired by his reading of the philosopher Ludwig Wittgenstein, Pincus's aspiration was to film the world without withdrawing from the world, to overcome or transcend the inhuman aspect of the role of the direct-cinema filmmaker by filming his own everyday life and thereby transforming filming itself into an everyday activity. And yet in *Diaries* conflicts inevitably emerge between the filmmaker's commitment to filming and the demands of others (wife, children, parents, lovers, friends, fellow teachers, students) who call upon him to acknowledge them as human beings separate from him—and from his film.

In McElwee's films conflicts also emerge between filming and living. Especially in *Sherman's March* (1986), McElwee's own grand epic begun a full decade after Pincus finished shooting *Diaries*, the film's droll narration is strikingly reminiscent of *A Happy Mother's Day* (1963), a signature work of his other great teacher, Leacock. In McElwee's *Sherman's March* and its sequels *Time Indefinite* (1993), *Six O'Clock News* (1996) and *Bright Leaves* (2003), however, the filmmaker speaks his own narration. And that narration asserts a comical perspective not primarily on the people he filmed but on himself and the role filming plays in his life, a perspective that the film reveals him to have lacked when he was living and filming the events we are viewing. In McElwee's films, as in Leacock's *A Happy Mother's Day*, the comical narration is itself undercut, or transcended, by the flashes of breathtaking beauty, and of emotional or spiritual depth, his camera reveals—or provokes—in the men and women he films.

The mysteries and paradoxes attending the act of filming and the at times vexing conflicts between the exigencies of filming and the demands of everyday life are among McElwee's abiding subjects. In the face of such conflicts, as the essays in this volume remind us, he rarely loses his light touch or his sense of humor, and yet there are serious undercurrents that give McElwee's films their unfathomable depth. In McElwee's films, for example, the fear of death is a pervasive theme; it is a key to the narcotic-like pleasure of filming ("When I look through a viewfinder," he says in *Bright Leaves*, "time seems to stop; a kind of timelessness is momentarily achieved").

Like Errol Morris, McElwee finds and tells good human stories that explore human nature and raise philosophical questions. That he finds his stories by filming his life as he lives it is part of the story a McElwee film tells. And in the telling he proves himself to be a true *writer*. All the book's essays on McElwee share this insight. Diane Stevenson, for example, suggests that McElwee belongs to the rich tradition of Southern writers (Erskine Caldwell, Flannery O'Connor, Carson McCullers, William Faulkner) for whom comedy and the gothic belong together, adding that his stories, like those of the modernist Faulkner, are also "stories about how stories are told." Equally fruitfully, Marian Keane links McElwee with Walt Whitman; Jim Lane, with modern autobiographical writers; Charles Warren, with essayists like Montaigne. For my part, I dwell at length on the way McElwee's narrations are written and, in a broader sense, on the way he "writes" his films cinematically, the way he composes them from the footage he has filmed. And in writing about McElwee's films, we all felt the need for prose capable of evoking their ever-shifting moods and emotions, and capable, at the same time, of acknowledging what remains fixed in the physiognomy of the world on film, what Cavell in *The World Viewed* calls "the reality of the unsayable" (Cavell 1979, 148).

Jean Rouch: The Filmmaker as Provocateur

Ross McElwee teaches at Harvard and lives with his family in Boston, but the world he is drawn to film is the American South, the world he left, his original home, which continues to cast its seductive spell over him. Like McElwee, Jean Rouch found himself divided between two worlds. His native France was the world Rouch called home, although he felt alienated there, while West Africa was the seductive world he was drawn to film. Whereas McElwee's films envision the South, where the Civil War is a living memory, as at once a higher and lower order of civilization than the North, in Rouch's films Africa emerges as a world unambiguously superior to his native France. In any case, Rouch's Africa, like McElwee's South, is a world cut to the measure of a filmmaker whose works meditate deeply on the camera's power to capture the enchanting life force of its subjects, and on its affinity with death.

Understanding Errol Morris to share his own preference for Anglo-American analytical philosophy, Carl Plantinga cites approvingly Morris's quip that one of the good things about living in Cambridge, Massachusetts, is that "Baudrillard isn't in the phone book." From Alan Cholodenko's reading of *Les maîtres fous* (1955), it is clear that Rouch was, or should have been, in *Baudrillard's* phone book. It would seem that Plantinga's Morris and Cholodenko's Rouch are on a collision course. Yet for all their philosophical differences, and despite the radically different formal strategies they developed, the challenge faced by Rouch *as a filmmaker*—and by McElwee too, for that matter—is precisely the challenge Plantinga understands Morris to have faced: How to convey, in the medium of film, the invisible in the visible, the reality of the unsayable?

Of the three filmmakers addressed in this volume, Rouch is at once the most famous and the most unknown. Within film studies, it is widely recognized that he occupies a unique and important place in the history of cinema. Yet most in the field have seen few if any of his films. Rouch's significance is generally taken to reside not in the artistic value of his films, but in the influence of *Chronicle of a Summer* (1961) on generations of documentary filmmakers—Errol Morris and Ross McElwee among them—and especially in his role as a missing link, as Richard Peña puts it, between the postwar Italian neorealists and the directors of the French New Wave, for whom his "ethno-fictions" were an inspiration and a major influence. Jean-Luc Godard once called *Moi, un noir* (1958) the greatest French film since the Liberation (see Rothman 2007, 13). It is in the mid- to late 1950s and early 1960s that Rouch had his greatest influence on the course of world cinema, and it is his films from that period—especially *Les maîtres fous* and *Chronicle of a Summer*—that have received most attention within film studies. Yet even those films have rarely been accorded serious *criticism*. Indeed, most of the best writings about Rouch's work have been by anthropologists, not by film critics or theorists. And they assess his films primarily as visual ethnography, not as cinema—as science, not as art.

For the likes of François Truffaut, Eric Rohmer, Claude Chabrol, Jacques Rivette, and Jean-Luc Godard, cinema was a religion. They aspired to follow the path of exemplary men of cinema like Alfred Hitchcock, Jean Renoir, Kenji Mizoguchi, and Roberto Rossellini. Except for the films of Robert Flaherty, Dziga Vertov, and the other documentary filmmakers he considered his cinematic ancestors, Rouch rarely if ever talked about films or filmmakers. His ambitions seemed incommensurate with those of the New Wave directors he inspired and influenced. And yet, for all his reluctance to claim to be an auteur, he was no less a *cinéaste* than they were. It is at once a premise and conclusion of Michael Laramee's essay on Rouch in this volume, and my own as well, that he strove to make immortal films, works of art of enduring value in and of themselves.

For a half-century, Rouch developed his cinematic practice primarily by filming the Songhay of Niger, whose possession rituals were the subject of his own ethnographic publications, and the Dogon of Mali—the people studied by Marcel Griaule and Germaine Dieterlen, his mentors in ethnography—whose rituals are spectacular triumphs of mise-en-scène. Rouch's work among the Dogon culminated in a series of films documenting the epic *Sigui* ritual staged every sixty years to commemorate the origin of death among human beings, and two feature-length films, arguably his cinematic masterpieces, *Funeral at Bongo: The Old Anaï* (1848-1971) (1972) and *Ambara Dama (To Enchant*

Death) (1974). The latter of these closes a circle: Rouch films the mask dance first filmed by Griaule in the 1930s, and in the narration Rouch speaks his teacher's words.

In "Jean Rouch as Film Artist," I argue that Rouch's films are philosophical, and they are personal and poetic, as surely as they are ethnographic. Their art is in pursuit of self-knowledge no less than ethnographic knowledge. Indeed, it is a main thrust of all five of this volume's essays on Rouch that within his films science, philosophy, and poetry cannot be separated. If Rouch's films quest for knowledge, they also aspire to transform our understanding of what knowledge is. They do so by demonstrating what becomes of the science of ethnography, and what becomes of the art of cinema, when they provoke each other to acknowledge that there are no fences that separate them. Rouch's films transform ethnography, with its claims or pretensions to know others with scientific objectivity, into an artistic practice no less rigorous for acknowledging the unknowable, the unsayable, the value of abandonment.

The aspiration of Rouch's art is to break down the fences—there are no such fences, he believed, in the African societies he filmed—separating what we know from the way we live. Rouch's way of filming, which he devoutly wished others to emulate, was also a way of thinking and living, one which embraced the magical, the strange, the fantastic and the fabulous and promised freedom from the alienation, the joylessness, to which Western society threatens to consign us. As I put it in *Documentary Film Classics*, "No less than Buñuel, Rouch believed that our way of life in the West has to change, that our lives cannot change unless we change, and that we cannot change unless we change our way of thinking. We have to awaken to, awaken from, the horror to which we have condemned ourselves and our world. We have to tear down the fences we have built, the fences we continue to build, to deny that nature exists within us as we exist within nature" (Rothman 1997, 101).

The new world his films herald is also an ancient world, Rouch believed, a world older than Western civilization. As his films envision them, the Dogon and Songhay villagers who perform the rituals he films are dwellers within that world. Transcending or overcoming the fear of death, their every gesture expresses what can be known, and acknowledges what cannot be known, about being human. How Rouch's films enable us to enter a world so different from our own is the question Daniel Morgan addresses in "The Pause of the World."

Of course, the ideal societies Rouch's films envision may themselves be dreams, myths, or fictions, as would be claimed by those anthropologists who impugn Griaule's methodology. However, the scientific validity of Griaule's findings is moot as far as Rouch's films are concerned. If the Songhay and Dogon societies his films envision are fictions, they are fictions that are "more real than the real," as Mick Eaton paraphrases Rouch, resulting in the revelation of a new truth "which is not the 'truth' of the pro-filmic event but the 'truth' of cinema itself" (Eaton 1979, 51). The idea that the world created or re-created on film is "more real than the real" leads Alan Cholodenko to invoke Jean Baudrillard's concept of the hyperreal in exploring the radical implications of Rouch's work.

No less than Errol Morris and Ross McElwee, Jean Rouch under-stood that the world on film always has an aspect of fiction, myth, or dream. The world on film is always transformed or transfigured by the medium of film itself. In Rouch's words, "Cinema is the creation of a new reality" (Eaton 1979, 52).

I would like to thank all of the authors who have contributed to this book. It is a great pleasure to be the editor of a collection of chapters when they speak with such lucidity, thoughtfulness, and eloquence.

I am also grateful to the editor of the Horizons in Film series, my friend Murray Pomerance, for his embrace of this project from the outset, for his patience in waiting for the manuscript to materialize, and for the well-conceived and well-realized anthologies he has put together, which make him a role model for editors who aspire to follow in his footsteps.

And I am, as always, grateful to my wife Kitty Morgan for the love, companionship, encouragement, and inspiration she has given me for so many years.

PART 1

Errol Morris: The Fog of Film

GILBERTO PEREZ

Errol Morris's Irony

THIS CHAPTER WILL FIRST CONSIDER the issue of authorial intrusion in documentary films. It will then go on to examine the special case of Errol Morris, a documentarian who keeps himself as much as possible out of the picture but still makes his implied presence felt, subtly yet unmistakably, through authorial irony.

We all know that documentary is never a straightforward record of reality, always a construction slanted in some way. Even so, documentary filmmakers are commonly expected to be self-effacing, to let the facts speak for themselves. Michael Moore, for example, has often been criticized by people who think that he puts too much of himself into his films and that this breaks the rules of documentary. But other documentarians, from Ross McElwee to Claude Lanzmann, also intrude into their films and make their presence central to them.

Unlike Lanzmann or Moore, Errol Morris lets the people he interviews tell their own stories with minimal interference from him. They do not even address him directly, rather, he has them speak into an interviewing machine he devised, so that they seem to be bypassing the filmmaker and telling their stories directly to the audience. Morris takes the self-effacement conventionally expected of interviewers to an unconventional extreme. He makes his interviewees into storytellers and gives them free rein to speak to us. But, though we are to pay them

13

sustained attention, we are not called upon to accept what they say. Unlike news commentators on television, who may be lying or dissembling but are presented as telling the truth, these storytellers, though they have a certain authority, are not to be regarded as authoritative. They are allowed to speak at length but left on their own, and we are left on our own to assess the truth of what they say. Behind them we sense an ironic author, an author who asks few questions and yet is felt all the while as questioning. This essay will look into the ways in which Morris manages this irony and the effect it has on us.

"Show, don't tell" has been a governing principle in much fiction since the later nineteenth century. That's what students of creative writing are usually taught, that the author must stay out of the picture, must set forth without comment the facts of the story (which may include a dramatized narrator, a character in the story made into the storyteller and entitled to comments and opinions while the author remains mum). This kind of self-effacing author may seem to be allowing the facts to speak for themselves, to be eschewing rhetoric. But facts never speak for themselves, and saying or implying so is always a rhetorical posture. It's a posture, a trope, for an author to hide behind his or her own fiction, to conceal the hand that constructed these characters and incidents, the mind that intended them to have a certain meaning and effect. The trope is called irony. It's ironic for the author of a story to pretend that the story says it all and that he or she has nothing to say. Northrop Frye links the hidden author to the *eiron*, the self-deprecating person, a prime example being Socrates, who pretended to know nothing in the famous brand of irony that bears his name. "The term irony," Frye writes, "indicates a technique of appearing to be less than one is, which in literature becomes most commonly a technique of saying as little as possible and meaning as much as possible" (Frye 1957, 40).

How does this apply to film? In a fiction film, as in a play, actors moving and speaking before the eyes and ears of the audience enact a story without the intermediation of a storyteller. The author is out of the picture not as a matter of irony but as a matter of course. An author may be implied, but it is always an author hidden between the lines, behind the scenes, behind the camera. (I should make clear that by "author" I don't mean an auteur but the agency, individual or collective, responsible for the arrangement of these images and sounds.) Fiction film may involve a kind of telling but is more about showing. Documentary film, on the other hand, is more about telling, more an account than an enactment. Proof of this is the frequent use documentaries make of voice-over narration and of interviews with recounting eyewitnesses. What a documentary shows is often merely an illustration of what it tells. But who is the storyteller? The interviewed eyewitnesses usually tell us only bits and pieces of the story. The voice we hear in documentary voice-over narrations is usually impersonal, authoritative but not authorial, not the voice of an author taking responsibility for these words. If in fiction films the author gives way to the actors, in documentary films the author normally recedes in favor of recounted facts supposed to speak for themselves. There is a rhetorical posture here, but it is the opposite of ironic, a pretense not to be less but to be more than one is, an attempt to give the impression of unassailable objectivity. As in most fiction films, the author in most documentary films is conventionally, rather than ironically, self-effacing.

But some important documentarians depart from such self-effacement and enter prominently into the picture. Ross McElwee comes forward as the author—and largely the subject—of his autobiographical documentaries, whose voice-over narration in a conversational first person is far from impersonal. Claude Lanzmann does not make films about himself, but he plays a central role in his films, and he makes his shaping hand as the author palpable to the audience. The two parts of his Holocaust documentary *Shoah* (1985) last nine and a half hours, and much of that length comes from the way in which Lanzmann, an assertive and insistent interviewer, asks the same questions over again and has things repeated for rhetorical emphasis. The former Nazis he interviews agreed to talk to him on condition they did not appear in the movie, but he filmed them anyway, and he shows us how he did it, with a camera and sound equipment hidden in a van, thus flaunting his disregard for their wishes and expressing his contempt for them. Polish peasants who lived near the Nazi camps, and whom he also holds responsible for what was done to the Jews, he treats with similar undisguised contempt, which the questions he asks them are calculated to bear out. And Lanzmann does not spare Holocaust survivors: He presses the reticent ones, those who find it too painful to talk about the awful experience they went through, until they break down in front of the camera.

Michael Moore has made the most popular documentaries ever (aside from IMAX spectacles and rock-concert movies). He is a performer in them, an actor who is also the author and who incarnates the author on the screen. McElwee, by contrast, isn't much of a performer, though the people he films, such as the women in *Sherman's March* (1986), often are. No doubt Moore's popularity has something to do with his presence on the screen as a character the audience can identify with and at the same time identify with the author. Already in his first film, *Roger & Me* (1989), Moore assumed his working-class persona—although he was born working class, this is all the same a persona he assumes—as the importunate little guy risking the big guy's rebuff and turning that against him, the little guy willing to look foolish and showing up the big guy. (Physically Moore is big, not little, but in our society the rich stay thin and the poor grow fat.) Both Moore and McElwee enlist our personal sympathy in a vein of comedy—Moore, more broadly, like a stand-up comedian. Lanzmann is of course very different—righteous and impervious to whether we like him or not, his rhetoric not one of ingratiation but of anger. That might be why his intrusion into his films hasn't met with objection as Moore's has: a comic persona is deemed inappropriate to the seriousness of documentary. But we ought to know that comedy is serious business.

In their different ways, Lanzmann and Moore break with the convention that the interviewer should not express a point of view, should not appear to be taking sides, but should stand back and let the interviewee have a say. Another part of the convention—which may be called the convention of objectivity, of the pretense of objectivity governing most documentaries—is that the interviewee, the talking head, should not talk for too long, that other interviewees should also have their say and that the voice-over narration should put it all in proper perspective. It's this other part of the convention that Errol Morris breaks with. He does not intrude into the picture. Quite the contrary: he conspicuously leaves himself out. He lets the talking heads in his films talk at sustained, uninterrupted length. Or to be more precise, there may be visual interruptions, brief blackouts, cuts, insertions, but the talking voice will continue as voice-over narration. And whereas the usual interviewee looks off to the side, talking to an interviewer whose presence offscreen we never forget, the interviewees in Morris's films always look straight into the camera, as if no interviewer were there and we in the audience were being directly addressed. Which is to say that these talking heads given center stage and allowed to talk on cease being mere interviewees and become full-fledged storytellers.

The title of the television series Morris did a few years ago is *First Person*. It's not his first person but that of his subjects, the storytellers who come before his camera and tell their stories to us. And it's not just that they speak in the first person—every interviewee does, of course—but that they look directly at us as they speak, that we, rather than the interviewer, are their second person. The first person isn't just in their words but in their eyes, in the way their gaze unswervingly meets ours.

One, for example, is a man who believes we can defeat death by having our bodies frozen and kept that way for as long as it takes for medicine to advance enough to cure the ailment we're dying from, at which point we'll be thawed and brought back to life. The man has tried this on his own dying mother, whose head he had cut off and frozen—whether she had just died or was about to die is an issue that has gotten him into trouble with the law—and who he figures will be resurrected many years hence in another body. Crazy, incredible, though this story may sound, Morris passes no judgment on the sanity or credibility of the storyteller. The man has the floor, and on his proposal for immortality, on the freezing of his mother's head, Morris takes no position, for or against. By inserting footage from *Frankenstein* (the man says he's always admired Dr. Frankenstein), or from Leni Riefenstahl's *Olympia* (the man talks about the beautiful bodies we'll all have when we rise from the frozen), Morris makes a kind of ironic comment. But mostly he withholds comment, and his irony lies mostly in his withholding of comment. It's the irony of the *eiron*, the man who pretends he knows nothing and has nothing to say. It's the irony of the self-effacing author.

Morris's storytellers may be considered unreliable narrators, not because they're liars, not because they're crazy, but because we can't be sure how far to trust them, because the ground on which to credit them or discredit them has been pulled out from under us. Morris may not endorse them but neither does he disparage them. His irony is not at their expense. Rather, it's directed at us in the audience, and it leaves us unsettled, in suspension. It's what Wayne Booth has called *unstable* irony (Booth 1974, 240–45). What are we to make of this wacky, self-assured man who would deal with our mortality through some amalgam of a religious faith in everlasting life and a faith in science and progress that has been prevalent in our culture? Or of an autistic woman who has a singular empathy with cattle, is able to put herself in their place, and as she says, not just imagine but really feel what that's like, and so is able to design more humane slaughterhouses? Morris's irony cuts both ways: these narrators may be unreliable, but he credits them enough to let them take over, to lend them in his films the authority of storytellers, which normally they wouldn't enjoy.

Morris's method requires subjects who open up before the camera and microphone and rise to the narrator role he gives them. In his feature-length films there is usually more than one first-person storyteller. An exception is *The Fog of War* (2003), in which he interviews Robert McNamara and stays with him all the way through. This may have been a mistake: McNamara, especially when it comes to the Vietnam War, is self-justifying and evasive, not a reliable but not a very interesting unreliable narrator either.

In *Mr. Death* (1999) the principal storyteller is Fred A. Leuchter, Jr., the son of a Massachusetts prison guard and a self-made and quite successful designer of electric chairs and other execution equipment, which he tells us about in the first part of the film. The film's subtitle is *The Rise and Fall of Fred A. Leuchter, Jr.*, and the first part recounts the rise, the second the fall, which occurred after Leuchter got involved with Holocaust deniers. He was approached by a German in Canada who had published a pamphlet claiming that the Nazi extermination of the Jews never happened. This German was being brought to trial for knowingly spreading lies, and his idea was that the expert in methods of execution would find evidence to support his claim and would testify in his behalf. This, Leuchter tells us, was an issue of freedom of speech. It was also a project the self-made engineer took on with the homespun American know-how that had always served him well. He went to Auschwitz armed with a chisel, dug into the walls of chambers where Jews were killed with cyanide gas, and collected some sample powder for chemical analysis. No cyanide was found in that powder. He testified at the trial (the German was convicted anyway) and published a report saying that Auschwitz couldn't have been an extermination camp. The fact, however, is that he didn't know what he was doing in his rash excursion into the camp. As a chemist explains to us: cyanide doesn't penetrate past the sheerest layer on the surface of a wall, and any remnant would have been diluted in that powder beyond detection.

This chemist is one of the alternative storytellers enlisted by Morris in this film. Originally, I gather, the plan was to let Leuchter tell the whole story and to have his version of it called into question by authorial irony alone. But irony, and especially unstable irony, is not something people can be counted on getting, and Morris felt it necessary to discredit Leuchter's Holocaust denial unequivocally, unironically. Apart from that, Leuchter is an unreliable narrator of the same sort as the various others in Morris's films, neither exactly trustworthy nor simply dismissible, somewhat odd and off-putting but with a story to tell that we want to hear. And the fall of Fred Leuchter—the way his business, his marriage, his life fell apart after he collected the samples and testified at that trial and published that report—is another story. Although in Auschwitz he was out of his depth (or his surface), he was nationally recognized for his expertise in capital-punishment engineering—maybe not the most commendable line of endeavor, but one in steady demand—and yet nobody would hire him any more. He was persecuted, it seems fair to say, for denying that the Jews were persecuted. And that is another irony.

2

Ira Jaffe

Errol Morris's Forms of Control

Poets, critics, and theorists have long examined the potential of film as an art—distinct from film as entertainment or as a recording of the world. Hence titles such as *The Art of the Moving Picture* (Vachel Lindsay, 1916), *Film in the Aura of Art* (Dudley Andrew, 1984), and *Film as Art* (Rudolf Arnheim, 1957, but composed of essays from the 1930s). While the topic is familiar, agreement as to the nature of cinematic art, as well as of art in general, remains elusive. Perhaps the most convincing claims about what art is, in any medium, focus on form or style, not just content, or better yet, speak of form *as* content, as Susan Sontag does in two famous essays, "Against Interpretation" (1964) and "On Style" (1965). In "On Style" she states, for example, "Knowledge we gain through art is an experience of the form or style of knowing something, rather than a knowledge of something (like a fact or moral judgment) in itself" (Sontag 1966, 22).

Although Sontag asserts in "Against Interpretation" that "cinema is the most alive, the most exciting, the most important of all art forms right now" (ibid., 11), the focus on form she advocates does not necessarily encourage the reception and production of a major type of cinema—the documentary. For as Bill Nichols states in *Representing Reality* (1991), the traditional function of documentary has been to provide an explanation or argument about the actual historical world. More than fiction film, then, with its mandate to create imaginary universes of sense, thought, and feeling, the documentary possibly discourages filmmaker and spectator alike from focusing on form or style, which in turn often means focusing on the film medium and apparatus, as distinct from the world and the arguments that are being represented. Even a documentary such as *Fahrenheit 9/11* by Michael Moore (2004), which highlights the importance of the camera, editing, sound, and the filmmaker, keeps the medium secondary to the realistic rendering of the external world. The referent, or what is being represented, not the style or mode of representation, remains primary. In Dziga Vertov's *The Man with a Movie Camera* (1929), on the other hand, form and referent seem more equal and intertwined.

Of the filmmakers celebrated in the United States today, possibly none has created films that challenge devaluations of form in the documentary more persistently than Errol Morris, whose recent work, *The Fog of War: Eleven Lessons from the Life of Robert S. McNamara*, won the Academy Award for Documentary Feature in 2004. Yet *Fog of War*, concerning the career of Robert Strange McNamara, secretary of defense for both Kennedy and Johnson during much of the Vietnam War, is considerably less challenging in its form, and in its experimental use of the film medium, than were previous films by Morris. That this fact has gone largely unnoticed in reviews and commentaries, which instead have focused on matters of content, such as whether Morris lets McNamara off too easily for what many regard as war crimes, might support the view that the audience for documentary, even more than for other types of film, focuses on content, particularly of social and political import, and neglects form.

The play of form has been important in most of Morris's films since *Gates of Heaven* (1978), his first major documentary, but it has been most prominent in Morris's two films just prior to *Fog of War*—*Mr. Death: The Rise and Fall of Fred A. Leuchter, Jr.* (1999) and *Fast, Cheap & Out of Control* (1997). To be sure, attention to form by either a filmmaker or an audience does not necessarily yield "art" or an "aesthetic experience," but the sensual and intellectual stimulation afforded by these two films of the late 1990s merits such dignified labels. In part this chapter aims to underscore the play and experimentation with form in *Fast, Cheap . . . and Mr. Death*, in contrast to the more conventional style of *Fog of War*. A further purpose is to consider *Fog of War* as a reversal of the two previous works: Insofar as distinctions between form and content are appropriate, one might contend that the explicit argument or content in *Fog of War* is more radical than in the previous films, while the form is more conservative. Indeed, the argument of *Fog of War*—its explicit, even didactic, interpretation of the actual historical world—might serve as an explanation and justification of the formal experimentation in *Fast,*

Cheap . . . and *Mr. Death* (both of which were part of the actual world when *Fog of War* was being made).

If style or form in Morris's films diverges from the documentary norm partly by foregrounding the film medium rather than the external world, it may be useful to venture a few general remarks about Morris's technical repertoire before exploring its aesthetic consequences in the two films preceding *Fog of War*. Obviously, numerous technical elements are deployed in Morris's stress on the display as distinct from the referent. Moreover, variations in these display elements often occur suddenly and without clear justification in his films. Color, grain, focus, and exposure shift unpredictably, for example. An image commences in fine grain, and within a normal range of color, then shifts to coarse grain, and to a narrow portion of the spectrum, either within a long take or following a cut. A person or object in color is preceded or followed by a shot of the same subject in black and white. Contrast and other aspects of illumination also shift in unconventional ways. Further, seemingly arbitrary changes occur in the camera's movement and angle of view. Extreme close-ups yield disorienting shifts of scale and perspective. As a result of changes in the rate of the film's movement through the camera, motion in the world viewed on screen slows or accelerates, and often turns hesitant or jerky. Superimpositions and other optical effects also transform the subject in front of the camera while foregrounding the medium. Indeed, as a result of the shifting deployment of such diverse elements, the subject frequently appears illegible, foreign, or unnatural. Further, the shifts of color, light, focus, speed, and so on often register, at least initially, as disturbances alien to the very surface of the film as well as to its narrative clarity, logic, and continuity. The disturbances register as excesses, eruptions of formlessness—random, inexplicable, ungovernable events exceeding the film's laws and boundaries. Often it appears that the film has gone out of control.

As is not unusual in documentaries, Morris's films incorporate excerpts from diverse "texts," including old fiction films, home movies, newsreels, science films, still photographs, and TV news and commercials. He also includes fragments and clusters of words, numbers, graphs, maps, and charts discovered in newspapers and in public and private documents. Further, images and sounds in his films originate in various formats, such as video, Super-8, and 16mm, as well as 35mm. Nevertheless, the disturbances to which I refer result primarily from how he shoots his own original footage, how he alters it and the found footage, and how, as much as anything else, he edits the final product. The disturbances in his films ensue from his manipulations, more than from the diversity of his quoted texts and sources.

Editing is vital to Morris's destabilizing manipulations—and repeated jump cuts and blank frames are key elements in his editing. They function to keep his films on edge—skipping beats and missing moments, precluding flow and continuity. Further, as in *Breathless* and other films by Jean-Luc Godard, jump cuts in Morris's films often occur in the image but not on the sound track; the unnatural discrepancy makes for a more jarring, unsettling sensation than occurs when picture and sound are jump-cut synchronously.

Aside from jump-cutting, Morris develops broader opportunities to edit image and sound in ways that generate counterpoint and discrepancy. One typical device is to cut from the shot of a speaking character to other images, while the character continues to speak in voice-over. Although the audience may expect the subsequent images to mirror or illustrate the character's voice-over words, Morris's images often skid away. If their whimsical course does not entirely abandon the words, the relationship at least becomes ambiguous, rippling with irony, play, and contradiction. Also sound rather than picture may take the lead in establishing a gap or discrepancy—an unexpected voice, noise, or strain of music may surprise the image and revise its import. Or a voice-over may refer to a particular person while several persons appear on-screen, leaving ambiguous which one is meant.

Morris's editing of images in relation to sounds in order to generate counterpoint, discrepancy, and ambiguity is but one aspect of his reliance on montage, a term that refers not only to the junctures between the picture and sound tracks but also, of course, to the junctures within each track separately. In all of Morris's work, perhaps the most extensive, omnidirectional montage occurs in *Fast, Cheap*, since this film's four main characters—the robot scientist (Rodney Brooks), mole rat specialist (Ray Mendez), topiary gardener (George Mendonca), and wild animal trainer (Dave Hoover)—live and work in disparate environments, and throughout the film, images and sounds of one overlap as well as displace images and sounds of another. Moreover, to this convergence on the screen of four separate worlds, *Fast, Cheap* adds other excerpts from live-action and animated motion pictures, which further expand the montage options. The result is a film considerably liberated in its choices and arrangements of images and sounds; from documentary norms of clarity, causality, and continuity; and from the usual adherence to the actual historical world. More than most documentaries and even most fiction films, *Fast, Cheap* relies on montage as defined by Miriam Hansen: "the composing and assembling of shots on the principle of contrast and discontinuity, which creates meanings the individual shots would not have on their own and that is capable of presenting a world that has no referent in empirical reality" (Hansen 2004, 39).

An account of images that elide rapidly into one another at the start of *Fast, Cheap*—many of them so rapidly as to be imperceptible—may further indicate the prominence of contrast, discontinuity, and referential mystery in Morris's montage. Equally characteristic of his work is the interweaving in this sequence of nature, technology, animal life, and human life caught up in a kinetic mix of play, struggle, and crisis:

1. Blade-like legs of a robotic figure advance across the screen on a broken surface of chopped ice or similar fragments in a black-and-white shot.

2. A bluish, indistinct mass moves in the direction and at the rate of the blade-like legs in #1. Then the indistinct mass registers as a dense haze; the grain in the shot seems exceptionally coarse. A human form emerges vaguely in the distant center of the image and moves a bit deeper into the indefinite background. (The form makes little progress perhaps because the shot is taken with a telephoto lens.)

3. A whooping, athletic individual (probably the vague form in #2) runs in the direction of the blade-like legs in #1. Attached to this individual is a large, two-dimensional skeletal form that sails beside him (between him and the camera), and then behind. The athletic individual continues to race across the screen and becomes identifiable as a clown in tight, striped garb (who, at least in long shot, bears a resemblance to the antic visual and performing artist Matthew Barney). Although the environment is bluish, the clown's body and attire are in black and white. Then diverse dots of brighter, warmer colors enter the blue, and the black-and-white clown tailed by the skeleton surges through the pointillist, rainbow-like colors.

4. The clown runs offstage (or beyond the arena) in the swelling glare of a huge light suspended above left. The shot is totally in black-and-white.

5. Creatures wrestle and cavort with one another. In extreme close-up at the start of the shot, they can pass for elephants, but turn out to be mole rats. The shot is in color, particularly orange and brown.

6. Large, insect-like robotic figures whose legs occupied #1 appear in a black-and-white shot. There is an indistinct grunt, moan, or similar sound originating in a human, an animal, or a machine.

7. Amid blue-and-white foliage outdoors, a human form moves across the screen (as did the robotic legs in #1 and the clown in #3). The foliage becomes less distinct, more abstract, as the camera pans.

8. Extreme close-up of a sunflower.

9. Two or three quick, indeterminate shots in black-and-white of abstract spiraling or winding compositions resembling tortuous skies and streets by Van Gogh, or coils of mud by Ana Mendieta. A woman screaming in alarm is heard over these imperceptible images.

10. Frightened woman and stunned men behind her—all of them faux African natives in an excerpt from a black-and-white Hollywood B movie. The hokey action and setting are visually sharper and clearer than any thus far in *Fast, Cheap.*

11. A menacing lion.

12. A white boy "gone native" picks up a spear.

13. Lion advances from screen right toward boy.

14. In shift to blue-and-white from black-and-white, sunflowers, probably from the topiary gardener's world as before, slant down from screen left toward the space occupied by lion in prior shot, as if to oppose the lion.

15. Return to African excerpt; sound of train's bell.

16. Slowly moving train in color in front of circus.

17-24. Opening credits.

This blizzard of images culminating in the opening credits lasts about one hundred seconds.

While pre-credit sequences in many films take mysterious, nonlinear paths, such a course persists throughout *Fast, Cheap.* For example, one sequence from the body of the film begins with the wild animal trainer on-screen, discussing the importance of bluffing, of not letting a lion know "you're scared or hurt," and proceeds as follows (the shots are in color, unless indicated as black-and-white):

1. Close-up of lion's face.

2. Excerpt from old movie of two lions attacking each other (b&w).

3. Animated cartoon of massive robot—devilish, with horns—holding a tiny young man in each metallic hand.

4. Animated cartoon of billowing smoke of explosion.

5. Four amoebic forms wiggle in center of screen, and then multiply (b&w). (By this point, wild animal trainer's voice-over has ended. Voice-over of robot scientist, perhaps foreshadowed by animated robot in #3, discusses evolution for the remainder of the sequence—mostly voice-over, but commencing with a close-up of him speaking.)

6. Close-up of robot scientist.

7. Indistinct section of bluish, whiskered, cat-like face connected to bluish tubular form.

8. Vehicle resembling an immense insect-like robot, bearing a man in a hard hat, emerges from garage onto street.

9. Close-up of green plant stem with bug moving slowly on it.

10. Indistinct, often blurred images suggest TV interference, a grid, a frame, fetal life, and then mole rats (b&w).

11. Overhead shot of vehicle, similar to that in #8, but topped with a kind of umbrella.

12. Excerpt from old movie of Clyde Beatty, the wild animal trainer's hero, attacking soldier or guard whose legs are bare and who wears a helmet and, affixed to his back, a pair of wings. Clyde starts to wrestle his opponent to the ground (b&w).

13. In laboratory, part of robot at end of metal arm or pole turns and rotates, thus continuing movement of struggling men in #12.

14. Blurred, whitish blob appears in black limbo, turns into whitish light, and then congeals into bulb-like mole rat which races backward (or in reverse motion) up into spiral of cave or tunnel.

15. Graceful animal with long tail bounds across open terrain and then soars into the air.

16. Robotic movement of two metal poles or legs attached to flat surface in laboratory.

17. Animated cartoon resembling live scene in #15. Graceful, giraffe-like, three-dimensional creatures with orange bodies, white legs, and immense tails race toward screen left.

18. Closer shot of action in #17: the creatures set foot on yellow ground between blue rocks; a robotic, umbrella-shaped entity appears in background.

19. A return to live action: gazelle-like creature bounds toward screen right.

20. In laboratory setting again, skeletal blue-and-white robotic entity bobs up and down, twists, and somersaults.

21. Three-dimensional animated creatures as in #17 leap ahead.

22. Motion of creatures in #21 is carried on by a single robotic entity in a corridor, probably outside laboratory observed earlier; a pair of human feet is visible behind robot.

23. Robot trots jauntily down corridor. Long tail, leash, or hose extends far behind robot to human figure following it, while four men await robot at end of corridor.

24. Excerpt from another old movie: Prehistoric monster's snout (screen left) enters barren plain under dark sky with clouds. Some houses appear low in distance (b&w).

25. Close-up of robot scientist.

26. Claws of monster as in #24 plunge through roof of house (as a mole rat might tear through skin of a human hand, according to the mole rat specialist at another moment in the film) (b&w).

27. Tilt down indistinct, faintly orange-colored human forehead.

28. Black birds fly in blue sky.

29. Green, blue, and black robotic entity advances with a camera or other viewing device mounted on it.

30. Blue-black robotic entity marked "USA" moves across lunar or planetary surface.

31. Robotic entity, probably same as in #30, but this time with large star visible on its side, ascends orange-brown hill.

32. Indistinct green-white motion on white ground or surface; robotic feet enter; more of robot with "USA" printed on it appears. By this point blue-black has joined green-white hues dominant at start of shot.

33. Vertical blue pole appears against tangled red background. Muzzled bear face enters from screen left, and roped or leashed bear ascends rolling barrel against red, white, and blue canvas background. Music swells to notes of triumph.

34. Blank black frame.

35. Lion mounts pedestal, returning *Fast, Cheap* approximately to where sequence began.

The robot scientist's words, which begin by shot #5, lend a degree of unity to the unusually diverse images juxtaposed in this sequence. "Higher-level intelligence, whatever that is," asserts the scientist, "is pretty easy once you have the ability to move around, hunt, chase. They're the tough parts." The scientist's emphasis on "the ability to move around" speaks to the ceaseless motion central to this sequence, bringing to mind Sal Paradise's remark in Jack Kerouac's *On the Road*: "We all realized we were . . . performing our one and noble function of the time, *move*. And we moved!" (Kerouac 1976, 134). Further, "the ability to move" levels the differences between the diverse types of existence—natural, animal, human, and technological—as every type (except for the voice-over narrator, whether wild animal trainer or scientist) appears similarly engaged in wordless motion. Also the evolutionary path to "higher-level intelligence" implicit in the scientist's words presumably embraces every type of life represented here. And the broad range of existence depicted—from simple cells to intelligent robots—demonstrates better than would a smaller sampling the extensive reach of practical science and evolutionary theory. Thus the diverse images are not without conceptual links. There are also narrative links, such as the quest to design robots and to explore distant planets. But no tight logic or causal chain makes any particular image, or its location, necessary or indispensable, and certain images, such as #10, 17, and 27, seem especially whimsical.

The incessant motion serves to connect the images but in the manner of a tornado swooping up all things in its path. As elsewhere in the film, play and jollity in this sequence sometimes veer into chaos and destruction, underscoring the structuring absence in the robot scientist's talk about progress. For while he stresses the ongoing evolution of mobility and intelligence, images of dumb violence and destruction, committed by humans or their movie creations and surrogates, rear up in ironic counterpoint.

Although the scientist evinces skepticism that "higher-level intelligence" amounts to much more than exceptional accumulation of motor and tactile capacities, he does not explain the human taste for devastation and chaos, for turning play into mayhem and reversing life's ascents. Further, the scientist boasts that he has designed his robots by forgoing aspects of control over them—leaving them free, for example, to stumble and move at will. But in noting such limits to his control, he scarcely comments on the ubiquitous counterpoint, overlap, and wrangling in Morris's films between representations of "control" and "out of control," logic and nonsense, knowledge and mystery, convention and experiment.

Unlike *Fast, Cheap*, *Mr. Death* has just one major narrator, Fred Leuchter, Jr. Its tempo is slower than *Fast, Cheap*'s, and its topic and tone are more somber. But it still resembles *Fast, Cheap* in key aspects of form or style and consequently poses similarly sharp contrasts to *Fog of War*. At one time Leuchter was to have been the fifth major character and narrator in *Fast, Cheap*, but his line of work seems closest to that of McNamara—as secretary of defense, if not as head of General Motors—since Leuchter devises ways of killing. A proponent of capital punishment who wants to make execution more humane and economical, Leuchter designs systems which kill by electrocution, lethal injection, and hanging in prisons throughout the United States.

He appears in the opening credit sequence, which, though more legible and comprehensible than the start of *Fast, Cheap*, is nevertheless strikingly unconventional for a documentary. As the credits roll, and lightning and thunder spread around him, Leuchter sits unflappably within the vertical bars of a huge cage or jail that resembles the lightning theater at Boston's famous Museum of Science. Relentlessly upbeat music counters the apocalyptic blasts of light, color, and noise. In a variation on the tension between "control" and "out of control," Leuchter remains unperturbed as well as unharmed at the center of the maelstrom. His Olympian composure alone seems to limit the racing electric claws of the storm, redolent of environments for creations of artificial life in films such as Fritz Lang's *Metropolis* (1927) and James Whale's *Frankenstein* (1931).

This opening credit sequence ends as it begins, without narrative or explanation. Among other things, it seems an exercise in "light moving in time," as William C. Wees entitled his book devoted to the "visual aesthetics of avant-garde film" (Wees 1992). In a manner one might almost associate with flicker films and other experimental cinema, with

Fast, Cheap, and with segments of fiction films, more than with typical documentaries, this prelude highlights primary elements of the film medium—light, color, motion, and sound. Like *Fast, Cheap,* moreover, it joins images and sounds of disorder to ones of calm and control.

After this opening, or invocation, the first scene of the film, which later I will compare to a similar scene featuring McNamara at the end of *Fog of War,* starts quietly: Leuchter appears driving a car, while his voice-over describes his goals as execution designer. Again, however, departures from documentary norms occur, and the materiality of film comes to the fore. For example, the scene begins in black and white, a break from the prelude's bursts of blue, white, and orange. The scene's third shot shifts to color, but the fourth returns to black and white, which persists for three more shots until the scene ends. A further oddity arises in the second shot, as the space in motion beyond the front windshield above Leuchter's hand on the steering wheel turns fuzzy and abstract, and its motion appears jerky and distended. This discrepant moment is succeeded by a shift to sharp focus and conventional realism in the third shot which, in addition to being in color, reveals one side of Leuchter's face and the upper portion of his body, rather than just the fragment of his hand on the steering wheel as in the second shot, or his bespectacled eyes in the rearview mirror as in the first shot. Another odd moment—reflexive and discontinuous—occurs at the end of the driving sequence, when the film goes totally dark and blank before a new shot of Leuchter appears, a medium close-up in color. Although now speaking directly to the camera, and seated in a studio rather than in a car, Leuchter, dressed in sport jacket and tie, continues on the same topic, in the same tone, as during the voice-over in the car prior to the visual interruption and change of scene. Evidently, he has been speaking from this studio while appearing in the car and in a sense may be considered to have been occupying two spaces at once—or to have been divided between them.

The eruptive, unpredictable qualities of Morris's filmmaking expand in this new scene that begins in the studio, and they possibly suggest split or multiple aspects of Leuchter's psyche as well as of his physical state. He evinces nothing less than poise and command as he faces the camera and discusses humane and economical execution. Then the film cuts to another room, one featuring an electric chair and related machinery, and here Leuchter's physical bearing changes. As he walks from one piece of execution technology to another, identifying each in turn, he appears increasingly unstable, not because of his own activity so much as maneuvers of the camera—along with jumpy editing and changes in the celluloid itself. The canted handheld camera, with the electric chair central in its view, sets the entire room at an angle from the start. Once

Leuchter plugs an electric cord into an outlet low in the wall, the camera
starts swaying more than is necessary to keep him and the action in frame,
yielding in tandem with the editing a sense of vertigo and disorienta-
tion. More drastic are the changes that occur when Leuchter announces
he will press the last button in the control console required to operate
the electric chair. The film shifts from color to black-and-white to high
contrast with deep shadows, and from a medium shot of Leuchter to a
close-up of his finger, viewed from the other side of his body, pressing
the button in slow motion. A longer shot of the finger completing its
action follows, in a slight temporal overlap with the previous shot. Both
Leuchter's voice and the room noise cease for these two shots. Then
the screen goes blank. When the image returns, it reiterates an earlier
moment in which Leuchter, prior to pressing the button for operation,
turned power on with a key. In the next shot he no longer holds the key,
however, and he starts to move away from the console. As he proceeds,
the slanting slow motion persists in high-contrast black-and-white and
now grain denser than before thickens the image.

This combination of cinematic effects exaggerates the turgid, ghoul-
ish aspects of Leuchter's appearance. He does not so much walk from the
console as drift off heavily through the murky air. His mouth opens into
a prolonged toothy grimace. His eyes are dazed, his face dark and bristly.
In voice-over (talking from the studio again, where he is shown twice in
color before the scene ends), he warns of sloppy electrocutions in which
excess current cooks the tissue of the "executee" and forces the "meat"
to come off, or in which the prisoner returns to life in twenty or thirty
minutes, but as a "brain-dead vegetable" to be killed again. While he cites
these hazards in the composed, reasonable voice of a person determined
to end them, his fiendish, unhinged appearance, along with the distorted
environment, possibly suggests other dimensions of his reaction.

Perhaps the expressionistic images reveal a Leuchter who is more
deeply horrified by the incidents described in his voice-over than his tone
of voice suggests—and who even identifies with the victims (elsewhere,
Leuchter reports having sat in an electric chair in his youth). Or the images
expose a Leuchter struck by the guilty revelation that, as no execution can
be civilized or delicate, he is monstrous to uphold capital punishment in
any fashion. Or on the contrary, the images reveal Leuchter to be either
a spectator or an executioner perversely thrilled by the incidents related
in his voice-over. The puzzle is not resolved. No authoritative narrator
steps in to clarify things. Instead, the cinematic disturbances resemble
random inkblots susceptible to multiple readings.

Apart from hinting at perceptions submerged within Leuchter,
the expressionistic images could represent aspects of the filmmaker's

viewpoint. Yet the first strong impression, as one views the film, is that the medium itself, distinct from both Morris and Leuchter, erupts like an outraged conscience to challenge the all-too-sensible equilibrium in Leuchter's voice and in his studio demeanor. How does a person or a society so calmly justify taking another's life, whether cleanly or not? What explains the human drive to kill or die? More generally, how do unspoken, unconscious, or inner drives shape Leuchter's outlook and behavior? While Leuchter himself does not voice such vital questions that seem to spring up along the edges of his words, the bulging, distorted images of him and his environs possibly summon the viewer to do so. Again, however, no authoritative voice steps in to mitigate the ambiguities and uncertainties.

A factor encouraging the illogical, though not unusual, sensation that the film itself, independent of the filmmaker, reacts to Leuchter is that Morris is not heard to say anything during the interviews, or at any other time, except for one short question to Leuchter at the end of the film. Nor does Morris ever appear on screen. Further, his "characters," such as Leuchter, do not appear to address him more than they do the camera. The film medium or apparatus often seems more prominent than the filmmaker. Leuchter in fact addresses the Interrotron, Morris's invention which, according to Philip Gourevitch, "uses two-way mirrors to project his face across the lens of the camera as he interviews people, so that his subjects address him eye to eye, and appear on film with maximal directness" (Gourevitch 2004, 34). The Interrotron adds to the interviewee's force and authority, allowing him or her to appear to address the audience, as well as the camera and filmmaker, eye to eye. On the other hand, Morris's authority and control accrue with his absence and mystery. Although he is eyed intensely by each interviewee, Morris remains foreign and immaterial, while the sensitive film in his control seems to the viewer tangible and immediate.

The flow of images and sounds in *Fog of War* is far smoother—markedly less volatile, complex, and ambiguous—than in *Mr. Death* and *Fast, Cheap*. To be sure, *Fog of War* incorporates several of Morris's standard manipulations, such as unpredictable jump cuts, blank frames, changes to fast or slow motion, and shifts of focus and camera position. Yet in *Fog of War* these measures are fewer and less intrusive than in the two previous films. Further, most changes of color and texture in *Fog of War* appear natural, a function simply of the variety of archival footage Morris deploys rather than of his inveterate tinkering with the image.

Another reason the advance of images and sounds in *Fog of War* seems smoother and clearer, though not necessarily more satisfying, than in *Mr. Death* and *Fast, Cheap* is that *Fog of War* largely rejects surprise and counterpoint in the relationship between picture and sound. Instead, imitation and redundancy are the rule. McNamara's narrative voice governs *Fog of War* even more than Leuchter's does *Mr. Death*. At crucial moments in the latter, especially after Leuchter is hired to look into the Holocaust, narrative agents other than Leuchter briefly take charge. These agents include historian Robert Jan Van Pelt, who counters Leuchter's denial of the Holocaust, and publisher Ernst Zundel, who pays Leuchter to investigate the stones at Auschwitz and to find Germany innocent of genocide. Since no comparable figures appear before the camera in *Fog of War* to support or challenge McNamara's storytelling, he alone provokes and explains the visual images, which, as indicated above, repeatedly illustrate his words.

Whether McNamara speaks of his marriage or the birth of his children; of victory celebrations at the end of World War I or economic failures and worker protests in the 1930s; of his role in the firebombing of Tokyo near the end of World War II, the expansion of the Vietnam War two decades later, or the push for safer vehicles at the Ford Motor Company between those wars, still photographs and archival movie footage conform to his words at every cue. Indeed, the synchronicity of word and image can be startlingly specific. As McNamara recalls General Curtis LeMay's conduct at a meeting during World War II, for example, he remarks that LeMay at one moment rose from his chair to make a point; precisely as McNamara says this, LeMay is shown rising from his chair.

The notion that agreements of word and image in *Fog of War* serve a style or form that eschews losses of clarity and control finds an echo in McNamara's first utterances in the film. *Fog of War* begins dryly and abruptly, free of the hullabaloo of *Fast, Cheap* and *Mr. Death*, with archival footage of McNamara standing next to a map of Vietnam and its surrounds and preparing to speak about the war. With his first words in this clip, which also inaugurate *Fog of War*, he asks the people gathered in the room whether they can see the map clearly or would like it lowered. Then he asks the TV crew whether it is "ready—all set?" Just moments later, stationed before the Interrotron for the start of his interview with Morris in the present, McNamara checks sound levels with the filmmaker, who remains offscreen, to be sure they can hear one another clearly. Morris replies that McNamara's volume is fine and proceeds to prod and question him from time to time throughout the rest of the film.

Hence Morris's response to McNamara's concern about audibility is to emerge from silence as never before in his films. In *Mr. Death*, *Fast, Cheap*, and *The Thin Blue Line* (1988), for example, his voice is heard just briefly and only at the end: a question to Leuchter in *Mr. Death* and to the wild animal trainer in *Fast, Cheap*, and a fragment of audiotape conversation with the young killer, David Harris, in *Thin Blue Line*. But although Morris remains offscreen in *Fog of War*, his voice attests to both his presence nearby and his intense engagement in McNamara's discourse. At times his voice serves almost as a reverse shot to McNamara's look. As a manifestation of the filmmaker's role and the space he occupies, Morris's voice contributes to the clarity and the reduction of mystery important to both McNamara and *Fog of War*'s form or style. The voice also serves to remind the viewer that Morris as filmmaker, not McNamara, determines the film's legibility and realism, goals that the two men share. Further, it is Morris who decides which of McNamara's utterances are to be highlighted as the "eleven lessons" to be drawn from his life. Despite the immense power McNamara wielded at the pinnacle of American business and government, Morris controls the film.

At a rare moment the interplay of word and image in *Fog of* War forsakes realism though not clarity. Still facing the Interrotron, McNamara states that toward the end of World War II both he and General Curtis LeMay behaved "as war criminals" when they approved the firebombing of Tokyo that killed 100,000 inhabitants in one night. Both men predicted they would be found guilty of war crimes if the United States lost the war. With this recollection, the image of McNamara's face freezes into a still photograph, while his words continue the voice-over with the question, "What makes it immoral if you lose, but moral if you win?" The shift to a freeze-frame and to an asynchronous relationship between word and image diverges from realism, but in order to deepen the clarity of a singular moment: a man who symbolizes global U.S. power has just confessed to an epic crime and to power's pollution of justice. The moment is too shocking for the film to proceed normally.

The question arises whether justice, possibly along with other qualities of civilized life, ever exists simply, clearly, absolutely, or only in a relative, ambiguous, compromised, and unstable condition. The film's clarity of form and technique seems designed to raise such complicated questions unmistakably. At least once, though, the film's clarity falters a bit, perhaps as a signal by the filmmaker of a lapse in McNamara's moral resolve that prevents him from admitting guilt about Vietnam as he has about the firebombing of Tokyo. The moment occurs during the excerpt of the ceremony in which McNamara finds he is too emotional, too choked up, to express in words his gratitude for the Medal of Freedom

President Lyndon Johnson has just awarded him following McNamara's resignation as secretary of defense.

In the present, on screen in the studio, McNamara speculates about what he would have said had he been able to: "Had I responded, I would have said, 'I know what many of you are thinking. You're thinking this man is duplicitous. . . . I want to tell you you're wrong.' " Then the excerpt resumes with Johnson and a military officer on screen. The president looks screen right, and the camera pans right to include McNamara in the frame. McNamara's voice then continues over the image of himself, the president, and the officer: "Of course, he had personal idiosyncrasies." The frame narrows to just the president and McNamara, as the latter says in voice-over: "He didn't accept all the advice he was given." The visual emphasis tilts toward McNamara, as the president looks at him while McNamara looks down at the medal. McNamara's voice-over continues: "On several occasions his associates advised him to be more forthcoming. He wasn't." Now McNamara and the president, rather than face the camera or each other, peer down at the medal. In voice-over McNamara says, "People didn't understand at the time. There were recommendations and pressures that would carry the risk of war with China and the risk of nuclear war and he was determined to prevent it." The image shifts to a close-up of the Medal of Freedom, slowly rotating as if on exhibit, while McNamara says in voice-over: "I'm arguing that he had a reason in his mind for doing what he did."

Has McNamara in this monologue been describing Johnson or himself? War critics had deemed both men duplicitous as well as idiosyncratic. And the film has presented a torrent of headlines, pictures, and cartoons from print media and television reviling McNamara. Indeed, the film has depicted opposition to him more graphically and extensively than it has opposition to Johnson. Moreover, in the moments just prior to the ceremony excerpt, McNamara in the present has sought to defend himself rather than Johnson. In response to Morris's voice-over question about responsibility for the loss of life during the Vietnam War, McNamara has replied, "It's the president's responsibility." Next, he has interpreted two photographs of himself in conversation with Johnson as demonstrating the tensions and disagreements between the two men, who were "poles apart" according to McNamara. Then he has told of his memorandum to Johnson urging U.S. withdrawal from Vietnam and has gone on to acknowledge that many people, including *Washington Post* publisher Katherine Graham, believed Johnson forced him from office. While it is possible that receiving the Medal of Freedom, or recalling that honor now, motivates McNamara to defend Johnson rather than himself, it is also reasonable to take "this man" considered "duplicitous" to be McNamara, not Johnson, and to understand McNamara as continuing to defend *himself.* Surely McNamara identified with Johnson's role in Vietnam, just as he had identified with LeMay's in the incendiary destruction of Tokyo. But he refuses to share responsibility with Johnson, perhaps because Johnson rejected him and let U.S. media and war protesters vilify him. His family suffered too, the ordeal probably hastening his wife's death. Further, Vietnam left McNamara, like his nation, isolated and defeated, as World War II had not. In voice-over McNamara concludes the scene by finally dropping the indefinite "this man" and "he," naming Johnson as the man who decided after the Medal of Freedom ceremony not to remain in office. Yet this conclusion does not entirely erase the question of who was accused of duplicity and who needed defending. That moment of moral and perceptual uncertainty lingers.

As already indicated, Morris's films often digress more than *Fog of War* does from conventions of clarity and realism, and consequently their style or form provokes greater uncertainty in the viewer. Characters in his films also experience perceptual uncertainty and ignorance. For example, in *Vernon, Florida* (1981) a man trains a jeweler's lens on a gem he has ordered by mail but confesses he does not know what to look for in evaluating it. Later in the film, another character is unable to identify the content of an image he has obtained with an opera glass attached to a camera lens aimed at the night sky. In *Thin Blue Line*, a possible witness to the killing of the policeman acknowledges that he may not have seen clearly in the dark. Scientist Stephen Hawking in *A Brief History of Time* (1991) faces myriad perceptual obstacles in his struggle to picture the universe. He also experiences uncertainty regarding the moral implications of his work. For the most part, however, neither moral nor perceptual doubt causes major characters in films by Morris to break their stride.

Often these characters are practical, can-do people—positive think-ers a bit like Phillip, the junior executive in the pet cemetery business in *Gates of Heaven* (1978) who refuses to use words like "can't." A number of these characters are problem-solvers who learn to master sectors of their environment. Leuchter deplores the pain and indignity, the burnt flesh and excess excretions of flawed executions, so he devises new machinery to solve the problem. Also, he does not dawdle on the documented hor-rors of Auschwitz when he gathers samples that eventually convince him no mass murder occurred there. Characters in pursuit of knowledge and control in *Fast, Cheap* appear similarly free of doubt and ambivalence.

More colorful and socially intelligent than Leuchter, they too devise ways to restrict or overcome unruliness, disorder, or formlessness, whether in shrubbery, lions, robots, mole rats, or people. The wild animal trainer, who has learned to guess correctly how a lion perceives the world, notes that to be successful "you have to experience an injury, you have to experience chaos." The topiary gardener prefers hand shears to electric ones, as they afford him tighter control of the details of animal forms he carves out of foliage and rebuilds after storms and insect attacks. The robot scientist foresees a time when the distinction between what is alive and what is a machine will become blurred and perhaps meaningless, but this potential confusion does not deter him or slow him down. Further, as indicated above, he accepts limits to his control over his robots, and refrains from worry that, as in the film clips Morris inserts into the scientist's account of his work, robots may eventually destroy people or otherwise get out of hand. The mole rat specialist discerns some fundamental bewilderment within human beings, "constantly trying to find themselves in another social animal," but he sidesteps this possible dilemma as he conducts his research with cheerful alacrity. It falls to McNamara, more than any other major character in Morris's oeuvre, to focus on ambiguity, indeterminacy, and disorder—qualities that mirror vagaries of form and style in Morris's earlier films, including the grand playfulness of *Fast, Cheap*—and to suggest that the tendency to repress, disclaim, or sidestep such qualities could now prove suicidal.

Billed as "Eleven Lessons from the Life of Robert S. McNamara," *Fog of War* mounts a series of didactic chapters, somewhat in the manner of early U.S. fiction classics such as E. S. Porter's films of social protest and D. W. Griffith's *Birth of a Nation* (1915) and *Intolerance* (1916). The lessons, or chapter titles, are:

1. Empathize with your enemy.

2. Rationality will not save us.

3. There's something beyond oneself.

4. Maximize efficiency.

5. Proportionality should be a guideline in war.

6. Get the data.

7. Belief and seeing are both often wrong.

8. Be prepared to reexamine your reasoning.

9. In order to do good, you may have to engage in evil.

10. Never say never.

11. You can't change human nature.

In stressing practical, rational conduct, a few of McNamara's lessons or imperatives, such as "Get the data," "Maximize efficiency," and "Be prepared to reexamine your reasoning," harmonize with the outlook of Morris's can-do, control-minded characters. But other lessons or observations, such as "Belief and seeing are both often wrong" and "Rationality will not save us," are distinctly less positive and sure-footed, as is the observation, "You can't change human nature." Also off-key are the embrace of contradiction and the acceptance of evil in two of the lessons: "In order to do good, you may have to engage in evil" and "Never say never." None of these exceptions to a logical positive outlook looms as large, however, as the exasperating contradiction underlying the lessons: "Human beings must stop killing other human beings!" exclaims McNamara. But how can they stop when "You can't change human nature"?

"Death may, in fact, be the underlying theme of the great majority of documentaries, as André Bazin hinted about the cinema generally," observes Bill Nichols in *Representing Reality* (Nichols 1991, 110). Ever since *Gates of Heaven*, the documentary about pet cemeteries that includes a socioeconomic excursus on reprocessing the byproducts of dead snakes, rats, monkeys, chickens, and mice, death has held a central place in Morris's films, as has killing. Swaths of *Vernon, Florida* focus on the killing of turkeys that a hunter complains are far less numerous than the circling buzzards. *Thin Blue Line* centers on the death-row prisoner Randall Adams and killer David Harris, while returning obsessively to images of the shooting and dying fall of a policeman. Noted also in the film is that Harris's four-year-old brother drowned right after John F. Kennedy's assassination and that a psychiatrist paid to assess which of those accused in death penalty cases were likely to commit more crimes was called "Dr. Death"—since his predictions spared no one. *Thin Blue Line* also includes archival footage of the slaying of gangster John Dillinger and speaks of bystanders collecting mementos of his fresh blood. While *A Brief History of Time* is free of killing, it is preoccupied with death. Hawking buckles down to his most serious scientific work only after learning he has a motor-neuron disease that will reduce his body to the condition of limp cabbage and end his life in 2½ years. Much of his research then focuses on the eventual death or collapse of the universe and the nature of black holes. As already indicated, prospects of death and destruction propel *Fast, Cheap*, in which they seem as typical of animal and natural life as of human existence. Only in captivity, for example, do mole rats live to grow old, says the mole rat specialist. He adds, "Stability is death," a remark that perhaps casts the film's intense flux and restlessness, its impression of matter in ceaseless motion, as a strategy to fend off death. In *Mr. Death*, Leuchter's obsession with killing and dying appears to be lifelong, originating in childhood visits to the prison where his father worked and where in 1957 the son first sat in an electric chair.

Although death and destruction abound in Morris's cinema, perhaps only in *Fog of War* does a major character fiercely resist accepting them as either routine or inevitable. A major reason, of course, is that McNamara confronts the prospect of nuclear war, in which human beings would kill other human beings on a far vaster scale than ever before in human history. He would concur with historian Bruce Catton's observation, "A singular fact about modern war is that it takes charge. Once begun it has to be carried to its conclusion, and carrying it there sets in motion events that may be beyond men's control" (quoted in Brooks 2004, 33). Further, McNamara not only lived through the Cuban Missile Crisis but before and after, during World War II and Vietnam, and facilitated more mass killing than any other witness or engineer of killing in Morris's work. Paul Celan's lines, "Whichever word you speak— / you owe to / destruction" (Celan 2001, 71), apply to parts of McNamara's career all too well. The former secretary of defense has reason not only to turn human nature around and stop the killing but also to atone.

He brings to this complex mission not only his experience of modern war, weaponry, and political power but also his immersion in qualities of modern life such as ambiguity, indeterminacy, disorder, uncertainty, and complexity that happen to inflect the form of Morris's more experimental films. McNamara suggests that recognition of these qualities as central to human experience would help deter humankind from waging war. In any case, such recognition informs McNamara's eleven lessons, which exist in sharp contrast to another list devised for human edification and success much earlier in U.S. history, Benjamin Franklin's thirteen virtues—highlighted in thirteen key words: temperance, silence, order, resolution, frugality, industry, sincerity, justice, moderation, cleanliness, tranquility, chastity, and humility (Silverman 2003, 82–84). Franklin's list, including the succinct fine print following each key word, posed distinctly brighter prospects than McNamara's. Unlike McNamara, the man who signed the Declaration of Independence and the new nation's Constitution did not declare that sight, belief, and reason were often unreliable. Nor did he assert that well-intentioned people might have no choice but to commit evil. And rather than say that human nature was unchangeable, he stressed its capacity for steady improvement. He knew firsthand the positive effects of focusing on a single virtue every four weeks of the

year. Franklin trusted that practical intelligence, along with diligence
and sociability, empowered human beings to control their destiny and
to set the world right. Probably McNamara shared Franklin's confident,
Enlightenment-like outlook when he taught business administration at
Harvard University from 1940 to 1943. But the young professor's confidence was eroded and ultimately exploded by his subsequent service
during World War II and later the Bay of Pigs, the nuclear standoff
with the Soviet Union over Cuba, and of course Vietnam. Indeed, *Fog
of War* charts his journey from one worldview—one world, one historical
moment, one self-image—to a radically different one. Presumably, it is
this wrenching journey—and not simply his responsibility for destruction
nor his consequent remorse and defensiveness—that has transformed him
and equipped him for his mission.

Transformed but also damned ("Damned if I do, damned if I don't,"
he says in response to Morris's question at the end of the film about
whether he takes responsibility for the deaths in Vietnam), McNamara
brings the zeal of the convert and the penitent to the task of spreading
the word about the shifting fog and indeterminacy of life and war, and
to counseling humanity about the wisdom of doubt and the legitimacy of
uncertainty. His outlook—call it "postmodern lite"—contradicts President
George W. Bush's creed of certainty and his ban on ambiguous perceptions and complex messages. In addition, McNamara's Vietnam-inspired
view that "We are the strongest nation in the world today, we should
never apply that power unilaterally" warns against the very approach for
which Bush has been criticized in Iraq. Nevertheless, *Fog of War* does
not explicitly explore this contrast between McNamara and Bush, though
Morris later created commercials critical of Bush during the 2004 presi-
dential contest. Instead, through McNamara's journey and his changing
vision, Morris explores philosophical questions about human existence,
knowledge, and morality in relation to the larger universe, as he has in
his films for more than twenty-five years.

More than any other Morris character, McNamara comes to reject his
old practices and beliefs and to espy a new reality—too new and complex
for his comfort. At the same time, like Leuchter and other characters, he
enters a social void where no home, family, friends, or colleagues are in
sight. Isolated, burdened, unredeemed, McNamara near the end of the
film quivers with humility (Franklin's thirteenth virtue), and invokes T. S.
Eliot, another witness of fog and death though McNamara does not say
so ("Unreal City, / Under the brown fog of a winter dawn, / A crowd
flowed over London Bridge, so many, / I had not thought death had
undone so many" (Eliot 1964, 53)). Informing Morris that he is about
to quote Eliot, McNamara states, "We shall not cease from exploring

and at the end of our exploration we will return to where we started and know the place for the first time."[1] His face brightens a bit, as he adds tentatively, "Now that's where I'm beginning to be." Earlier in the film McNamara evinced a touch of modesty about his reputation in business and public service for being a master of material reality, a man poised with all the data and answers, but now he presents himself as a novice struggling to discern what is real, a pilgrim awkwardly aware that signs of truth and progress may prove illusory and void.

When, as noted earlier, Morris raises questions of responsibility for the deaths in Vietnam and McNamara responds that he will be damned regardless of his answer, their exchange most likely occurs in the studio, though it is heard as McNamara on-screen drives silently alone in his car. Unlike a comparable scene of Leuchter driving alone at the start of *Mr. Death* while his words from the studio are heard in voice-over, the picture in *Fog of War* undergoes no odd, unpredictable changes of color, texture, or tempo. Here as elsewhere, *Fog of War* is less tricky cinematically than *Mr. Death*. Nevertheless, at a moment of decisive loss and defeat, McNamara seems to dissolve into a void of smoke or fog, much as Leuchter turns into thin air in *Mr. Death*.

The turn for McNamara occurs shortly after images of his resignation as secretary of defense, the fadeout on the Medal of Freedom, and his statement that Johnson "concluded that he couldn't continue" as president. McNamara then states in front of the camera in the studio: "I'm very sorry that in the process of accomplishing things I made errors." On a blank screen his eleventh lesson appears: "You can't change human nature." Thus both McNamara and his president have been driven from power; McNamara has admitted mistakes and apologized, and his eleventh and concluding lesson has provided scant hope of a better future. The next shot presents McNamara as a nondescript citizen walking outdoors in slow motion away from the camera. In voice-over he states, "We all make mistakes." As he recedes, a large white-shirted pedestrian, his back to the camera, appears in the foreground, quickly filling the left half and full height of the frame, and proceeding in the same direction as the former secretary of defense. In extreme soft focus, the blurry whiteness of the stranger's shirt becomes a thin, filmy sea that envelops and drowns the diminishing figure of McNamara, positioned near the center of the lower half of the frame, as the shot abruptly ends. McNamara's erasure is complete in the next shot, a shift to black and white, in which an infantryman in the left half of the frame charges toward the camera through the dense smoke of battle. Other soldiers soon appear, but at first there is no one else. The lower central area of the frame that was occupied by McNamara toward the end of the prior shot is now empty except for the formless smoke; it is as though he has turned into opaque air. In a ghost-like and heartsick voice-over, he states, "There's a wonderful phrase, 'the fog of war,' " and cautions that war's complexity—"all the variables"—overwhelms human understanding.

Leuchter does not admit error as McNamara does, but by the end of *Mr. Death* he too is heartbroken. Ostracized for asserting in multiple forums that no mass murder of Jews occurred at Auschwitz, Leuchter finds no one in the United States who will employ him or buy his products. Prison after prison turns him down. His estranged wife, who honeymooned with him in Auschwitz while he pried samples from the death-chamber walls to be chemically analyzed in North America, throws him out of their house, indicating she will not object if she does not see him again. (His mother stopped speaking to him well before his marriage.) Just about penniless, Leuchter travels to Los Angeles in pursuit of a job offer. When his prospective employer cannot pay for his lodging, Leuchter is locked out of his hotel room, and his rental car is taken away.

In voice-over Leuchter explains about the hotel room and car, while on screen a door appears with a small window in its upper half through which a long, narrow hotel corridor is visible. At the distant end of the corridor stands a rectangle of soft white light, possibly daylight bleeding through a tall window. Except for this opaque rectangle, toward which the corridor walls converge, color, light, space, line, and texture are relatively sharp and clear. However, these visual elements change radically when Leuchter enters the corridor through the door with the small window. Although the camera's stationary position behind the small window seems unchanged, the image becomes blurred and compressed, and the hazy colors and forms merge together. Observed through the door's window, Leuchter walks toward the previously distant white rectangle that now, more curved and dilated, presses against him like every other aspect of the environment. He proceeds indistinctly like a phantom, fading in and out of the imbroglio of color and light. When the shot ends his head and upper body are absorbed almost entirely by the whiteness ahead.

In various senses, Leuchter is rendered immaterial in the next scene as well. Having stated in voice-over in the corridor that he was dropped off on a freeway when his rental car was taken away, he now stands in a black-and-white shot at the edge of a freeway while cars race by, and he remarks in voice-over, "It's pretty tough when you're out in the middle of nowhere all by yourself." In the next shot, in color, Leuchter walks on the edge of a road against traffic. He is in much softer focus than the automobiles, almost like an apparition superimposed on the vehicles and on the white dashes marking the traffic lanes. He appears most ethereal and fragile as he passes through the left foreground out of frame in the shot's final seconds. During these closing instants, a character, possibly Van Pelt, describes Leuchter's plight, in voice-over: "He'd been destroyed as a human being. . . . I frankly am surprised he didn't commit suicide. . . . He had no idea of what he was blundering into. . . . He wasn't putting his name on the line because he had no name. He came from nowhere and he went back to nowhere."

Neither Leuchter nor McNamara crosses permanently into immateriality. However, both individuals commute cinematically between corporeal and incorporeal existence, and both confront not only radical changes of fortune but also harrowing shifts in their understanding of reality and of their place in the world. Both individuals negotiate between seemingly opposing realms—clarity and ambiguity, certainty and doubt, order and chaos, control and its absence, form and formlessness—that intermingle throughout Morris's films. A judge in *Thin Blue Line* reverently cites the thin blue line that in his view divides the world of the police from the realm of chaos. But along with the intermingling of seemingly opposing qualities, Morris's films entail the blurring and crossing of lines. This may be why Morris questioned in an interview prompted by the growing box-office success of documentaries whether a clear divide exists between documentary and fiction: "Movies are movies," he said simply (Waxman 2004, B5). In any event, although Susan Sontag cautions against society's insistence that art be useful, there is no denying the potential gain in sociopolitical as well as aesthetic understanding from cinematic art like Morris's, in which form as well as content exposes and dissolves borders that repress rather than delineate truth.

Note

1. Eliot's precise words in "Little Gidding" are: "We shall not cease from exploration / And the end of all our exploring / Will be to arrive where we started / And know the place for the first time" (Eliot 1980, 145).

3

CARL PLANTINGA

The Philosophy of Errol Morris

Ten Lessons

G IVEN THE FULL TITLE OF Errol Morris's celebrated 2003 film about Robert McNamara, *The Fog of War: Eleven Lessons from the Life of Robert S. McNamara*, it is easy to mistakenly assume that the lessons enumerated in the film are McNamara's, and at least one critic has done so (Hoberman 2004, 20–22). McNamara later complained that the eleven lessons were not his but Morris's, but Morris insisted that they had legitimately been culled from McNamara's life and words. Perhaps in an attempt to placate McNamara, the film's subtitle about the eleven lessons does not appear anywhere on the cover of the Sony Pictures Classics DVD. In addition, among the DVD's special features is listed "Robert S. McNamara's Ten Lessons," lessons straight from the horse's mouth and introduced in his recorded voice and words: "the eleven lessons are not my lessons. I've prepared ten lessons, and I'd like to show those to you now."

In a similar way, this chapter presents ten lessons culled from the words and films of Errol Morris. These are not Morris's lessons, but nonetheless, I claim, they have been legitimately culled from interviews, lectures, and of course Morris's fascinating documentary films. Together they constitute what I have called Errol Morris's philosophy. What do I

43

mean by that? To my mind, Errol Morris is the most remarkable documentary filmmaker working today. What makes him so, in part, are his interests in philosophy and anthropology—in philosophical anthropology. Morris doesn't merely find and tell good human stories but stories that raise philosophical questions or through which Morris explores human nature. His interest in philosophy is long-standing. In 1972 Morris enrolled in the PhD program in philosophy at Berkeley. He spent at least two years there and received an MA, but finding the program to be "a world of pedants" (Singer 1989, 43), he never finished his PhD and left the program. Morris has never lost his interest in philosophical questions, however. As Morris reports, "Someone who worked here once said, perhaps uncharitably, that I was not interested in a story unless it contained a first-semester philosophy question. There is definitely some truth to that" (Grundmann and Rockwell 2000, 6).

My ten theses are not all statements of philosophical positions or claims, although many are. Some are lessons on how to use the film medium to explore the mental landscapes that are Morris's chief interest. My hope is that Morris will be happier with these ten lessons than McNamara was with his. If not, I will allow him to present ten lessons of his own. Maybe even eleven.

1. Objective Truth Exists; Truth Can Be Known; Truth Is Difficult to Know

Over and over again in interviews, Errol Morris has affirmed his belief in the existence of mind- and discourse-independent truth. Such a belief is also apparent in his films. Consider some of what Morris has said. *The Thin Blue Line* (1988) presents the story of Randall Adams, a man who was arrested in Dallas, Texas, for the murder of policeman Robert Wood during a traffic stop late one night. Adams was prosecuted, convicted, and sentenced to death, sometime after which he was fortunate enough to draw the attention of Errol Morris. Morris turned his camera on the various personalities who believed Adams to be the murderer and/or were willing to testify to that effect. The film presents diverse claims and motivations for making them, weaving a tapestry of competing and conflicting stories about the case. Some critics called the film "*Rashomon-*like" in its portrayal of the event as nonspecifiable, discourse-dependent, and purely subjective. Morris disagrees: "For me there is a fact of the matter, a fact of what happened on the roadway that night. . . . Someone shot Robert Wood, and it was either Randall Adams or David Harris. That's the fundamental issue at the center of all this. Is it knowable? Yes, it is. We have access to the world out there. We aren't just prisoners of our fantasies and dreams. I wanted to make a movie about how truth is difficult to know, not how it is impossible to know" (Moyers 1989). At the end of the film, Morris presents an audio-taped interview with David Harris, the young man who had been with Randall Adams on the night of the murder. Harris indirectly confesses to the crime. In this and in other ways, Morris strongly implies that there is a truth of the matter. Harris is the actual murderer and Randall Adams is innocent.

Take another example, this time from Morris's brilliant film *Mr. Death: The Rise and Fall of Fred A. Leuchter, Jr.* (1999). Leuchter, a lonely fringe-dweller with a BA in history, had eked out a living designing and renovating execution equipment. After meandering into the orbit of revisionist historians, or Holocaust deniers, he made a trip overseas to Auschwitz to perform a series of experiments designed to determine whether the gas chambers at that concentration camp were actually what they were purported to be. After performing a series of questionable experiments that were later called meaningless by the very technicians who analyzed his data, Leuchter concluded that the gas chambers at Auschwitz had never seen gas in sufficient quantities to kill anyone. This resulted in *The Leuchter Report*, a booklet that has become a prized document of Holocaust deniers around the world. In return for his experiment and testimony, Leuchter received various sorts of attention, including invitations to speak at the conventions and conferences of Holocaust deniers.

Given the example of the murder of Robert Wood in *The Thin Blue Line*, one might expect Morris to take a similar position on the truth of the gas chambers at Auschwitz and on the legitimacy of Leuchter's experiment. And he does. Morris uses the testimony of Holocaust historians and scientists to question Leuchter's experiment within the film, and moreover, often undermines Leuchter's credibility by showing the man in the context of bizarre and expressive shots featuring the strobe effects of bursts of electricity and the accoutrements of a mad scientist. Morris also provides an explicit perspective on the matter in an interview: "In his own dream world, Leuchter is a scientist conducting important, authentic research. In reality, he is a history major practicing as an engineer with no scientific background and conducting a grossly inadequate and flawed series of unsound, unscientific tests" (Grundmann and Rockwell 2000, 2).

Dream worlds versus reality. Fantasies versus the real world. Lies versus facts. Morris consistently affirms these binary oppositions. For Morris, it is at times an abdication of responsibility to cease trying to get beyond the lies, fabrications, and self-serving personal fables that are characteristic of human discourse, to get behind them to the truth of the matter. In the Randall Adams case, District Attorney Doug Mulder had learned of and then suppressed evidence of Adams's innocence because as D.A. he had a vested interest in seeing the man convicted of murder (Singer 1989, 63). These cases not only illustrate the necessity of distinguishing truth from fabrication, they also show the degree to which human beings lose interest in the truth or are hopelessly misled in their attempts to find it. As Morris says, "Today, I believe there's a kind of *frisson* of ambiguity. People think that ambiguity is somehow wonderful in its own right, an excuse for failing to investigate. What can I say? I think this view is wrong. At best, misguided. Maybe even reprehensible" (Morris 2005a).

2. As an Epistemology, Philosophical Realism Is to Be Preferred to Postmodernism

I began with this thesis about truth and knowledge because Morris has been celebrated as a postmodernist filmmaker and *The Thin Blue Line* as a "postmodern documentary." As Linda Williams writes, he borrows techniques from the fiction film (thus putting into question the fiction/nonfiction distinction, one of the binary oppositions disliked by postmodernist theory) and engages with "a newer, more contingent, relative, postmodern truth" (Williams 1998, 382). But planting the flag of postmodernism on any Morris film is questionable. Williams is right to note that Morris cannot be legitimately held to dismiss the existence and pursuit of truth. But there is no reason to believe that the truth Morris pursues is merely contingent and not necessary, merely relative and not universal. For Morris, the truth may be something contingent and historically specific, like "Randall Adams is innocent of the murder he was accused of." But there is nothing in Morris's films or words that denies the existence of necessary truths. Judging by his own words, Morris does not believe that truth is relative or subjective, but rather independent of mind and discourse. Thus, for example, much of the testimony revealed in *The Thin Blue Line* is not presented as truth, but is strongly implied to be fabrication. And Morris's explicit claims in interviews and innumerable implications in his films about the hopelessness of the human situation are not meant to be relative claims, but claims about universal human truth. Human fallibility isn't limited to Fred Leuchter or to the many small-town eccentrics Morris interviews for *Vernon, Florida* (1981). It is characteristic of the human race.

Morris has said that his sympathies lie with "American analytic philosophy" in part because this is his educational background. He also suggests that one of the good things about his hometown of Cambridge, Massachusetts, is that "Baudrillard isn't in the phonebook" (Grundmann and Rockwell 2000, 6) Morris identifies himself with philosophical realism, the view that reality exists independent of observers. Realists believe that theories are successful to the extent that they correspond to reality, to what really exists. And realism often contains an ethical commitment to embrace what is real, however unattractive such reality might be. As Morris says, "Truth is not subjective. . . . You don't take an audience survey" (ibid.).

Unlike many postmodern theorists, Morris makes a distinction between ontology (the study of being, or what exists) and epistemology (the study of the nature and origin of human knowledge) (see Blackburn 2005). To believe in truth is not to claim that the truth is immediate or transparent. We can have access to the truth through representations, which may themselves be illuminating or misleading. They are illuminating to the extent to which they lead to the truth, misleading to the degree to which they do not. In this sense one can believe in an objective reality (an ontological issue) and still question whether humans have complete, partial, or absolutely no access to it (an epistemological issue). Thus some realists are skeptical of many claims to knowledge, as Errol Morris is, while still believing in objective truth.

3. Human Attempts to Know the World Are Typically Riddled with Error and Misunderstanding, and Are Sidetracked by Self-interest and Willful Ignorance

If Morris's ontology squares badly with postmodernism, some aspects of his epistemology are more amenable. Morris has thus called himself "the anti-postmodernist postmodernist" (Morris 2005a). We have already seen the ways in which Morris can be said to be anti-postmodernist. He is allied with postmodernism, however, in his skepticism about the possibilities of human knowledge and belief in the plasticity and naiveté of human belief. For Morris, humans are constitutionally incapable of understanding themselves or the world around them. Thus when nothing immediate is at stake, for example, the guilt or innocence of a man on death row, Morris takes deeper interest in the stories people tell and the web of beliefs they weave than in whether those beliefs are true or false. Morris seems to think that most of them are false.

What McNamara says about war in *The Fog of War* applies to other realms of human experience: "What the fog of war means is war is so complex it's beyond the ability of the human mind to comprehend all the variables. Our judgment, our understanding are not adequate and we kill people unnecessarily. . . . We see incorrectly or we see only half of the story at times. . . . Believing and seeing; they're both often wrong."

For Morris, however, human epistemic fallibility extends beyond the ability to understand war or the origins of the universe (as in *A Brief History of Time*, 1991). At some level persons are fundamentally confused about more mundane matters as well. Thus Morris delights in showing us the old man in *Vernon, Florida* who insists that what appears to be a tortoise is actually a gopher, or the couple in that same film who claim with straight faces that the sand they brought home from White Sands National Monument has been growing (more on this below).

Morris has a strong misanthropic streak, as can be seen in *Gates of Heaven* (1980), his film about two competing pet cemeteries, the people that run them, and their customers. His perspective on the marketing tactics used by the Harberts, owners of Bubbling Well Pet Memorial Park, is subtly but unmistakably ironic. As Cal Harberts says in one of Morris's characteristic interviews, "We created the Garden of Honor. And in this garden we will bury a Seeing Eye dog or a police dog killed in the line of duty at *no* cost—*if* it's killed in the line of duty. And for anybody else who wants to share this garden then we created a price which amounts to more than any other garden that we have." Morris also trains his camera on Florence Rasmussen, an older woman whose celebrated monologue meanders unexpectedly and nonsensically and contradicts itself on several occasions. This seemingly irrelevant interview made the final cut not merely because it is humorous, and not merely because it illustrates Morris's pessimistic view of the human condition, but because Morris thinks that humans often deserve to be laughed at, as I will discuss further in the tenth thesis below.

The eleventh lesson in *The Fog of War* is this: "You can't change human nature." As Morris says, "It tells you that all of the other lessons are valueless, that the human situation is indeed hopeless" (Morris 2005a). And it is hopeless (if also amusing) for Morris not because there is no objective truth, but rather because human beings, in their fallibility and hypocrisy, are typically unable and/or unwilling to discern truth. Given Morris's view of humans as "just a bunch of apes running around" (Singer 1989, 39), his pessimism is unsurprising: "What's so interesting is this idea that we can possess absolute, certain, infallible knowledge. Of course, this is utterly ridiculous. Who do we think we are? We are some kind of grossly self-deceived primate at best" (Morris 2000, 82). Yet for Morris the search must continue: "We investigate, and sometimes we find things out and sometimes we don't. There's no way to know in advance. It's just that we have to proceed as though there are answers to questions. We must proceed as though in principle we can find things out—even if we can't. The alternative is unacceptable" (Morris 2005b).

4. Humans Construct Frameworks of Belief— Fables or Dreamscapes—to Make Sense of Their Lives and Their World

Errol Morris's films are not first and foremost about politics, religion, history, or science. They are about people, and especially the content of and motivations for people's beliefs. Morris makes strategic use of the filmed interview (see Lesson #8) in part because he is fascinated by the mental landscapes of his subjects. In *Fast, Cheap & Out of Control* (1997), Morris chronicles the obsessions of four men with, respectively, mole rats, robots, lion taming, and topiary gardening. Speaking of George Mendoca, the gardener, Morris says, "Mendoca claims that hand shears are better than electric shears. Do I really care if this is true or false in some absolute sense? No. It's irrelevant. What you care about in that movie is the character's investment in his belief. It's his dreamscape, his subjective world which is at issue" (ibid, 83). Morris is proud that *The Thin Blue* line helped to exonerate Randall Adams. Truth matters. But in many cases, the truth is less interesting than the human dreamscapes that provide the bizarre and somewhat morbid topography of Errol Morris's work.

We can see this clearly in Morris's short-lived television series *First Person*, which aired on Bravo in 2000 and on the Independent Film Channel in 2001. Typical episodes of this series present extended interviews with remarkable persons, remarkable not necessarily for their great achievements or exceptional talents but for an odd obsession, an unusual way of looking at the world, or some other quality that distinguishes them from the great sea of human "normality." "The Killer Inside Me" features Sondra London, who fantasizes about being carried away by the Grim Reaper on a black stallion and whose current romantic interest is a man convicted of slaying five college students. In "I Dismember Mama" we meet Saul Kent, a pioneer in cryonics—the technique of freezing humans beings for later thawing in a future where advanced medicine will enable their lives to become extended and their identities changed. And we meet Temple Grandin in "Stairway to Heaven," an autistic university professor who empathizes with cattle in order to design "humane" methods of slaughter. In each case, Morris is most interested in how his subjects think about the world.

Morris is fascinated by what motivates humans, by the self-invented fables by which persons order their lives. And these fables, of course, are often in Morris's estimation patently false. "What I find scary," he says, "is that our capacity for belief is so plastic, we can convince ourselves of anything" (ibid.). Laurie Calhoun puts this well:

Errol Morris is keenly aware of the degree to which *we find ourselves with our beliefs* (Calhoun's emphasis), and these beliefs sometimes rest upon flimsy evidence. Sometimes the only real "reason" that we believe something is that we happen to believe it (we no longer even know why), and our cognitive manner of dealing with the world into which we have been in some sense thrown is essentially conservative. (Calhoun 2004)

The persona Morris takes on in his films differs somewhat from film to film, ranging from a bemused and sympathetic, yet somewhat aloof admiration, as in Morris's clear respect for Stephen Hawking's intellect in *A Brief History of Time*, to pity and fascination, as might characterize his perspective on Fred Leuchter in *Mr. Death*, to the subtle but readily apparent derision Morris has for the small town eccentrics of *Vernon, Florida*. Morris is often fascinated by the story itself for what it reveals of its teller's mental landscape. But he will occasionally provide a firm estimation of its truth or falsity. He says that *Mr. Death*, for example, "is a movie about denial. Denial about the obvious, denial of self, denial of death, denial of the Holocaust. But at its center, it is a failure to see the world, to see reality" (Grundman and Rockwell 2000, 5).

5. Once Established, Personal Fables and Other Beliefs Become Intractable

Fred Leuchter suffered a good deal from his affiliation with Holocaust deniers and his "experiment" in Auschwitz. One might legitimately wonder if all of the criticism, loss of work, and ostracism has caused him to rethink his views. In *Mr. Death*, one of the only times we hear Errol Morris's voice is when he asks Fred Leuchter if he has ever considered that he might be wrong about his experiments and findings with regard to the gas chambers of Auschwitz. He replies that he is "beyond all that," and that once the experiments were performed and his conclusions reached, he decided what he believed and apparently never looked back. On seeing the film and in conversations with Morris himself, Leuchter was confronted with all of the counterevidence that to most viewers seems quite compelling. Yet Leuchter persists in his views. In *The Fog of War*, Morris similarly asks Robert McNamara, a much more imposing figure, whether all of the criticism of and mass demonstrations against the Vietnam War caused him to change his thinking. McNamara's response: "I don't think my thinking was changing. We were in the cold war, and this was a cold war, uh, activity."

Errol Morris has an explanation for this hardening of beliefs and belief systems. In regard to this issue, Morris invokes one of Richard

Feynman's books (Morris doesn't specify which one) about his involvement with the Manhattan project. Feynman initially worked on the Manhattan Project with severe misgivings and only because he thought that if Germany were to develop the bomb before the Americans, the world would be in grave danger. After the war ended, however, Feynman's initial justification disappeared, and yet he continued to work on the project. Feynman writes in retrospect that he should have reconsidered. As Morris says, "I think what Feynman is saying . . . is that in order to live we make decisions, and to re-examine those decisions constantly isn't possible. You can't function as a human being if you're constantly re-evaluating your actions" (Cronin 2004, 21).

6. Given the Tenuous Condition of Humanity with Respect to Knowledge of Self and World, the Truth-seeker Should Ask Questions and Practice Epistemic Humility

It would be fair to ask of Errol Morris how he believes a documentary filmmaker, or anyone else, should approach the pursuit of truth, given his views on human nature. If humanity is prone to error and self-deception, and if the proper attitude toward reality is one of epistemic humility rather than brash confidence, how must one go about making claims in documentary films? For Morris, we move closer to the truth not by making brash assertions but only by asking questions and entertaining multiple perspectives. In *The Thin Blue Line*, Morris interviews numerous persons with varied perspectives on the crime that is at the heart of the film. What becomes apparent is that human testimony is tenuous indeed, but that the motivations that lie deep within are nonetheless fascinating. If Morris's best estimation of the truth of the matter emerges, it does so only after one wades through a thicket of fabrications and half-truths, some of which are espoused by people of the utmost sincerity. Morris doesn't explicitly affirm truths but rather allows apparent truths to emerge more subtly in a gradual fashion.

In *A Brief History of Time*, Morris alters his usual sardonic perspective to grant Stephen Hawking a more sympathetic, even optimistic hearing. Yet in the film the great physicist makes some rather startling statements: "We can figure out most of what has happened in the universe since the first split second, but all the really interesting stuff occurred in that original instant, which remains a mystery; to understand it would be to look into the mind of God." Well, really? And when Morris tries to visualize what it might be like to fall into a black hole, or to have time begin to move backward toward creation (where we see a spilled coffee cup "unspilling," "unfalling," and righting itself on a table), one gets the sense that for Morris, all of Hawking's claims are infused with a certain what-if quality. As Morris says, "if my movies are any good, it's because they're full of unresolved questions you can keep thinking about" (ibid.).

Morris relates a telling story about the old couple in *Vernon, Florida* who insist that the sand they brought home from White Sands National Monument has been growing. When watching this film, one senses Morris's ironic amusement at such naive delusions. Yet years later, he says, an audience member told Morris that the sand from White Sands consists of gypsum, which expands when it takes on moisture. If it were transported from a dry environment like White Sands in New Mexico to the high humidity of Florida, it might very well expand. This makes the claims about growing sand more plausible.

7. The Filmed Interview Is the Best Tool to Discover and Represent Mental Landscapes

Morris has said that Freud had his couch, while he has his Interrotron. The Interrotron, a tongue-in-cheek name for a serious piece of filmmaking technology, allows Morris to film interviews in which the subject appears to be speaking and looking directly at the camera rather than off to the side. When Morris filmed *Vernon, Florida* and *Gates of Heaven*, he would put his head just to side of the camera lens while conducting interviews. The Interrotron, essentially a chain of modified teleprompters that allows both interviewer and interviewee to address each other down the central axis of the camera lens, corrected all that. The result is what Morris has dubbed "the birth of true first-person cinema" (Gourevitch 1992, 53). In Morris's films, the use of the Interrotron provides a sometimes unnerving concentration of the face, with the subject staring and speaking directly into the camera. Morris often will cut to extreme close-ups that typically feature an eye, sometimes composed with other parts of the face.

With the arrival of the Megatron, which supersedes the Interrotron, Morris can use up to twenty cameras to record every movement and twitch of his interviewees. It is as though Morris would like to interview the subjects' minds or souls directly but must be content with this material manifestation of the head and face.

Morris rejects the idea that technology impedes intimacy, citing the examples of the telephone and email. The Interrotron and Megatron create intimacy, he believes, by giving spectators a more detailed representation of the human face. The human face has long been recognized as one of the essential features of all of film. The early Hungarian film theorist Béla Balázs wrote that the close-up is foundational to the cinema because it shows us the human face that hearkens back to prelinguistic communication, "the expressive movement, the gesture, that is the mother-tongue of the human race" (Balázs 1972, 42). Human responses to the face, whether it is photographically represented or actually present, are powerful, and the face can be remarkably expressive of interior states.[1]

Morris became interested in the interview while a graduate student at Berkeley, where he interviewed mass murderers as research for his unfinished dissertation on criminal responsibility and the insanity plea. Morris has been interviewing people ever since, and the interview is his most important filmmaking technique. The filmed interview provides an account not merely of what was said, as does an interview recorded on the printed page, but also how it was said. The manifestation of language in voice, gesture, facial expression, and posture contribute greatly to the value of the filmed interview, and make it one of the essential tools of the documentary filmmaker. This is especially true for a filmmaker such as Errol Morris, who is less interested in the surface features of the visual world than in the interiority of the human mental landscape.

8. Spoken Words, Written Language, and Other Visual Symbols Are Sources of Both Illumination and Mystification

Given the importance of interviews in Morris's work, it is not surprising to learn that what is said in the interviews is the central structuring principle in his films. Morris's interviews are the script upon which everything else is based. His reenactments illustrate what is said. His use of footage from old movies likewise illustrates what is said. Morris's questions, sometimes heard on the soundtrack, are often responses to what was said previously. The structure of his films is rooted in what is said in the interviews.

Morris is interested in more than *what* is said; he is also fascinated by how people talk, about how they express their inner world through language. Language is the imperfect means by which the persons who inhabit these mental landscapes communicate with each other. Through language we learn about each other and the world. Although I do not know of an instance in which Morris directly addresses the issue of language and reality, it would make little sense of him to deny the benefits of language in the pursuit of truth, given his position on epistemic realism and the place of representation within that epistemology.

Yet for philosophical realists like Morris, nothing guarantees that representations will lead to truth; they may just as easily lead to lies and distortions. In much of his work, Morris seems fascinated with written language and other visual symbols not as guarantors of truth but almost as fetish objects that have a material significance of their own, or that might lead to misleading fixations on framing ideas or concepts. Morris began to infuse his films with language and symbols in *The Thin Blue Line* and has been doing so ever since. In *The Thin Blue Line* Morris punctuates the dozens of interviews with shots that illustrate the visual detritus of memory—newspaper headlines and stories, license plates, diagrams of the murder site, maps of Dallas, police reports, television listings from *TV Guide*, motel signs, court drawings, the personality test of a psychologist ("Dr. Death"), street signs, and the keys of a typewriter.

Sometimes these serve the basic function of informing the spectator of important dates or other required information. More often, however, Morris seems to be commenting on the nature of memory itself as built on isolated and tenuous bits of visual images, words, and symbols. Morris often cuts to extreme close-ups of words or phrases isolated from their contexts, for example, "stopped for," "oh, my gosh," "guilty," "no description." He also includes the grainy and indistinct photographs of various persons as they are reproduced on newsprint. What is interesting is that the closer the camera gets to these reproduced photographs, the grainier and less distinct they become. Perhaps this is a metaphor for the search for truth under many circumstances.

9. The Exploration of Mental Landscapes Requires Film Techniques That Are Creative, Intrusive, and Which Manipulate and/or Alter Visual Reality

It is well known that Morris rejects the call of many cinéma vérité filmmakers to remain as unobtrusive as possible in the making of a documentary, as though she or he were the proverbial fly on the wall. Where cinéma vérité filmmakers called for the unobtrusive and unmanipulated capture of the reality before the camera, Morris films staged events, constructs and carefully lights sets, and uses old movie footage to illustrate the interior lives of his subjects. Morris has criticized *cinéma vérité* for assuming that correct technique would "guarantee truth," to which Morris responds that no technique guarantees truth, and in fact, nothing guarantees truth. The *cinéma vérité* practitioner might respond that she or he never assumed that to be the case and that Morris's criticisms are somewhat unfair. At the heart of the issue, in my opinion, is not that one method naively promises truth but rather that the particular methods of *cinéma vérité*, which highlight the visible surfaces of the world and exterior events, are ill-suited to explore the invisible mental landscapes that fascinate Morris. It is for this reason that Morris favors the interview as a key to his inner exploration and examines the use of language as a key to interiority.

If film is essentially a sensual medium, relying on images and sounds that are processed by the spectator in ways similar to extra-filmic perceptual reality, then the challenge facing Morris is to find ways to represent interiority using a medium that favors the exterior. His predominant method is to use visual images to illustrate the interior life of his subjects. For *The Thin Blue Line* Morris staged various versions of Robert Wood's murder to illustrate the testimony of various witnesses. Careful to note that none of these staged scenes is meant to represent the truth, Morris has steadfastly claimed that what they do illustrate is the subjective testimony of the witnesses. For *A Brief History of Time*, Morris constructed a set to appear like Stephen Hawking's office rather than use Hawking's actual office. The final shots of *Fast, Cheap & Out of Control* were shot in a topiary garden with a crew of over forty, using rain towers, cranes, and other equipment. As Morris relates, a friend remarked, "Well, you may be a fly-on-the-wall, but it's a five hundred ton fly-on-the-wall" (Slattery 1997). For Morris, inner truth—mental landscapes—is not best discovered by respecting the surface features of visible reality. Various creative techniques are best suited to represent and suggest such landscapes.

One consistent hallmark of Morris's style is his use of archival footage and clips from old movies and television to illustrate the testimony of his subjects. The most famous of these is also one of the earliest. When Morris interviews Emily Miller, a notoriously unreliable witness in the case against Randall Adams, she reveals a desire to "be the wife of a detective or to be a detective." Morris illustrates this testimony with shots from *Boston Blackie*, a black-and-white TV detective show. In "Mr. Debt," an episode of *First Person*, Morris interviews lawyer and consumer advocate Andrew Capoccia (at the time of this writing in prison for fraud and theft), who presents himself as a champion of the consumer in the face of threatening corporate giants. Morris uses uncredited footage from an old swashbuckler, as a swordsman hacks his way through a throng of attackers. Morris asks him if this is a David and Goliath story, and he replies that it is. Morris cuts to scenes of David fighting Goliath from an uncredited film about that Biblical story.

It is certainly plausible that images from movies and television provide some of the flora and fauna that litter our mental landscapes. Morris says that these clips are designed to delve into the interior lives of his subjects, or what he calls "the Whitman's sampler inside our brains" (ibid.). Yet the footage is typically from campy older films that suggest an aura of the ridiculous. Some of the footage is designed as a kind of neutral commentary on the testimony being presented, but much of it clearly undermines the testimony in its association with farcical images from B films and television. It might be objected that while this found footage is humorous, its value as an illustration of the subjects' actual mental landscapes is tenuous at best. Yet it does fit with Morris's skepticism and pessimistic view of the human epistemic condition.

10. The Human Story Is a Tragicomedy

Morris was criticized for what some saw as his sympathetic treatment of Robert McNamara in *The Fog of War*. Alexander Cockburn, for example, calls the film a "cop-out" and finds it easy to see McNamara as an evil mass murderer (Cockburn 2004, 9). For Morris, however, all of humanity is blinkered, hypocritical, deluded, and self-serving. Perhaps McNamara's faults are exaggerated and his evil deeds compounded only because he was put into a position of military authority during a time of war. Perhaps Morris believes that if any of us deserves a fair hearing, then McNamara does also. Or perhaps Morris believes that the issues of guilt and responsibility for the deaths that occurred during the Vietnam War are not as simple as Cockburn believes. Yet although Morris clearly disapproves of much of McNamara's past behavior (during the Vietnam war Morris had been a protester), he treats the man with a modicum of respect. (As I mentioned above, he agreed to let McNamara add ten theses of his own on the special features section of *The Fog of War* DVD to assuage McNamara's criticism of Morris's eleven theses in the film).

Morris's two earliest films, however—*Gates of Heaven* and *Vernon, Florida*—are widely thought to ridicule their subjects. There he turns his camera, for example, on an enthusiastic turkey hunter with particularly bad storytelling skills, a country preacher whose scripture for his sermon is the word "therefore," and a pet owner who sings a duet with her dog. One senses Morris's amused disdain on the other side of the camera. Morris's response to this charge of ridicule is worth quoting at length:

[I]n many of my earlier films, I was told that I was setting people up for ridicule. I used to defend myself—usually, by denying it. Now, I am less excited about doing so. Properly considered, filmmakers in general and documentary filmmakers in particular should not be creating ads for humanity. "*Wow. Look how great the human race is. I never thought that being human could be so wonderful*" [Morris's emphasis]. Nor should I be protecting my subjects from themselves. If they are ridiculous, why can't I show that? Does it make the other humans nervous? Am I writing ad copy for some kind of television program on Neptune on why the human race should be allowed to continue? Do I have to show us to our best advantage? (Morris 2005a).

A column on Morris's website "The Grump" reveals Morris at his most misanthropic. There he explains that he is a "secular anti-humanist" because "religion is pretty nasty and so is mankind." In another column, Morris notes that when confused about human behavior, simply imagine that the people in question are gorillas or big monkeys. He says he finds this to be very helpful: "Once we have dispossessed ourselves of the notion that we are rational, consistent or even make sense, then we are in a much better position to analyze our own behavior and the behavior of others. Big monkeys. That's what we are. And by that I mean no disrespect to monkeys."[2]

Not only are humans nothing more than big apes, but Morris believes that we are apes destined to come to a bad end. Morris has a long-term interest in morbidity—in murder (*The Thin Blue Line*), pet cemeteries and pet owners' beliefs about what happens to animals after they die (*Gates of Heaven*), mass deaths during wartime (*The Fog of War*), what would happen to someone if she or he were to fall into a black hole (*A Brief History of Time*), and execution (*Mr. Death*). In his online column "The Grump," in an entry entitled "The Last Dingdong of Doom," Morris writes about the 1949 Nobel Prize banquet speech given by William Faulkner. After questioning the meaning of Faulkner's beautiful but enigmatic language, Morris quotes the author: "Our tragedy today is a general and universal physical fear so long sustained by now that we can even bear it. There are no longer problems of the spirit. There is only the question: When will I be blown up?" "Hear, hear," Morris responds. Then he answers Faulkner's question: "Soon, very soon."[3]

Beginning with *The Thin Blue Line*, Morris's films show more sympathy for humanity. Has Morris become more sympathetic, or simply more politic? For whatever reason, his later works definitely allow his sympathies for his fellow primates to emerge. Despite his misanthropy and pessimism, Morris is not without what Adam Smith called "fellow-feeling," the compassion or pity humans feel when confronted with the pain or suffering of others (Smith 1984, 5). Thus Morris has spoken often of his care in the treatment of the foolishly self-deceived Fred Leuchter in *Mr. Death*, whom he describes as "a completely benighted human being who still deserves our sympathy" (Singer 1999, 39). Morris shows us Leuchter's most vehement detractors as some pronounce judgments with a quick readiness to identify and locate pure evil in the man. Shelly Shapiro says of Leuchter: "There is no slippery slope for Mr. Fred Leuchter. The man is an anti-Semite. There are hate-mongers in this country, and he's one of them." After having learned something of Leuchter's biography and the complexities of his personality, such pronouncements seem not only simplistic but void of the sympathy Morris clearly takes toward Leuchter.

Morris is proud of having exonerated an innocent man in *The Thin Blue Line,* and his skeptical treatment of the witnesses for the prosecution (such as Emily Miller, mentioned above) show where his sympathies lie. His use of Randall Adams's two original defense lawyers (Edith James and David White) is pertinent here, since Morris clearly takes their side in a collective sadness about Randall Adams's conviction and death sentence. As the accumulated evidence of Randall Adams's innocence becomes convincing, Morris shows us David White revealing that this case has affected him so deeply that he will quit practicing trial law. The placement of this revelation lends it Morris's imprimatur, as though White's reactions have the director's full support. For Morris, the human condition is both laughable and hopeless, yet human beings ought to battle injustice and pity its victims.

As a master storyteller and perpetual student of humanity, one imagines Errol Morris turning his camera-microscope on his subjects. He has an amused look on his face as he discovers yet more evidence of the weaknesses and oddities of the subjects being "Interrotroned" or "Megatroned." Yet Morris realizes that he is also one of those benighted primates and is able to treat his subjects not solely with disdain or indifference but, in some cases, as a sympathetic observer and even a collaborator in the tenuous search for truth and justice. There is more than a hint of sadness and pity here. The story of humanity, for Morris, is not merely a dark comedy but a tragicomedy.

Notes

1. For more on the use of the human face in film, see my "The Scene of Empathy and the Human Face on Film," in Carl Plantinga and Greg M. Smith,

eds., *Passionate Views: Film, Cognition, and Emotion* (Baltimore: Johns Hopkins University Press, 1999), 239–55.

2. http://www.errolmorris.com/content/grump/grump8.html, (accessed October 16, 2006).

3. http://www.errolmorris.com/content/grump/grump6.html, (accessed October 16, 2006.

PART 2

Ross McElwee:
I Film, Therefore I Am

4

DIANE STEVENSON

Coincidence in Ross McElwee's Documentaries

UR CULTURE BELIEVES IN CAUSALITY and does not believe in coinci-dence. Theorists have attempted to define narrative in terms of cau-sality, as if there were no narrative connections other than those of cause and effect. But in the ancient story it was by coincidence that Oedipus killed his father and married his mother. In a work of today such a play of coincidence is thought implausible, the notion of fate or destiny mostly discredited. The naturalistic novel made use of coincidence to express a social and biological determinism, but in our time any kind of determinism, any sense of life as foreordained, is regarded as an out-moded way of thinking. Our empirical age looks down on coincidence, finds it contrived, unconvincing, smacking of metaphysics.

Documentary is nothing if not empirical. We may tolerate co-incidence in a far-fetched comedy, in a tale of the fantastic, but in a documentary? And yet in his documentaries Ross McElwee avails himself of coincidence and succeeds in making it work. What kind of storyteller is he? What does this way of telling stories have to do with the storytelling of Southern writers who kept up the narrative tradition of coincidence? How does it relate to the very different tradition of documentary filmmaking? How does it fit in with the way McElwee makes documentaries in the first person, with the filmmaker entering prominently into the film?[1] These are questions I take up in the discussion that follows.

When I first watched McElwee's *Bright Leaves* (2003), a film in which he tells the story of his great-grandfather and the tobacco industry in the South, I was struck by the role coincidence plays in it. The only other Ross McElwee film I had seen was *Sherman's March* (1986), his best-known work. I remembered the repeated, but apparently offhand, references to Burt Reynolds in that film, which reach a climax near the end when, as it turns out, the movie star and the documentary filmmaker happen to be in North Carolina at the same time and happen to meet—or rather, a meeting is made to happen because they happen to be in the same place at the same time. McElwee takes advantage of his chance and finagles an encounter. He doesn't really manage an interview; he is shooed off by guards, but through sheer bluff, he gets close enough with his camera so that he and Reynolds are together in a place off-limits to almost everyone else. He has made it to an inner circle, and the two of them are there, coincidentally if not intimately. This coincidence is the stuff of fiction, not of real life. It's the stuff of contrivance, not documentary. Still, it happens.

After repeated mentions of Burt Reynolds's name, he appears in the flesh—implausibly, yet as if invoked. Or not exactly in the flesh. Let's put it this way. After repeated mentions of a name indicating a real person, there appears an image associated with the name: an image that represents the real person of that name. Two representations or signs for Burt Reynolds, each indicating a real Burt Reynolds but neither one giving us the real Burt Reynolds: one is a word, the other is an image, a documentary image. After all, in his movie McElwee did not walk up to a screen showing a clip from a Burt Reynolds movie or, for that matter, a home movie of Burt as a child, two different representations entirely; he walked up to Burt Reynolds occupying the same time and space as Ross McElwee at that place in that present. Watching the film we are not, of course, presented with Burt Reynolds in the flesh in our present. We are dealing with representations, and what is striking about McElwee's documentaries is the number of ways he makes them signify without breaking conventions that would take us out of the documentary sense of reality—and into the world of fiction. Not even an inordinate cropping up of coincidence does that.

Let me give you the dictionary definitions (*Merriam Webster's Collegiate Dictionary*) of "coincide," "coincidence," and "coincidental."

- *Coincide*: to occupy the same place in space or time; to occupy exactly corresponding or equivalent positions on a scale or in a series; to correspond in nature, scale, or function; to be in accord or agreement; also, any of these occurrences.

- *Coincidence*: the act or condition of coinciding; the occurrence of events that happen at the same time by accident but seem to have some connection also.

- *Coincidental:* resulting from a coincidence; occurring or existing at the same time.

McElwee's meeting with Reynolds was a coincidence: the two came together by accident but seem to have some connection also. That is, it happened that Reynolds was in North Carolina, but there is also the way in which the design of McElwee's film gives his meeting with Reynolds a connection, a meaning.

"Coincidence" carries the sense of accident, chance, happenstance. But when coincidence becomes part of the design of a work it carries the sense of fate, destiny. (And often in fiction, the sense of fate or destiny carries with it a sense of the uncanny.) Coincidence as happenstance fits into documentary: this is the way things happen in real life, by accident, without design. But a documentary film is not just a record of random events, what happened to happen; it is also an arrangement of events into some kind of design that connects them together and gives them a meaning. It is McElwee's task as an artist—an artist documenting life—to reconcile coincidence as happenstance, as chance, with coincidence as design, as fate or destiny.

At the beginning of *Time Indefinite* (1993), McElwee—who hadn't been able, or hadn't been ready or willing, in *Sherman's March* to find a woman to settle down with—finally gets married, which is something his father had always wanted. And then McElwee and his wife are expecting a child, which is also a fulfillment of his father's wishes. Unfortunately, his wife has a miscarriage, and his father dies, suddenly, right after. Is this coincidence as happenstance, or coincidence as destiny? Somehow in McElwee's film it works as both. His marriage and child—the child he and his wife eventually get to have but his father doesn't live to see—are a reconciliation with his father that only comes about after his father's death. This is tragic but also fitting. That was the way things happened, and it seems meaningful that they happened that way. To McElwee the actor, the participant in his own life, they happened that way by chance. To McElwee the filmmaker, the writer, the narrator, they have a connection, a meaning.

This leads me to a coincidence central to all of McElwee's work: in his person coincide roles normally played by different persons in the making of a film, the roles of cinematographer, sound man, editor, director, writer, actor, and agent in the story. McElwee the actor, the participant in events, may have met Burt Reynolds by happenstance or may, by happenstance, not have had a child until after his father was dead and buried. But McElwee the writer, the narrator, the shaper of the film, seems to have designed the meeting with Reynolds and the reconciliation with the father that comes too late—or if he hasn't designed it, at least he has incorporated each event into the design of the film so as to make a connection, a meaning.[2]

It's important to remember that McElwee is a writer. His voice-over narration may come across as unobtrusive, in part because of his soft Southern delivery. The images may appear to dictate the words. The images themselves may appear to be following only a roughly sketched-out program with plenty of room for improvisation; nothing appears written in stone. Yet the writing is precise, even elegant—not only the writing of the voice-over narration but the arrangement of things in sequence, which is also a kind of writing. Like the images themselves, apparently casual, the writing is precise and elegant.

Ross McElwee is indeed a writer.

Many of the formal terms for talking about films come from literary studies: first-person narrator, point of view, author (auteur), narration, omniscient narrator, reliable narrator, unreliable narrator, comedy, melodrama, etc. But there is another set of terms for discussing film, terms that come from production: camera, camera angle, cut, lighting, actor, director, producer, studio, editor, scriptwriter, and so on. The two vocabularies do not make a comfortable fit (perhaps like making Old English conform to Latin grammar, it never really works out). The coincidence in McElwee of the roles of cinematographer and writer, actor and narrator makes these roles clearer, more visible to us in the audience than they normally are. Instead of these different roles being confused, they're made easier to sort out. There's clarity on both sides of the equation—the film side and the literary side. This is in part because each of the roles McElwee plays has a discretely assigned spatial and temporal place.

When McElwee stands behind the camera, he is in the place of the person making the movie in two of its aspects: cameraman, and soundman. What he sees the camera sees; what he hears the sound system picks up—because it's in his hands (or rather, it's electronically synchronized with his camera). During the filming he also plays a third role from behind the camera: as a kind of interviewer, as someone who interacts with the people he is recording.

When McElwee stands in front of the camera, he has either set up the camera to film himself, and is sitting in front of it alone, or he has aimed the camera at a mirror or a reflecting window. He speaks to the audience in a voice that resembles the voice-over narration, but this voice comes to us from the time of filming rather than the later time of editing and organizing the film, which is the time frame of the voice-over narration. Sometimes he sits on a bench, say, or walks through a bit of landscape—with pumpkins and, unexpectedly, a yapping dog—and this is filmed by someone else, perhaps even a crew, because in the yapping dog take, we see him signal "cut." During filming, his role in front of the camera is different from his role behind the camera, as well as from his role later on as editor and voice-over narrator.

For the most part McElwee is the observer and narrator, but some-times he takes a more active part in events, as when he pushes one of his girlfriends in *Sherman's March* to explain why she gave him up in favor of someone else. His voice-over narration frames the footage, perhaps unflatteringly as he attempts to make a case for himself by forcing her to make a better case for the other man. Offhand, I can't remember any other scene in which we see him play such a blatant part, except perhaps for the scene with Charleen in *Time Indefinite* when he encourages her to go ahead and spread the ashes of her husband over the waters near her house. McElwee's principal role as observer or narrator frames or mediates his other activities.

There is a literary intelligence at work here, and one that throws interesting light on literary matters and the semiotics of representa-tion and, not least of all, genre, although not much room will be given here to the latter, very interesting topic. Investigations of issues like representation have often been biased toward the verbal and against the visual. Theorists of art who worked from a more evenhanded, less verbally slanted semiotics do come to mind—the art historians E. H. Gombrich and Erwin Panofsky, for example. Michel Foucault, however, isn't on the list. In his famous essay "This is Not a Pipe," his semiotics was not up to his subject's, the painter René Magritte. Magritte knew that the visual, too, was a language, and Foucault, depending on the linguist Ferdinand de Saussure, who was understandably interested primarily in verbal signs, wasn't receptive to and didn't see Magritte's play with perspective. Magritte treated perspective as a convention, a sign like any other: a representation. Foucault took perspective as real (that, at least, is what his essay implies, and how it reads). Thus he missed Magritte's visual and as well as verbal puns. Like Magritte (and unlike the more limited Foucault) McElwee plays with representation.

Let's return for a moment to the meeting of Ross McElwee with Burt Reynolds. The two coincide in more than one way, not only in coming together in space and time but in the fact that they're both

Southerners who have moved elsewhere but are now back in the South, and that they're both in the movies, both actors who act in films they direct. How does this translate into fame and celebrity? Reynolds has the bigger share. He encounters his fans with apparent reluctance, and also charm. This is not the same Reynolds that McElwee catches up to in the restricted, off-limits area later on. Reynolds is not as eager and kiss-happy now. He's ready to be left alone. In the conventional documentary sense there isn't much payoff here. Reynolds doesn't stamp his foot, shove, or pout. Nor is there mutual recognition and male bonding. Not much revelation at all. Reynolds simply watches as McElwee is escorted away. The real impact of the scene is the coincidence itself.

An extreme of coincidence is doubling: one man disguised as another runs into his original; a twin runs into his or her twin. This is a very old technique in comedy, when the coincidence in time and space raises issues of identity: Who are these characters? What are their places in society? This indeed happens with Reynolds and McElwee. They are doubles of each other, and there is something comical about their coincidental meeting—comical in part because we are aware of the discrepancy between Reynolds' role (and popularity) in American film culture and McElwee's, and the joke that McElwee plays by being the empowered stalker, empowered because he is the director of a movie that Reynolds is only acting in—however involuntarily. He is both who he is, a filmmaker, and who he is in reference to Reynolds, another groupie grasping for an autograph or, in this case, a picture. But the tables really are turned. The carnival reversal is true. The joke really is on Reynolds, and doubly so because McElwee has admitted that at least half the joke is on him, and here we have part of a Southern tradition, the tradition we have tended to call Southwest humor, the country bumpkin who takes in the city slicker by pretending to be what the city slicker sees, a country bumpkin. We are still in the realm of representation, and how representation gets played out, and what that has to do with society and its hierarchical valuations and violations.

In *Bright Leaves* Gary Cooper is a double of McElwee's great-grandfather: in a Warner Brothers melodrama called *Bright Leaf* (1950) Cooper plays a character McElwee thinks was inspired by his great-grandfather. The joke here is on McElwee when it turns out that the character was actually based not only on McElwee's great-grandfather, the good guy of family lore, but also on the bad guy of family lore, the Duke tobacco baron who drove McElwee's great-grandfather out of business. As for the meeting between Reynolds and McElwee, let's ask again, who is mirroring whom? In what role? What kind of joke is this? Who is the butt of the joke? Because McElwee is self-deprecating, he calls the joke down on himself, but because of his humility he can't be further humbled, so the joke can only be on Reynolds. Even though in *Bright Leaves* the joke is on McElwee, still it works in his favor because, just as in *Sherman's March* our sympathy lies with McElwee rather than Reynolds, so in *Bright Leaves* our sympathy is with the great-grandfather who lost out in the capitalist tobacco game and the spread of cancer to the Duke baron. McElwee muses on a lost fortune, but there's compensation: less guilt. And this parallels the racial theme that runs through his films—how you, a white Southerner, love and need the South but must also face its legacy of slavery. It's a tough subject to narrate. (It's a tough representation to investigate.) Faulkner, at the close of *Absalom, Absalom*, offered one solution: an unreliable narrator repeating several times something like a double negative, "I don't hate the South." McElwee's narrator is more detached. He doubles up his subjects—the South with family, friends, and lovers and with filmmaking, throwing in along the way (along the road) lots of apparent digressions, apparent coincidences that comment back and forth, making of his personal films complicated rhetorical feats—both verbally and visually.

McElwee is sensitive to arrangements of place, literally and metaphorically, including arrangements of caste, of class, of race. *Backyard* (1984) is a story both about his family and about a black couple who works for his family and whose place is in the kitchen and in the backyard. His grandmother sings a song about a "pickaninny" whose "mammy" consoles him because the white children won't play with him by telling him to keep to his own backyard, to stay in his place. His grandmother's racism is blatant; she sings an overtly racist song. In the next generation, in his mother's relations with her black servant, the racial paternalism seems more benign but is still marked by the same divisions and still expressed in the same spatial terms, the kitchen and the backyard. There are complex doublings here. Let's try to sort this out.

Constance Rourke, best known in American studies for her influential book *American Humor*, had this to say about Edgar Allan Poe: that he took doubling from comedy (familiar to us from Shakespeare) and turned it to a different use in his gothic stories, and she described these stories as on the "brink of psychological discernment." A three-quarter century after Rourke, we more commonly associate doubling with gothic storytelling, with genres like horror, science fiction, and mystery and suspense, though we still enjoy the mistaken identities of comedy. Of course, the founders of psychoanalysis, like Rourke and like us, also went to gothic stories when they wanted to ponder doubling. E. T. A. Hoffmann features in both Otto Rank's "The Double" and Sigmund Freud's "The Uncanny." But Rourke was right to bring comedy into the mix. She considers Poe in a tradition of American humor. McElwee belongs to a tradition of Southern comedy and he belongs to a tradition of Southern gothic, and the two belong together—we've seen it in regional writers like Erskine Caldwell, Flannery O'Connor, Carson McCullers, and William Faulkner. When modernism is added to the mixture, as it certainly is with Faulkner, additional repetition and coincidence, though of another kind with another purpose, pop up. The stew gets thicker, and the question of representation gets more urgent. Let's suggest that by coming along later, McElwee was spared that particular urgency—that anxiety. But McElwee's stories, too, like the modernist's, are stories about how stories are told.

So far, the coincidences I have talked about in reference to McElwee's films have veered on the spatial side of things rather than the temporal. His films usually proceed in chronological order with clearly specified flashbacks. But alongside this linear progression in time, there is another sense of time connected with customs and ceremonies of family and community, and coincidence is built into this communal, cyclical, repetitive time. Let me just mention one scene in *Bright Leaves*, the last ever Tobacco Parade, the 150th, because ever after it is to be dubbed the Farmers' Day Festival. It's no longer possible merely to celebrate tobacco; the cancer it causes is too controversial an issue. So the harvest celebration has to have a makeover, a name change, and the small town where the parade takes place and McElwee takes his camera is trading in one name for another. The floats pass by and also the tobacco queen and her maids—a long series of beauty queens in a long line of open cars. They sit on top of the back seats. The oldest comes first, so they are staggered by size. They get smaller and smaller (so do their crowns), a perspective line leading back as they proceed forward.

The paved road, the cars, the straight route they take is a curiously modern symbol for an old agricultural festival: a clash of two ways of counting time: one progressive and linear, the other seasonal and cyclical. McElwee points out the lawn mowers, the kind you sit on and drive, performing a precision drill. They are drawing circles in the road, a counter to the other straight-ahead lines. Could one of these have been the mower, McElwee asks, that displaced the headstone of his great-grandfather—a small headstone in contrast to the huge and ornate Duke tombs—in the graveyard he and his cousins visited earlier in the film? And somehow we have come full circle—back to his great-grandfather, back to death—a recurring theme in the film—and back specifically to the discussion of that gravestone's displacement and the discussion that it must have been a mower that did it: through this, another, if minor, coincidence.

Notes

1. Nanni Moretti (*Caro Diario*) is another writer-filmmaker who makes first-person autobiographical films. He acts in his films; he supplies the voice-over narration, but in other ways the production of his films is like the production of ordinary films. It's the simple fact that McElwee does everything himself (or almost everything) that complicates what he does.

2. Conventionally, a novel, a play, or a poem is seen as the work of one author; a movie is seen as the work of many. When the French critics at *Cahiers du cinéma* began looking at classic Hollywood cinema as auteur cinema, they shook things up. By assigning clear narrative jobs to specific filmmaking jobs, and thus creating a coherent formal vocabulary for speaking about narrative in film, and doing it, of all places, in documentary filmmaking, McElwee has shaken things up again.

5

MARIAN KEANE

Reflections on *Bright Leaves*

I F WE DIDN'T ALREADY KNOW IT FROM *Sherman's March* or other of his films, we have only to look at *Bright Leaves* to see that Ross McElwee is completely charmed and disarmed by any group of pretty Southern women: consider the spell cast on him by the beauty parlor students or the beauty queens. And we learn again from *Bright Leaves* that he has a gift for presenting people in their uniqueness, and for appreciating human beings so much that they remain intact as *subjects*. His achievement in presenting human beings is extraordinary in the medium of documentary film, where people often remain unnamed, for example, and seem to exist in the world of the film as if suspended from their relation to their actual lives. McElwee's filming of human beings—the way he films them—sheds light on his procedure for studying *Bright Leaf*, the 1950s Hollywood movie that seems to be based on his great-grandfather's life, in which he searches for evidence of human truth of the stars who performed in the film. Or if this claim seems to be a stretch, then I ask only that you think about the relation between McElwee's presentation of human beings throughout *Bright Leaves* and the way he pays attention to, and the questions he asks of, the moments of *Bright Leaf* he incorporates, surely as subjects for study, within his own film.

McElwee's films now compose an oeuvre and call for being studied as such, for their connections to and revelations of each other. *Time Indefinite* made us aware of the weight Ross felt upon the birth of his son, Adrian, one year after the death of his father. *Time Indefinite* ends on an optimistic note (a close up of Adrian as a baby that Ross's wife Marilyn comically dubbed "the gerbil shot"), but one can sense that Ross feels deeply that he is his son's connection to his grandfather and that life had handed Ross the challenge of not only becoming a father but of representing his own father at the same time.

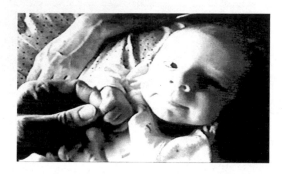

My feeling at the end of *Time Indefinite* was, when I first saw the film, and remains now, after successive viewings, that the filmmaker wishes to find a way of his own to do what his father was doing so vividly when, on a sunlit deck during the family's summer vacation, he held a baby up in the air.

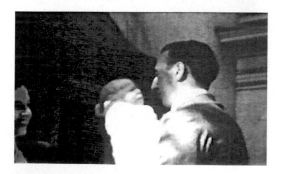

"My father could do this all day and never get tired," he says over this image. It is not this particular gesture Ross wishes to perform, or so I have always thought. It is what this particular gesture showed about his father, in relation to his children and grandchildren—the happiness of it, the confidence of it, the fun of it, the strength of it.

Bright Leaves picks up where *Time Indefinite* leaves off. It poses the question of how the filmmaker is going to connect his son to his

North Carolina legacy; it asks whether film can be a medium of life, by which I mean—and I admit this is a cloudy idea—a medium both in the aesthetic sense and in the spiritual sense. Can film provide a vivid enough accounting, representation, or expression to enable us to make real contact with a time, a way of life, and most importantly, people now gone? The question is complicated—as complicated as the question of what film is, what filming is, what film viewing is.

The issues *Bright Leaves* raises with regard to filmmaking center on the reasons Ross McElwee films, and his reflections on this question constitute the central meditations of the film. The issues of film viewing are addressed throughout the film in several ways; for the moment, suffice it to say that the filmmaker presents explicit and implicit accounts of how to view film images. The most explicit lesson in film viewing occurs when he studies *Bright Leaf* for signs of "home-movie content" or "authentic emotion." This sequence is one of many that offer guidance, I think, for viewing *Bright Leaves*.

In pondering such questions about film as a medium, *Bright Leaves* engages—partly as metaphor, partly as a kind of replacement for the home-movie footage Ross and other family members have shot, and partly in high contrast to documentary film as a form—a classical Hollywood film that contains or deploys all the things home movies or documentaries do not: a director, a screenwriter, the wizardry of Hollywood, the magic and accomplishment of movie stars, a made-to-order musical score, melodramatic emotions and gestures. *Bright Leaf* is also a black-and-white film—possibly its most obvious difference from *Bright Leaves*.

The passage that, to my mind, most overtly focuses and externalizes the subjects and procedures of *Bright Leaves* is the sequence of Ross filming at his North Carolina hotel—the sequence in which that snarky rat makes its cameo appearance. The passage, as it progresses, cuts to footage of Adrian learning to tie knots and so recalls the earlier home-movie sequence of the father patiently teaching Ross's brother Tom to tie sutures. There are differences in the scenes: Ross' father is teaching hands-on; Ross is watching Adrian and not teaching hands-on. How can the two be compared? Perhaps in response to this, in the next sequence Ross takes Adrian on a film shoot and demonstrates how to clap the microphone to create a slate that is essential to editing, a further phase of filmmaking.

Within *Bright Leaves*, the motel sequence is preceded by the scene in which Ross recovers from Patricia Neal's flat rejection of his "little theory" that *Bright Leaf* contains "home-movie content," revelations of the real lives of the human beings who appear in the film, even as it surrenders to the "wanton, melodramatic power [and] shimmering beauty" of Hollywood studio production. For the second time in his film—the

first being when he was studying *Bright Leaf* in advance of his meeting
with Ms. Neal—the filmmaker allows the Hollywood movie to flood
the screen of his movie. It is an important gesture in *Bright Leaves*, one
that all but obliterates Ross as director. Later in the film, though, when
he learns that *Bright Leaf* actually has no direct (or at least intentional)
connection to his great-grandfather's life, *Bright Leaves* takes a downward
turn, too, in the sequence of Ross's visit to the tobacco museum, where
the mannequin of a disturbingly angry nurse dominates the cigarette rolling machine on display. When Ross turns to *Bright Leaf* at that juncture,
the Hollywood film becomes a horror film—an image of a dark, twisted
world in which his great-grandfather has been converted from hero into
monster, a dyad fused with the historical villain, Mr. Duke. For the filmmaker, *Bright Leaf* has undergone a metamorphosis from a romantic home
movie in which his great-grandfather pursues justice, into a nightmare.
It is not surprising, on some level, that he moves from this reflection
to the Duke Chapel and films the marble statues atop the sarcophagi of
the Duke patriarch and his son.

The motel sequence is prompted, within the film, by Ross's immersion in *Bright Leaf*. For the first time, at this juncture, he views it as
nothing personal, as bearing no relation to his own project as a filmmaker
or to his theory of film. This is, so to speak, the ground on which he
finds himself as he starts out, once again, to film. The sequence that
follows is a meditation on why he films, why he films at all.

To start finding out why he films, to discover his sources and resources, the filmmaker pursues his ostensible other subject, smoking and
its grip on people, by filming a cleaning woman at his motel—a smoker
of long-standing, it turns out, who notes sweetly that she has divulged
a secret to Ross: her age. (Just for the record, I wouldn't divulge mine,
even if Ross McElwee were filming me.) This brief exchange in many
respects invokes the tradition of *cinéma vérité* in which Ross works (i.e.,
filming what's right there). By opening with a close-up of an ashtray
being wiped clean, the exchange subtly sustains the recurring motif in
Bright Leaves, the suggestion that the legacy that history has left to this
filmmaker is garbage (e.g., the storing of junk even more useless than the
junk in the junk store in his great-grandfather's former building).

Following his exchange with the cleaning woman, Ross begins a
meditation on his filming. "It doesn't matter what I'm filming," he says,
over a long shot of the parking lot and the evenly spaced trash cans
that punctuate the motel portico. "Even shooting around a hotel can be
an almost narcotic experience," he adds, over a shot of a single white
trashcan squarely in the frame, the image compositionally bisected by a
wooden post and filmed in very clear light.

"I mean, I don't want to force an analogy, but, come to think of it, for me, filming is not unlike smoking a cigarette." We view the back of a parked car, gleaming in the sun. These three images deliberately challenge the idea that only Hollywood films can provide shimmering images; the consistent element of these shots is, in fact, the light in them. The film cuts to a shot of the sky, taken from inside a car. The image contains small red lines cutting horizontally through the frame, interposed between the camera and the billowy clouds floating on the pale blue sky. "When I look through a viewfinder, time seems to stop. A kind of timelessness is momentarily achieved."

The epicenter of the motel filming sequence is the shot that shows Ross filming in mirror reflection. The shot is a kind of play on Velasquez's famous painting *Las meninas*, and rightly enough, the most explicitly Vertovian image in the film. In it, we see Ross to frame left, his head blocked from view by the camera as he looks through its lens, to a point inside his motel room. In the center of the frame, we view a mirror reflection of the image we view, in a rectangular frame within

the frame.

I don't know how Ross managed this shot, but however he was able to take it, or make it, the question remains: Where can we say this image comes from? And what does it mean that it emanates from the filmmaker and also shows him projected back onto his own camera? How can we not understand this shot to announce that this film comes from, and projects, Ross himself?

What Ross says to us at this juncture is, "Just fooling around here, playing with exposure, depth of field, mirrors, trying to see how many special effects can be created without the use of special effects." He speaks these words as his reflected image in center frame goes out of focus and returns to focus as his camera zooms in to a close-up. "I mean, I don't even notice the large rat that's about to slip by in the background there."

Probably most of us wouldn't notice the rat if Ross didn't mention it. But it's worth noting that *he* notices the rat only when he looks at the footage later, a fact that underscores the experience of filming as he describes it elsewhere in the film—that filming encourages, or involves, a kind of trance (Jean Rouch calls it a *ciné-trance*), an absorption so complete that time seems to stop. This entrancement is an alternative to—or better, a response to—the entrancement that, as he notes, he experiences while watching a Hollywood film. It makes him oblivious of everything that does not involve the act of filming. Over the zoom/refocus gesture, the filmmaker says, after a pause, "When I'm on the road, shooting, I sometimes imagine my son, years from now, when I'm no longer around, looking at what I have filmed. I can almost feel him looking back at me from some distance point in the future, through these reflections and these reflections that I'll leave behind." Halfway through this speech, he cuts to the shoe-tying scene.

So Adrian is now, metaphorically, the "returning gaze" figured in the reflection of the mirror shot. And Ross displaces onto Adrian the mystery his own work is to himself, as the filmmaker imagines his son examining his father's footage in the future, when Ross is "no longer around" (as in a sense, Ross wasn't around when he succumbed to the fullness of the Hollywood film). Why *does* he film? What—as Vlada Petric asks and, as Ross tells us, his own father used to ask—does Ross's filming of all these shots *mean*? What is he going to *do* with them?

At this juncture, fact is, Ross doesn't really know. Over the image of Adrian and his knots, Ross says, "I'm sure Adrian won't remember the day we filmed this," melancholically envisioning his own erasure from the world and the mysteriousness of the legacy of the film images he has made and will leave behind. "I mean, I don't even remember the circumstances, what happened just before this shot or just after. "Apparently Adrian was learning to tie his shoes and apparently I just wanted to preserve the moment. . . . As usual I didn't film this for any particular reason. Just a little scene. Just a little moment."

The filmmaker cuts back to that shot of his reflection in the mirror visible in a rectangle, and of himself visible behind the camera, and returns, via a zoom, to the original long shot set-up. The scene of Adrian is bookended by the single shot of Ross zooming in on his reflection, which is projected toward us, out of the film. If we understand the zoom in on his reflection to provide a way into himself, into the subject of his filming, then we might also say that what he finds, as his subject, is his son. Although what he shows us in the knot-tying sequence is a time past, Ross also imagines it as viewed from a time future—and not just our time future, right now, but long from now. He imagines his films to present images from which he is entirely absent; he imagines, perhaps, leaving something like a heap of garbage, or an assortment of junk, enigmatic and obsessive, for his son to sort through, to try to fathom its meaning.

But this film's investigation of the meaning of filmed images—what they are, what they do, what they don't do—is complex. Consider, for example, the filmmaker's poignant discovery that although he wishes that "the sheer weight of these images" of Adrian playing in downtown Boston "could somehow keep him from growing up so fast, slow the process down," filming, of course, "doesn't slow anything down." Filming doesn't have any effect on real time. Of importance is his characterization of filmed images as having "weight," which I understand to be both tangible and intangible.

The "thing" here, for me, is what the filmmaker calls "the sheer weight" of the images. I have tried, thinking and writing about *Bright Leaves*, to stay away from sentimentality, though I know, as we all do, the "sheer weight" of the images we have taken and stored in bookcases and drawers. Images that wait for some further placement. Images we don't recall the circumstances of the taking. Images. "The sheer weight" of images."

This is a deep moment of the film for me, this singling out of the "sheer weight" of its images. I am a typical photograph-taking parent. I am not Ross McElwee, laden with so many images of "nothing moments" in the past, filmed or photographed for no reason. What *are* "nothing moments"? Moments that could be meaningful, could be memorable, could be "something"? How do you tell the difference?

But I am avoiding the topic. The hard job of a *cinéma vérité* filmmaker is to decide what is worth remembering and what is not—what is to be left on the editing room floor. So I note, first, that a whole thesis could be written on the ways Ross McElwee imagines himself in other people's skins or lives or views. Just as he imagines Adrian viewing all his footage in the future, right after this interior/exterior moment, he imagines his great-grandfather standing outside the massive Duke tobacco factory; over the shot of the castle-like building, he says, "I can imagine how my great-grandfather must have felt like a foot soldier standing outside a heavily fortified hill town."

The motel sequence identifies the filmmaker's trance in filming, his crisis in making films, his concern that each of these images of "just a moment, just a little moment," that might not come to anything, might not add up to an answer to the question Vlada Petric poses at the end of that hilarious and amazing sequence when he asks Ross, "What do you *do* with" images of "life caught unawares?". Even Vlada, who constitutionally and ideologically opposes classical Hollywood films and so sees very little value to *Bright Leaf*, acknowledges that there are documentaries that succeed, that "transcend [merely] documenting an event and [achieve] ontological authenticity, as Vertov said." Vlada declares, citing one of his favorite filmmakers, that documentary film is "Life caught unawares." (If only I could replicate beloved Vlada's *accent!*) "But then, what do you *do* with that?" Ah. Yes. For all of Vlada Petric's criticism of the bourgeois film, he asks how one makes life qua life, life "caught unawares," *dramatic.* (This is not a problem if you happen to *be* as wonderful and vivid as Vlada Petric; he is a master of the dramatic as life qua life. Even his *dog* was dramatic. Me? I am afraid I am hopelessly—especially in Vlada's view—bourgeois and even more helplessly nondramatic.)

It seems to me that this question hits home with Ross when he recalls that his father asked it of him, too. This reminds me that the place the filmmaker locates himself and declares himself to be thinking—this is an important image, and an important activity—is McElwee Park. I love that he shows us himself *thinking.* I love that he gives us an *image* of thinking. Poor philosopher that I am, I find it thought-provoking that he is alone in that place. The thought it provokes is that Ross wishes someone else would come along: He wishes his father would appear; that is the conversation he is missing, the conversation he is hoping for.

That thought returns me to *the* question of the film: What makes Ross McElwee's work meaningful? In singling out this question, and focusing my answer on fathers, on fatherhood, on connections, I am omitting much that is of importance in the film, such as the complex connections between smoking, the narcotic of it, and filming. He could take issue with me on this score, although he is such a gentleman that he would only gently tell me I've missed the point.

Recognizing that I may be missing the point, I will jump to the film's concluding sequences: the one with the boat on the ocean and that day-moon above it, and then the sequence of Adrian saving the life of that tiny fish he holds in his hand and runs toward the ocean to save. The first seems to be the "big ending" of the film, the "big picture" ending. After watching *Bright Leaves* closely I found myself—and I wouldn't say this if it weren't overwhelming—worried that the filmmaker was crossing a line here, inserting too much "home-movie content" into a Big Movie. I won't deny that I want only the best and brightest for Ross McElwee. But my worry was that I was too connected to an image of a wonderful boy in a swimsuit running toward the ocean; not *my* ocean—that's the Nantucket Sound—but some ocean and running that incredible, awkward, rushing run of a little boy. My son is one of those boys, so I cautioned myself. I paused about my relation to this set of images.

And taking caution, I thought about it. As it happened, I was reading Carl Jung at the time, and in the first chapter, there was an epigraph from Walt Whitman. After this reading and thinking, this became clear:

Bright Leaf (Cooper) + *Bright Leaves* (tobacco) = *Leaves of Grass*

Bright Leaves stakes *everything* on its last shots. You have to see them as not sentimental. The very last shot of Adrian, running away from the camera to the beach, to save the fish—well, that's Ross's son. That's the kid who isn't going to kill the fish but save it, and this is the father who's going to film that moment, but not direct it.

As for the Walt Whitman connection: I've always thought *cinéma vérité* at its best naturally connects to Whitman, the best "ordinary" poet and philosopher of America's romantic, and fully personal, quest for meaning. Not all *cinéma vérité* lives up to Whitman, to be sure, however it aspires to. (Yes, if aspirations were horses, beggars would ride.) But in the nexus of Whitman and James Agee (*Let Us Now Praise Famous Men*) lies the hope for authenticity, for originality, that gives *cinéma vérité* in America—the "capturing" of reality on film—its meaning or, I want to say, its soul, its place of origin. Any course on documentary film should assign Whitman and Agee, no matter how hard these writers are to teach. Documentary films are no less hard to teach; America is no less hard to put into images.

As for my connection of McElwee with Whitman, I ask only this: That you think for a moment of the specifics of Whitman's poetry, its specifics of physiognomy; its singing, as he calls it, of faces, and places, and the New America; its understanding of the courage needed to tell a tale—one's own tale—carefully; and then, this: The feeling "or ambition to articulate and faithfully express . . . uncompromisingly, my own physical, emotional, moral, intellectual, and aesthetic Personality, in the midst of, and tallying, the momentous spirit and facts of immediate days, and of current America—and to exploit that Personality, identified with place and date, in a far more contemplative sense than any poem or book" (Whitman 1926, 44). All I know is this: If each of us undertook every day, in every encounter, to find something of value in everyone we meet, as Walt Whitman did, and as Ross McElwee does, our world would be changed and deepened.

A. O. Scott in a *New York Times* feature called *Sherman's March* the "founding document of narci-cinema" (Scott 2004, 10). The usually astute Mr. Scott missed the point of Ross McElwee's work. *Bright Leaves* is no more narcissistic than *Leaves of Grass*. Walt Whitman made poetry, out of—what? *What?* When there was no America for Whitman to call America, still he wrote. Where was that place of which he sang? Where else but here? Where does an artist go? *Bright Leaves*, lovingly, shows us that we all wish to be the stuff of dreams, of Hollywood films enacted by the incredibly gorgeous Gary Cooper and wonderful Patricia Neal. Ross McElwee was lucky enough, for some months, to live in this wonder, and live in it as a filmmaker, an artist who is so gifted that he can make his own tale of life the stuff of movies. The stuff of his dreams becomes the stuff of life, and vice versa. It's not that Ross or his family or his friends are movie stars. It's that the medium of film makes possible a way of picturing oneself that allows, perhaps requires, the allegorical; *Bright Leaves* tells a tale that needs to be told. In my father's lawyerly lexicon, this is called "intangible property."

6

JIM LANE

Drifting in Time

Ross McElwee's *Time Indefinite*

D AVID MacDOUGALL WRITES:

> A person I have filmed is a set of broken images: first, someone actually seen, within touch, sound and smell: a face glimpsed in the darkness of a viewfinder; a memory, sometimes elusive, sometimes of haunting clarity: a strip of images in an editing machine; a handful of photographs; and finally the figure moving on the screen, of cinema itself. (qtd. In Taylor 1998, 25)

Early in *Time Indefinite* (1992), Ross McElwee shows us a series of home movies taken by his uncles. We see the little boy Ross receiving his "first kiss," a visual staple of cinema, from a local neighborhood girl. We watch his father and mother standing outside a church after his christening. In voice-over, McElwee explains his fascination with watching the home movie footage. Not only does the footage allow him access to moving images of his now-deceased mother, it also inspires an aesthetic pleasure. The filmmaker explains that the interchange of light and shadow and a shaky handheld camera factor into a powerful remembrance. McElwee goes on to say that viewing his parents in this manner, noticing their genuine happiness and slight camera shyness in combination with a home-movie representation, is "stuff difficult to reenact."

This moment places the film autobiographer squarely within the lineage of his family documenters or, as McElwee later calls them, "family archivists." His observations also imply that these moments, "stuff difficult to reenact," provide documentary, and perhaps especially autobiographical documentary, its uniqueness. That we cannot reenact these moments without losing something in translation demands that we confront the very nature of documentary as it stands apart from reenactment (*read*: fiction). On the other hand, the two most striking aspects of McElwee's preestablished autobiographical persona, desire and obsession with death, visually marked by the "first kiss" and his deceased mother, respectively, suggest that these moments can be stepping-stones for a playful self. The film presents a subject willing to write and rewrite himself, in the face of documentary evidence—a self-conscious gesture perhaps more aligned with fiction than nonfiction.[1]

McElwee's autobiographical self, embedded in the home-movie fragments, initiates an autobiographical pact with the viewer by resuscitating McElwee's past in tension with the film's present tense, a discursive intervention of self-examination. This self, borne from images long ago, "of cinema itself" as MacDougall might say, announces that through the continued filmmaking process the family archive will develop and the autobiographical self will shift in relation to that.

Since documentary can appear to preserve the historical moment forever and since it can on many levels provide answers to questions that haunt the filmmaker, McElwee proceeds to let his camera explore the world to find answers to certain questions. In film-sequel fashion, *Time Indefinite* philosophically investigates the filmmaker's relation to the haunting questions of death (or conversely the meaning of life) and the filmmaker's desire, initially explored in *Sherman's March* (1986). The latter gives way to his opening engagement to Marilyn. As a detached viewer of his family at its annual reunion in North Carolina, McElwee occupies the familiar inside/outside locus afforded the son who did not follow in his father's footsteps, moved to the North, grew a beard, and became a filmmaker. As his grandmother seems to acknowledge later in the film, however, his marrying Marilyn is a welcomed step in the right direction, but he still needs to lose the beard and maybe the camera.

A deep irony sets in for McElwee as the pursuit of romantic love comes to an end and familial acceptance begins. Like so many docu-

mentarists coming out of this post-direct-cinema autobiographical tradition, he has for quite some time committed his camera to filming what
he calls "everyday life"—the stuff that would be "difficult to reenact."
This position is rooted in a commitment to documentary that espouses
the filmmaker's inherent connection inside and out to what he is filming. Despite his commitment to this approach, once he is engaged to
Marilyn and subsequently endorsed by his family, he has trouble filming
everyday life. This is succinctly summarized in McElwee's confession
that it is easier to make his film about the Berlin Wall, something
far away, than the one we are watching about things close to the filmmaker. His core commitment to documentary is destabilized by his
familial stabilization.

With his engagement to Marilyn, McElwee's cinematic pursuit of
desire, initially established in *Sherman's March*, finds fulfillment. Not
soon after, however, the question of parenthood—"Does Ross want to
have children?"—fuels his return to exploring his immediate world. A
potential burden is now displaced onto his future offspring depicting a
familiar McElweeian anxiety about the future and his place in it.

Consequently, McElwee forges the underpinning of the autobiographical tension to know himself and his world in the face of
overwhelming uncertainty about parenthood. Marked by the childhood
death of his younger brother, McElwee is simply not certain he wants
to be a parent, suggesting that he wants to avoid putting himself in
a potentially vulnerable position once occupied by his own parents.
Caught between external demands and internal recalcitrance, he seeks
the sage advice of his mentor and jettisoned narrator of *Sherman's March*,
Richard Leacock.

As Leacock prepares a dinner of red snapper, he admits that marriage really never was for him because he has a "roving eye." The initial
admission of Leacock's propensity for multiple dalliances gives way to
a profound metaphor for the film. The "roving eye" is never still and
the noted direct-cinema filmmaker, who developed a new, frenetic vision
of how cinema can view the world, reactivates McElwee's post–direct-
cinema eye once again, enabling Ross to film the everyday world.[2] The
scene ends on an unsettling note, however. McElwee frames the dead
snapper gazing into the camera, reminding us of the earlier scene, later
reprised, in which we see an innocent boy stomping a fish to death on
a North Carolina pier.

The pier scene is one that has stayed with the film autobiographer
and brings him back to his own childhood when his father taught him
how to catch and kill fish. Troubled by the practice and forced to ask

metaphysical questions about the fish's soul, the young McElwee eventually gave up fishing with his father yet clearly has never forgotten these moments from his early life. Years later, with his cinematic patriarch Leacock, McElwee implicitly announces that he is willing to engage himself in the practice of filming everyday life again, but the specter of death, marked by the lifeless gaze of the fish, seems never to be far away. McElwee's roving eye, his inquisitive camera, constantly seems mitigated by the structuring absence of death and its consequences.

During the dinner scene, we also see in full relief the intractable nature of human feelings as they fully impose themselves on film autobiography. As McElwee continues to examine himself and the world around him, the film's hold on real time unravels, giving way to an emotional timeline in which we can move from the past, present, and even future in a moment. The indefinite nature of time, almost being out of time, also establishes cruel dichotomies for the autobiographical subject. McElwee celebrates his love of Marilyn but is warned of divorce. The question of becoming a parent is undercut by memories of his brother's childhood death. Later, with the uncanny cluster of his grandmother's and father's death and his and Marilyn's miscarriage, McElwee observes that two generations before him and one ahead have vanished, a powerful observation and a grief-filled reminder that despite the noble project of his filmed autobiography, life and death get in the way. Similar to the way the biography of Sherman gives way to autobiography in *Sherman's*

March, McElwee's journey takes unexpected turns in *Time Indefinite*. Much like a story.

Autobiographical theorist Susana Egan has observed that modern autobiographers often revel in the potential for living life "like a story" (Egan 1999, 87). Here, McElwee fully embraces these possibilities. Devaluing neither the authentic nature of documentary moments nor the potential fictional play of a posterior reinterpretation of those moments, living and filming life like a story, and further like a story that involves performance, fully engages the ostensible opposites of nonfiction and fiction, opening up fruitful possibilities for film autobiography.

Charleen most fully encompasses this dynamic. Ross acknowledges that Charleen needs him to film her and Ross needs her to film—revealing a relation in which performance and storytelling engage across the view of a film camera. Friendship, trust, and love evolve, deepening the autobiographer's sense of self and his place in the world. Moreover, Charleen provides a welcome distraction for Ross. He does not have to dwell on his own immediate life issues yet still can find a place in which his humanity can come forth.

Perhaps the most performative set of self-interactions occurs in his North Carolina family home when Ross has come back in the summer after his father's death. Echoing the post–costume-party scene in which Ross speaks to the camera dressed as General Sherman in *Sherman's March*, Ross directly addresses the camera sitting in the very same chair we have seen him using years earlier.

Ross has spent some time away from his wife and home in the North, visiting friends and family in the South and ruminating over the impact of his father's death. In this scene, the present-tense main character, speaks directly to the camera and the posterior narrator's voice-over intrudes occasionally on the soundtrack serving to critique or even undermine what is being said on camera.

The on-camera Ross states, "Everything begins and ends with family. I don't know, some part of me resists that idea. I mean there's so much conflict in family especially between the generations. You drive your parents crazy. They drive you crazy. And then suddenly they're dead and you're stunned and heartbroken. I mean, first you're twisted by their lives and then you're twisted by their deaths. And then you grow up and do the same thing to your own kids."

At this juncture, Ross's voice-over interjects, "So as I am sitting here talking to my camera my mind starts to wander, and I begin worrying that I've gone off on the wrong track. I mean, sure, our family and I had our differences, but we did all love one another. That's actually the problem. You get bound up in family and then everyone in it starts to die and the pain just goes on generation after generation. But I just can't sit here and talk about all of this. It's just too depressing."

The on-camera sound comes back up on the soundtrack as Ross says, "I don't know. Once you get sucked into the vortex of family there's no way to get out except to die." The voice-over humorously counters, "I wish the camera battery would die. I mean what about spiritual things? Talk about the soul!"

Fidgeting in his chair and struggling to find the words, Ross continues, "I mean maybe there is an afterlife. I mean, I think that we might actually have a spirit or soul that lingers on in some form after we die, sort of lasting out over the centuries gradually fading until there's nothing left. Kind of like radioactive waste, but I think basically when you die, you die."

The voice-over emphatically declares, "God, how desolate! I've gone over the edge. What about love?" The following on-camera monologue directly answers the question. "Of course, you can fall in love. You can live with someone. You can marry them. I'm in love with Marilyn. I'm happy we're married. I can't wait to see her again. But it seems like the thing to do would be not to complicate this notion of love with family."

The voice-over concludes, "So sitting here staring at my camera, I've somehow gotten trapped in a kind of morbid, metaphysical feedback loop and to say the least I need to break out of it. But still there are these questions that won't go away. It's all very complicated." The on-camera monologue concludes, humorously echoing, "It's all very complicated."

As Susanna Egan has argued, contemporary autobiography may be uniquely shaped by the autobiographer's experience with trauma. This tends toward experimentation with autobiographical form itself, including one of the most recent autobiographical forms, film and video. McElwee has thrown himself fully into this formal experimentation in this scene of direct camera address. As the protagonist, author and narrator, his place within the text seems assured despite expressions of uncertainty about the project along the way.

His self-mocking voice-over is perhaps less a narration and more a reaction, which serves to undermine the genuine sincerity that appears to be captured in the original filmed scene. Through the formal after-the-fact play of his voice-over, and the inherent performative aspects of the voice-over itself, a method developed by McElwee and some of his colleagues at the M.I.T. Film Video Section, the filmmaker exposes an extraordinary gap between the moment of filming and its far later incorporation into a completed film. Momentarily, the viewer may be forced to question the sincerity of much of what has transpired. However, as the scene unfolds, characteristically overlaying humor onto pain, we realize that film autobiography presents extraordinary expressive means to explore the self across time in a brief moment. Again, even as McElwee in the shot attempts to assess things so far, his other voice, perhaps written and recorded years later, reconsiders the very assessment. Yet each holds significant weight in relation to questions raised.

His referencing *Sherman's March* by using the same scene set up should not go unnoticed. This reference within a self-reference creates a continuity of tension and resolution between father and son. In *Sherman's March*, Ross tries to keep his voice low, trying not to wake his father who could be looming authoritatively off-camera. Earlier in the *Sherman's March*, the father has questioned the value of making the film Ross is working on. This fully informs the father's off-screen presence in the scene for it seems that if the father had been wakened by Ross and entered the room to see his son talking to the camera dressed as General Sherman, the father's suspicions of the film's worth would be confirmed.

In *Time Indefinite*, with his father truly absent and the house apparently vacant, Ross assumes the off-camera presence himself in voice-over, transferring his father's critical point of view onto his present point of view. There is an extraordinary reflective movement from father to son here. Despite Ross not sharing his father's taste in clothes, as seen earlier in the closet scene as Ross reminisces that his own wardrobe of black was in stark contrast to his father's choice of plaids and colors, the larger point is made. Dissolving the boundaries of time and death itself, Ross comes closer to his father's perspective on his son in a complex interaction of voice, exploring the ways in which we might change over time and in relation to new life events.

In his discussion on film sequels, Todd Berliner argues that "at the same time a sequel calls to mind the charismatic original, it also recalls its absence, fostering a futile, nostalgic desire to reexperience the original aesthetic moment as though it had never happened" (Berliner 2001, 108). The sequel, *Time Indefinite*, deliberately replays the earlier Oedipal scene from *Sherman's March* and seems to have a similar relation to its much more widely viewed predecessor. The later scene, fully aware of its own artifice and arcane referencing to the earlier film, sheds itself of Ross's earlier life concerns and acknowledges the more deeply felt pain and loss that typically comes later in life. As *Sherman March's* lesser known sequel, *Time Indefinite* builds a thickly layered autobiographical subject that echoes much of the earlier subject but builds and points much more confidently, if not somewhat more soberly, to a future more deeply connected to the past.

Toward the final section of the film, McElwee presents old footage from his own family archive in which his father and mother appear in the family kitchen with perhaps a brother. They don't seem to be doing anything unusual. The scene appears to be another moment of "everyday life." McElwee in voice-over states that this is footage he has looked at many times and edited many times attempting to "massage the footage back to life." This precedes the final section that involves the birth of his son. Here, it seems that before we embark on the answer to the film's opening question, "Can Ross be a parent?" we must go back into the past. We must consider the past before we ponder the future. Like Charleen's old house, which was rebuilt from ashes, the film slips through time, providing another necessary affirmation despite all trepidations. This moment evokes David MacDougall's observation:

> Film gives us the bodies of those we have filmed, yet those same bodies dissipate or are transformed before our eyes. I want to try to grasp the sense of this—if not to find the person among the phantoms, then perhaps to find some reasons for my puzzlement. If images lie, why are they so palpable of the life between us? I want to look, sometimes sidelong, at the spaces between the filmmaker and the subject: of imagery and language, of memory and feeling. These are spaces charged with ambiguity, but are they also the spaces in which consciousness is created? (qtd. In Taylor 1998, 25)

Through filmic manipulation and unflinching commitment, McElwee's autobiography emerges as a gloss of human consciousness, allowed to traverse the family archive unfettered by generational or temporal constraints. Autobiography seems to be the completely appropriate discourse to build McElwee's new edifice. Founded on death and unfulfilled desire, the family archive emerges as a testament to the commitment of "the roving eye." Never satisfied, always searching and questioning, McElwee's project continues to blend contradictory, intrasubjective voices creating powerful generic hybrids founded in the documentary tradition.

Notes

1. For an excellent overview of performance in cinematic autobiography, see Nadja Gernalzick, "To Act Or To Perform: Distinguishing Filmic Autobiography." *Biography* 29, 1 (2006): 1–13.

2. Leacock's admission stands in striking contrast to the position he takes in fellow M.I.T. documentarist, Ed Pincus's, groundbreaking autobiographical documentary, *Diaries: 1971–1976* (1980). In a party scene late in the film, Leacock emphatically tells Pincus that he would not want to make the kind of autobiographical work that Pincus is producing because, as a public figure, there are things in Leacock's life that could be "very embarrassing" to disclose.

7

CHARLES WARREN

Surprise and Pain, Writing and Film

I N LOOKING FORWARD TO WRITING THIS chapter and in giving it, first, its title, I wanted to set myself up to give thought to what it is that appeals to me in Ross McElwee's films—to the very particular and acute sense of anticipation I feel when a new film of his comes along and I am about to see it, and to the qualities of his films that, so far, always bear out this sense of anticipation. I do think of McElwee as a writer, though as someone who is a thoroughgoing filmmaker and whom I cannot really imagine doing his work and coming across purely in the medium of writing. What does this mean?

In saying surprise, I want to point to a quality I think of as peculiar to writing, especially to such work as the essays of Montaigne—a linear movement forward and along where each idea or expression or registration of feeling seems to give birth to the next without knowing what that next might be. Or to put it differently: one thing is there, and a new thing seems simply to happen to the first, to come to it out of the blue, like an access of grace, and to make a connection, so that the making of connection is itself interesting. The "Apology for Raimond Sebond" begins with some thoughts on the limitations of knowledge, then after a few sentences moves into reminiscence about Montaigne's father and his entertaining of learned men at his house. Soon the essay is caught up in reflection on Martin Luther's effect upon the unlearned populace, where we sense admiration as much as alarm. Then Montaigne comes back to his now deceased father and his not-to-be-denied request that Montaigne translate into French Sebond's *Natural Theology*, a book Montaigne has reservations about. He briefly evokes his role as intellectual advisor to ladies who read Sebond. Then the essay is off on its hundred pages and more of speculation about the human condition, with memories and pictures from life and personal reflection, and odd bits of knowledge coming in from many sources, each as if remembered suddenly due to some thought that has just been written down, the whole adding up to what has often been taken as the intellectual inspiration for Shakespeare's *Hamlet*.[1]

The reader taking up such work knows that what is in store is a journey, a movement forward where feelings are stirred and the mind is illuminated, again and again, and one does not know precisely where things will go, though there will be moments of looking back and recouping, circling and drawing an emphasis. It is not a series of random events: the making of connections keeps a thread spun, a golden or silver thread, from starting out until stopping. Whatever such work has to give, whatever it adds up to, must come through this linear, experiential process.

By pain I mean seriousness, weight, the coming up against fact. In reading Montaigne or, for me, viewing a McElwee film, one is not entering an escape world, opening oneself to a sequence of purely delightful surprises. One comes, again and again, to recognitions of life in its imperfection, even messiness, and to hard ideas, ideas that are struggled for and that offer to recast life, to cope with it better through understanding, but that admit they cannot fully get a hold on life, comprehend it and settle it. Going to a McElwee film I look forward to humor and to marvelous images, to discovery of intriguing people, and of course each time to more of Ross, as he presents himself. And in all this I know there will be a periodic coming to earth, life taking hold. I will be sobered.

Near the center of *Time Indefinite* Ross and Marilyn, newly married, now expecting a child, shop for a baby's crib and linens and an electric breast pump. The camera stares at these strange-seeming objects and takes in the friendly saleswoman and her recital of mounting costs, as Ross and Marilyn undergo a Walker-Percy–like humorous/anxious encounter with the consumer world and suburban values, feeling pressed to accept it all. Ross seems especially put upon, unseen, only his muted voice coming from behind the camera, addressing Marilyn, "I find it difficult to breathe." Without resolution to this, there comes news of Ross's grandmother's death, with older film footage of her singing outdoors in

autumnal light—and this seems to usher in Marilyn's miscarriage on New Year's Eve, upon which Ross looks to his physician father for a rational consolation that is not forthcoming. Then suddenly there is news of the father's altogether unexpected death, and the film is cast into a mode of serious reflection it could not have expected and which is never overcome, despite the continuing discovery of marvels in life.

I do not want to spend time on qualification. Of course, there is surprise in a good deal of film, in painting, in music. And there is formulaic and predictable writing, some of it powerful and valid (Homer, in a sense?). Important to what I am thinking about here is linearity, movement, one surprising thing happening after another, the surprise overturning the work and casting it in a new direction. And surprise in music and in most film—even documentary (more of this in a moment)—comes within a structure important to grasp. McElwee films suggest structures, even comparison to established genres, such as romantic comedy.

I am not trying to draw lines between categories. The categories blur. I am just trying to develop an idea of something, as I see it, real and essential to a Ross McElwee film, that it moves as does certain writing, unpredictably, thinking on its feet, going forward without being sure where, and not spinning out its own fancy, but allowing itself to be brought up short by life and even thought about life as it were from the outside. This particular conjunction of film and writing, in McElwee, might help to think about a larger question or, as I see it, what is in our time a triple question, where the categories may be separable but not the questions: what is writing? what is film? and indeed, what is philosophy?

Stanley Cavell, a writer and a philosopher, asks at the end of his magnum opus *The Claim of Reason*, "Can philosophy become literature and still know itself?" The knowing itself, the unstoppable reflection that will not be co-opted by anyone's agenda, the radicality, seems crucial here. If literature comes to life with this reflectiveness, where are we as between literature and philosophy? Earlier Cavell argued in *The World Viewed* that film was born in a crisis of skepticism and that it exists as a way of reflecting on the sense of loss of contact with the world and as a means of trying to reconnect and to learn what connection can be that is not the possession that would satisfy a skeptic. Where are we as between philosophy and film?[2]

Let us narrow in on McElwee's procedure and see how it illuminates these questions. Is the unpredictable quality in his work, the surprise, which I take to be like that of writing, due to the films' being nonfiction, taking the world as it comes and reflecting on it stage by stage? Not altogether. Many documentaries feel planned and logical and all too well possessed of shape. One of McElwee's teachers, Ricky Leacock (who appears in *Time Indefinite*), wrote a famous brief manifesto, "For an Uncontrolled Cinema," (Leacock 2000, 76–78), and Leacock's own films, or I would prefer to say his shooting, his filming, have a wonderful quality of surprise, attending to the world as it changes. Leacock's filming seems to answer to Pier Paolo Pasolini's ideal, expressed in his theoretical essays, of a world that flows on unceasingly and registers itself on film in its totality.[3] Leacock has the eye for this. Toward the end of *A Happy Mother's Day*, at the official luncheon for Mrs. Fischer (mother of quintuplets) and then at the town's celebratory parade, Leacock's camera moves or zooms to find children playing, showing off, delightfully countering the overall staid and formal atmosphere of the proceedings. Marching in the parade, children, adolescents, even adults find their ways of anarchic self-expression within the parameters of formal activity—a drum majorette has more than usual bounce to her step, a middle-aged man waves his arms wildly as he plays the drum. The feeling of the film is of life continually calling the camera's attention to itself.

But I do not take Leacock to be a writer in the sense I am talking about. I miss reflection—not what Cavell attributes to the very medium of film, its meditating on our closeness to and distance from the world—Leacock has that in plenty. But I miss the saying of something, the quality of speaking. Of course, Leacock avoids spoken commentary, something crucial to McElwee's films, something McElwee has developed in a most distinctive way and made an art of. But the saying something, the speaking, in film is even more a matter of structuring, of deciding what to include and what to omit, of deciding what to put next to what other thing, what transitions to make, how to build or to let an extended argument take its way. One has the impression that McElwee shoots a good deal of film over time, whether in pursuit of a general idea like tobacco culture or stories behind the evening news, or not in pursuit of anything, just keeping up with life as it happens, as with

the material for *Time Indefinite*, and that he then works long and hard
sorting and arranging, juxtaposing and structuring, all the time developing his voiceover commentary and carefully timing it with the images.
The succession of experiences for the viewer, the encounters, the ideas,
one opening unpredictably into the next, is something *achieved*. And
this is not a hoax. Ross McElwee's films are honest. One feels that he
writes—shooting, editing, developing a commentary—from a take on the
world and from an active mind. One's feeling is not that he constructs
a simulacrum of writing.

I think of Jean-Luc Godard as a writer. And Godard said long ago
that, for him, his written essays and his filmmaking were two versions
of the same activity (Godard 1986, 171). Godard works mostly—there
are some striking exceptions—within the realm of the scripted film, with
actors and made-up stories and characters, without voice-over commentary. The quality of surprise, movement with surprise, saying something,
reflection, admission of pain, is due to structuring. Who could predict
that Nana/Anna Karina in the middle of *Vivre sa vie* would dance out by
herself an entire loud jukebox number, while her pimp talks to an associate instead of taking her to the movies? It is a gesture of protest against
her life and at the same time a gesture of taking delight in herself. With
the long dance Godard bends the expected and usual pace of narrative
to his own voice, and to Karina's. Of course, in a Godard fiction there
is an important element of nonfictional observation of the world, the
surprising world—those are the real Paris streets in *Vivre sa vie*, that is
Karina almost more than a created character. Perhaps any writing will
have such an element of nonfictional observation, of pure appreciation
of the world as found. (D. H. Lawrence objected that philosophy after
Plato was not writing, meeting life at every turn, as do Plato's dialogues
[Lawrence 1972, 520]. Godard's filmwriting, like McElwee's, is a matter of a certain kind of writing mind making a conjuncture with film,
through shooting, editing, forming. And it is not the mind of Godard
the person or McElwee the person at issue. I am more inclined to the
idea that the film—in the case of these two filmmakers the conjuncture
of a writing mind with the medium of film—*is* mind, that the film has
a mind of its own.

One more comparison will help to narrow in on McElwee. Consider
Chris Marker, another master of the voice-over commentary, certainly a
writer, perhaps a philosopher. In *Le joli mai* and *Sans soleil*, Marker has his
beautiful, reflective commentary spoken by someone other than himself,
in these cases a woman, and someone who never appears on-screen, and
the effect is to cast the words onto a level of pure ideas, consistent—on-
tologically, we might say—and final, for all their complexity and admitted

self-contradiction and even ephemerality. Simone Signoret's voice at the end of *Le joli mai* reflects on freedom as we get views of a prison and of the Paris streets; Alexandra Stewart's less familiar voice in *Sans soleil* reflects on the bitterness of history, after a presentation, with archival footage, of the political career of Amilcar Cabral in the Cape Verde Islands.

McElwee's commentary, by contrast, does not so much give us a person as through the personal open a variety of levels of engagement with the viewer. We do not get the whole Ross, and sometimes see and hear a Ross on-screen in counterpoint with rather another Ross speaking in voice-over. The sense of a person, which is not the sense of a whole and delimited person, makes us feel that the words mean more than we can see, that someone, someone other, is affected by what this someone is talking about. We feel that the words go in more than one direction, that we are being given ideas and something below or beyond the level of ideas, which cannot wholly be made out, but which we are also invited to respond to, as we are to the ideas. I am reminded of the first time I heard Stanley Cavell lecture, many years ago, when with the force of a salutary nail driven into the head, he looked me in the eye, as it seemed, and reiterated that for Wittgenstein reflecting on what J. L. Austin, in the title of a famous essay, termed the problem of "other minds," the crucial consideration was the mystery of another's pain.

Time Indefinite, like Bergman's *The Seventh Seal*, begins at the shore, here the land and a long row of dwellings on the left, set against the vast sea and an enormous sky, suggesting human life confronting what is beyond human life or comprehension, or what is bigger or stronger than life—perhaps death, or a wonderful transcendence. The beautiful colors, not like Bergman, draw us into the depths of the shot, though across the foreground falls the shadow of the fishing pier from which the shot is taken.

Ross McElwee, filming the world, is a fisherman, a hunter, like Nanook, or in William Rothman's account, Flaherty himself filming Nanook, hunting him, or like Peter and Andrew, called to be fishers of men, to save them.[4] Ross is ambivalent, to say the least, about fishing, as he explains when the film returns to this pier and its activities in ten minutes or so. And as he explains almost immediately, he has misgivings about filming, something he feels called, compellingly, to do, and yet something that seems to set him apart from life. We will see film of various kinds and qualities, made by various people, in the course of *Time Indefinite*, and it will become a pressing issue, what it is that film does with life, or does for life. The impossibility to disentangle film from life, or film imagination from life, is a great concern of *Bright Leaves*, as it is of Godard's 2004 film *Our Music* (*Notre musique*), where "our music" is film and is at the same time the dialogue necessary between persons, actually separate persons, in order for life to be lived.

The vista of beach, most unlike Bergman's, becomes quickly recognizable as a comfortable American resort, not too far north, so that it is in a way no surprise, with a cut, to be thrust into the midst of a McElwee family party on a beach cottage porch, where Ross and his friend Marilyn will announce their engagement—a party dominated by Ross's father, who does not like all the filming going on and yet at one point asks to wield the camera. Ross calls his father "the one who keeps these reunions going" (*read*: "these montages," these films, this film). *Time Indefinite* is, among other things, a film about paternity, the seed of life, the seed of film. But in a way the family party is indeed a surprise, because this footage comes to have a certain double aspect: it is a home movie, where we are intent on the people and a certain real time and place; but with the handheld camera very steadily panning left and right, a sort of fresco or mural is created where amiably chattering people become pure film figures, animated shadows, a little ghostly, the effect compounded by Ross's voiceover putting things at a distance. There is a *frisson* of reminder that these real people, so full of life's joys, so unabashed in their Southernness, are living up against that beyond suggested in the film's opening.

Flashes of black indicate a camera battery failure and give us the opportunity to see film of various kinds in short order: the present scene in failing light and with a camera wildly turned about as the photographer grapples with his problem; a wholly black stretch with sound; substitute video footage taken by Ross's stepmother. We are given opportunity to think about what becomes of people—mortal people—on film, and about whether any film is the right film or whether more than one kind of film is better. The interruption allows Ross to explain himself a bit as a filmmaker, with his compulsion to film daily life, and allows, as I would like to put it, the film itself to remember, to wash over us in a series of passages that seem to come from a more-than-human, stronger-than-human, somehow other-than-human center or source: footage of Ross's brother and father at an earlier time, Ross's sister talking in a canoe, Ross with his older friend Charleen and her arranged date for him in Charleston—moments we may recognize from *Backyard* and *Sherman's March*, life become film become film yet again—and then Ross on vacation with Marilyn, film, he tells us, as a mode of love.

Did the camera battery failure really happen? It is so opportune for dealing with what Ross introduces as his father's contra-filmic "Freudian force field," as well as for opening the episode of various passages of film. If it did not happen, it would make the film seem airier, more aesthetic, less open to admit fact. I think one has something more than the two alternatives of thinking either that the battery failure happened, or that Ross manufactured it for the sake of making his film. Wise literary criticism has maintained long since that writing can be sincere even though we are not sure about the writer.[5] *Time Indefinite*, all things considered, has us accept the battery failure as an assertion of reality, and this is not the same as the suspension of disbelief whereby we take in a fiction. To be suspicious of the battery failure and to turn this against the film would be a destructive act, uncalled for. Writing, and film, will give us plenty of signals when it is good to be suspicious. There are no rules for this. And we can never get it wholly right.

The film returns after its memories to the family reunion—hush-puppies are frying—and the film is drawn—Ross is drawn—to the pier, first down below where we see it stretch out to the horizon like the Golden Gate Bridge in Hitchcock's *Vertigo*, another film about romantic love, images, loss, intimations of what lies beyond life—though there are no babies.

We go up onto the pier and witness fishing, and launch into Ross's wonderful monologue encompassing his childhood questions to

his father: "Does a fish have a soul? . . . Does God take all the dead fish into heaven? . . . If it's an aquarium, who cleans it? Do angels clean it? . . . Why does anyone or anything have to die? What's the matter with staying right here?" These questions stick, and align themselves with the whole inquiry of the filmmaker, of the film, first to last, and with film's "impulse to preserve," as filmmaker Robert Gardner calls it, taking the phrase from Phillip Larkin.[6] Film is given something of Emerson's open-eyed authority of boys, and Thoreau's sunlight that is morning and mourning.[7]

On the words, "What's the matter with staying right here?" a man throws the waste part of a cleaned fish off the pier, and the camera follows his gesture, looking out to the shoreline and surf and eventually turning down to stare at just the churning sea—the beyond, heaven, the void, annihilation that perhaps gives new life. The sea with its reflecting surface and constant motion, its unseen depths that we posit or believe in, suggests the screen and the very medium of film.

In *Time Indefinite*'s important monologue midway through the film, back at the pier after the shocking sudden death of Ross's father, Ross tells of his anger at death's periodic visits to his immediate family over the years, taking a younger brother, their mother, Ross's unborn child, and now his father—and speculates on this as the source of his compulsion to film life. Life goes to annihilation. Perhaps this can be the death and rebirth of life on film, life in film's "time indefinite," as Ross puts it later, picking up on the apocalyptic phrase from the Bible, which we hear and see read to Ross at the front door, the threshold, of his father's house by a Jehovah's Witness.

After the earlier view from the pier down into the sea, a cut gives us the lovely image of hands shucking ears of corn, a parallel to the fish cleaning, an image of vegetable life like that of animal life undergoing preparation for the transfiguration of giving nourishment, of being feasted upon—and with a glare at the camera on the part of Ross's father, the film is once again washed over by old footage, this time the ghostly images taken by Uncle Fred or Uncle Nate, now appearing in otherworldly partial color, of Ross's parents long ago and Ross as a child.

Ross's father's painful glare seems to produce these images as a flight away, an alternative. At first, it is the day of Ross's baptism, the subjection of an infant to the ritual of death by water and rebirth. The camera's look off the pier and down into the ocean a few minutes ago, its

beginning of a plunge down, seems now carried out on this occasion of baptism. The new life here—the young mother, now dead, the youthful father and the infant, in shimmering light, for a moment in slowed motion—is a life of film. Then there is the toddler Ross receiving his first kiss from a toddler girl and going back for another, twice. If anger at death drives filmmaking—anger as the push for life, or toward life—then so does eros drive filmmaking. Or rather, anger at death, or desire for death and its transfiguration, desire for death's life, *is* eros. Such entanglement of eros and death is the ultimate "Freudian force field." Over all these images Ross speaks of his having been bred to filming through so much early exposure to film. The images, more than the words, tell us what film and exposure to film are.

The flight of fancy, into the past, into strange images, into a lost reality, comes to earth in Cambridge, Massachusetts, and preparations for Ross and Marilyn's marriage, and the film takes its way through things that happen—marriage, fatherhood, deaths, births, reunions. One wants to go on with the film, moment after moment. What is writing for? To be read.

Notes

1. I am looking at a few pages (368–70) of E. J. Trechmann's translation, *The Essays of Montaigne* (New York: Modern Library, 1946). T. S. Eliot's 1919 essay "Hamlet and His Problems" acknowledges J. M. Robertson and other scholars of the time who were connecting Shakespeare's play back to Montaigne's essay. The Eliot is reprinted in *Selected Essays*, new edition (New York: Harcourt, Brace and World, 1964), 121–26.

2. Stanley Cavell, *The Claim of Reason: Wittgenstein, Skepticism, Morality, and Tragedy* (Oxford: Oxford University Press, 1979), 496. The relation of film to skepticism is the abiding and overall concern of *The World Viewed: Reflections on the Ontology of Film* expanded ed. (Cambridge, Mass.: Harvard University Press, 1979 [1971]).

3. Pier Paolo Pasolini, "The 'Cinema of Poetry' " (1965) and "The Written Language of Reality" (1966), for example, reprinted in Pasolini, *Heretical Empiricism*, ed. Louise K. Barnett, trans. Ben Lawton and Louise K. Barnett (Bloomington: Indiana University Press, 1988), 167–86, 197–222.

4. William Rothman, *Documentary Film Classics* (New York: Cambridge University Press, 1997), 14–15; Gospel of Matthew 4:18–20.

5. See, for example, F. R. Leavis, "Reality and Sincerity" (1952), reprinted in *A Selection from Scrutiny*, ed. F. R. Leavis (Cambridge: Cambridge University Press, 1968), 248–57.

6. Robert Gardner, "The Impulse to Preserve," in *Beyond Document: Essays on Nonfiction Film*, ed. Charles Warren (Hanover, N.H.: Wesleyan University Press/University Press of New England, 1996), 169–80. Gardner elaborates on

the idea in his book *The Impulse to Preserve: Reflections of a Filmmaker* (New York: Other Press, 2006).

7. Ralph Waldo Emerson, "Self-Reliance" (1841), in *Emerson: Essays and Lectures*, ed. Joel Porte (New York: Library of America, 1983), 261; Henry David Thoreau, *Walden; or, Life in the Woods*, ed. Robert F. Sayre (New York: Library of America, 1985 [1854]), 587. Thoreau's concern with acknowledgment of loss that is at the same time an opening to a new dawn, a concern that builds to the book's concluding sentence, is a major theme of Stanley Cavell in *The Senses of Walden*, expanded ed. (San Francisco: North Point Press, 1981 [1972]).

8

WILLIAM ROTHMAN

Sometimes Daddies Don't Talk about Things like That

IN ROSS MCELWEE'S *BRIGHT LEAVES*, Vlada Petric, the noted film theorist and historian, asks the filmmaker behind the camera, with a great display of contempt, why he is so attached to *Bright Leaf* (the Hollywood film from the 1950s, which Ross believes to be based on the ultimately failed struggle by John Harvey McElwee, his great-grandfather, against the patriarch of the powerful Duke family). Vlada is no less contemptuous of Ross's answer; "It's because Gary Cooper plays the role of my great-grandfather."

For dear friend and longtime colleague Vlada, such a fact is "merely contextual." The only thing that matters is that *Bright Leaf* is uncinematic, has no value as a film, and thus is unworthy of attention in Ross's film. Thus it is on principle—and also because he is such a ham—that Vlada responds with comically exaggerated yet also genuine sarcasm. "So *what?*" Not responding in kind to Vlada's sarcasm, Ross answers, "It's an example of a fiction film becoming a documentary, a kind of home-movie film." Not accepting this answer, Vlada asks Ross, "How are you going to insert, incorporate, the sequences from *Bright Leaf?*" That Ross doesn't deign to answer this question suggests that he quite simply *has* no answer.

Then has Vlada bested Ross in a battle of ideas about the very film Ross is making? But *is* there a conflict between them? Isn't Vlada's real goal not to vanquish Ross but to provoke him—to challenge him to make as *cinematic* a film as possible, one worthy of the great art that Vlada, God bless him, loves as much as life itself? And the gratifying fact is that Ross does, indeed, rise to this challenge, as this sequence—alongside so many other great sequences in *Bright Leaves*—attests. That is, Vlada's question is also the film's question, asked of itself, as it were. And the sequence itself, placed as it is in the finished film, at once poses and answers this question by demonstrating, exemplifying, strategies that Ross employs throughout *Bright Leaves* for incorporating sequences from *Bright Leaf* in provocative, illuminating, and playful ways.

For example, when Vlada utters his contemptuous "So *what?*" there is a cut from this confrontation, or mock confrontation, to the decidedly melodramatic moment in *Bright Leaf* at which Donald Crisp, Gary Cooper's antagonist, slaps Cooper, who refrains from striking back, not wishing to stoop to his adversary's level. This cut suggests an equivalence between the two encounters—as if Vlada were a villain whose dismissal of *Bright Leaf* is an uncalled for slap in the face of Ross, a man too virtuous for his own good. Of course, *Bright Leaves* presents this suggestion jokingly. But the film is punctuated with such "jokes," not all meant to be funny, perhaps none meant *simply* to be funny.

When Ross adds, in defense of his interest in *Bright Leaf*, that it's "an example of a fiction film becoming a documentary, a kind of home-movie film," this doesn't overcome Vlada's skepticism. Not only does Vlada find *Bright Leaf* uncinematic, but he also implies that the two films cannot mesh because fiction is one thing, nonfiction something altogether different. But Ross inserts sequences from *Bright Leaf* into *Bright Leaves* precisely to meditate on the ambiguous, paradoxical relationship between the two. The two films couldn't be more different, yet there is a level at which they can be viewed, or imagined, as converging.

Part of what makes this possible, as Ross suggests, is the fact that there is a kind of home movie—nestled within *Bright Leaf*, as within any so-called fiction film. Ross's conversations with his film-buff cousin, resonating with the interview with Patricia Neal, *Bright Leaf*'s co-star, for whom Gary Cooper was the great love of her life, make clear that *Bright Leaf* can be viewed as *Patricia Neal*'s home movie, or Gary Cooper's, for that matter. But insofar as Ross views it as telling his great-grandfather's story, Ross sees or imagines it as a kind of home movie, or at least document, of his own family—his own self, insofar as he identifies with John Harvey McElwee, his mythical, and real, ancestor.

In *Bright Leaf*, Patricia Neal played Gary Cooper's love interest. However she may deny it, her "real" identity was—is—inextricably bound up with that of her character in the film. Just as there is a documentary nestled within every fiction film, there is every fiction film nestled within every documentary. That *Bright Leaves* has a fictional aspect is not an idea Ross expresses to Vlada or to anyone in the film. Nor is it a point he makes in his narration. But it's an idea central to the Vlada sequence and to *Bright Leaves* as a whole.

As Vlada is expostulating grandly on his theory of cinema, Ross, exercising his prerogative as filmmaker, abruptly mutes Vlada's voice and says in voice-over, "As we circle the block for the fifth time, I find myself wondering how I managed to get myself into this situation, bound in a chair and lectured at close range by a rabid film theorist."

This gagging of Vlada in mid-sentence, combined with his own exasperated tone, conveys the impression that Ross is "closing the iron door" on this "rabid film theorist," altogether dismissing his ideas. And yet—among all the vivid characters *Bright Leaves* presents to us, Vlada steals the film. And since Vlada commandeers Ross's camera, making Ross film him from a wheelchair with Vlada pushing him backwards as they speak and thus controlling the camera's movement, and since his express purpose is to make the resulting footage more kinesthetic than it would be without this camera movement, doesn't the fact that these shots succeed so spectacularly in "supporting," "expressing," and indeed "enhancing" Vlada's "mentality" (to use Vlada's words) confirm the very ideas about cinema that Ross seems to be dismissing?

Nonetheless, Ross, speaking to Lawrence Rhu in an illuminating *Cineaste* interview, cites the Vlada sequence, which would make no sense in a fiction film, as exemplary of the value of filmmaking that aspires to capture "life as it happens, unaware of itself" (Rhu 2004, 10). Vlada insists that "ontological authenticity," as he calls it, is only one element of cinema; the mere recording of events is not, in and of itself, cinema. This is true as well for Vlada's beloved concept of the kinesthetic. He recognizes, after all, that even a Hollywood film as "uncinematic" as *Bright Leaf* employs devices—high-contrast photography and elaborate tracking shots, for example—that make the film kinesthetic to a certain degree. Vlada's problem with *Bright Leaf* is that Michael Curtiz, the film's director, simply lacks "cinematic vision," that he fails to *integrate* the devices he uses, fails to *do* anything with them to make the film rise to the level of true cinema. Vlada goes on to say that some documentaries, such as Dziga Vertov's, succeed in integrating their devices and thereby transcend the mere photographic recording of reality. The question, Vlada insists, is what you *do* with such footage.

Immediately upon Vlada's uttering of these words, Ross rings down the curtain on the sequence by cutting to black—as if the filmmaker is acknowledging that despite appearing to dismiss these words, he takes them as a challenge. Thanks to Vlada, the interview footage is "kinesthetic." That, by itself, doesn't make it cinematic. If Vlada commandeers Ross's camera, Ross's film commandeers Vlada's question: What does the film *do* with this footage? How is it integrated in the finished film?

In *Bright Leaves*, as in *Sherman's March*, *Time Indefinite*, and *Six O'Clock News*, Ross's narration is composed and recorded during post-production, but it is written—with exceptions that prove the rule—in the present tense. ("As we circle the block . . . I find myself wondering . . ."). Although the footage may have the power to jog the filmmaker's memory, his authority is always open to question, at least in principle, when he claims in this way to speak for his past self. He is not exempt—no one is—from theatricality, wishful thinking, or denial.

For us, viewing the film, the time of Ross's speaking of the narration is the past, not the present, just as for Ross, speaking his voice-over, the time of our viewing is neither the past nor the present, but the future. In any case, the narration, written as it is in the present tense, systematically elides these temporal gaps—the gap between the time of shooting and the time of editing; between the time of editing and our time of viewing. Eliding these gaps, creating for his films a "time indefinite," is, indeed, one of Ross's principal strategies for fictionalizing his nonfictions, or for acknowledging that films by their very nature are forever blurring, or denying, or transgressing, the "boundary" between nonfiction and fiction. By eliding the temporal gap between shooting and editing, the narration also elides the gap between Ross's situation when he was shooting (when he broke his silence only to address or respond to others in his presence) and his situation when speaking his narration (when he is responsive to events in the past and addressing viewers who are not now in his presence).

These strategies have especially profound implications because a McElwee film characteristically presents itself as a narrative of a journey of discovery, one which is also a journey of self-discovery undertaken by the filmmaker—his quest to change. But if by making the film the filmmaker succeeds in achieving a change so traumatic as to be tantamount to death and rebirth, such a change cannot be marked by a narration in which he speaks for—speaks as—his "old" self.

In *Sherman's March*, Ross's voice, both as a character and as the film's narrator, conjures or projects the persona that has become familiar to us of Ross the skeptical, slightly neurotic filmmaker, at times comically obtuse, whose redeeming virtue is the fact that so many women worthy of being filmed find him worthy of filming them. The ending of *Sherman's March* implies that Ross has not really changed, and intimates that he never will. The Ross whose life revolved around filming his futile attempts to create a life for himself, and the Ross who composed the film from the footage that Ross shot, are positively the same guy. In his narration, Ross can speak for the film because the film speaks in his voice.

Sherman's March confesses—in part ironically—that the film's success marks the filmmaker's failure. But *Bright Leaves* marks the filmmaker's achievement. Ross, the character, is still the likable, slightly bumbling figure he cut in the earlier film; and the narration is spoken in that character's voice. But that figure is no longer the "real" Ross, if he ever was. The filmmaker has changed, *Bright Leaves* declares (although his sense of humor, thank God, has survived the sea change).

In *Bright Leaves*, Ross, both as character and as narrator, still speaks in his "old" voice, but that voice no longer speaks for the film. Rather, the film speaks for the filmmaker. And it speaks in its own voice, in the language that Hitchcock liked to call "pure cinema." *Bright Leaves* finds its voice not so much in the individual shots out of which it is composed—those shots were taken by the "old" Ross—but in the ways it uses those shots, integrates them in the finished work. *Bright Leaves* does not exemplify Vlada's claim that for a film to be truly cinematic every shot must be "kinesthetic," must provoke viewers to "feel something in their body, in their muscles." *Bright Leaves* sets the bar higher. Every shot provokes viewers to "feel something" in their minds, their hearts, their souls. Whether or not he would ever admit it, even Vlada has to be pleased.

In the passage immediately following the Vlada interview, Ross returns to McElwee Park, the comically minimal monument to Ross's great-grandfather set up through the efforts of a Mr. Lackey, a self-appointed local historian. Viewed from a distance, with the camera set on a tripod—let kinesthesia be damned!—Ross enters the frame and sits on one of the two benches. Nothing happens. Ross says, in voice-over, "I just sit for a while, perhaps waiting for someone to come along and enjoy McElwee Park with me. And, while I'm waiting, I think about what Professor Petric said about transcending the mere photographic recording of reality, how elusive this can be in documentary."

In *Sherman's March*, Ross sets up shots of himself to allow him to speak directly to the camera. Here, lost in thought about the elusiveness of transcendence in the world on film. When this shot was taken, was he really thinking about transcendence as he sat alone, in this comically untranscendent spot? Is this a moment of fiction? We have no way of knowing. Does it make a difference?

At one level, the shot speaks for itself, makes an ironic point about the inadequacy of the world's acknowledgment of Ross's family, and makes that point *cinematically*, we might say. At another level, Ross's voice-over invites us to think—with him?—about transcendence and where it may be found, if it may be found, in the "real" world and in the world on film. Is *this* a moment in which transcendence is achieved? And is Ross really alone? Are we not enjoying McElwee Park with him? McElwee Park, I take it, is one of the film's metaphors, no doubt joking, for itself.

We are perhaps already lost in Ross's thoughts, or our own, when without warning there is a cut to a shot we may not at first recognize—although we have seen it before—of the modest old brick building that was once John Harvey McElwee's factory. As the handheld camera peers through a window covered by a metal grate, into the murky interior, Ross's voice-over continues. "And as he also said, even if you succeed, then what do you do with it?" The camera moves closer to the grate. The shadow of the filmmaker can clearly be seen, moving with the camera's movement, as Ross adds, "I mean, that's what my father would always ask me. What will you do with all this footage you're shooting around the house?"

These words here explicitly tie Vlada's question to the one Ross's father was forever asking him and connect both with the elusive goal Vlada characterized as "transcending the mere photographic recording of reality." When Ross's father asked him what he was going to do with the footage he was shooting, he had no answer, just as he had no answer for Vlada. But from these striking, mysterious cuts and those that follow, it may well dawn on us that Ross has arrived at an answer—an answer that is not put into words but demonstrated, exemplified, by the sequence itself in its place within the finished film.

When the camera peers into the murky factory-turned-storeroom, it reprises a shot that concluded a sequence in which a Mr. Lackey shows

Ross the old factory building, which Lackey was instrumental in preserving. Over that shot, Ross remarks "I guess I should be grateful to Mr. Lackey's preservationist efforts on behalf of my family. But what exactly is being preserved here? What's being passed down?" By reprising the earlier shot, the film ties together—again, no doubt jokingly—Lackey's "preservation efforts" and *Bright Leaves*—as if Ross's film, too, is a "preservation effort" on behalf of the McElwee family. Then what, exactly, is "preserved" in *Bright Leaves*? What is being passed down?

The earlier shot peering into the factory-turned-storeroom is followed by a fade to black and then—in a magical transition—by a shot of a young boy at the seashore, wading in a shallow pool of water under a pier, gazing into the little net he is holding to see if he has succeeded in catching a fish in it, as Ross says, in voice-over, "This is my son, Adrian, on the Carolina coast, during one of our trips down here for a family reunion." When he adds, "My parents used to bring *me* here every summer when *I* was a boy," Adrian looks directly into the camera.

The reprise of the shot of the factory-turned-storeroom is followed by a cut to Mr. Lackey scrubbing its brick wall, and then—in another

magical transition that transports us to a different place, a different time, a different world—again to Adrian, looking thoughtful, as Ross says, in voice-over, "My father died when he was relatively young, before Adrian was born, and I've always been sad that Adrian never got to know his grandfather."

This is a rare moment when Ross's voice-over, although in the present tense, acknowledges—and perhaps overcomes or transcends—the gap between the time of his shooting and the time of his recording of the narration. That his father died before Adrian got to know him is a fact that made Ross sad, makes him sad, will always make him sad. This feeling ties together the "old" Ross, who voices it in words, and the "new" Ross, who expresses it cinematically, movingly but wordlessly, by cutting to a lovingly framed close-up of Adrian—this is another magical moment—that brings this breathtaking sequence to a close.

Enabling his son to get to know his grandfather, this sequence declares, is what the film is committed to "doing" with this footage. But again, what knowledge, exactly, is *Bright Leaves* to preserve and pass down to Adrian? What makes this such a pointed question is the fact that in a sense Ross and his father never really knew each other. That much we know, do we not, from *Sherman's March* and *Time Indefinite*?

So Ross's sadness that Adrian never got to know his grandfather is also Ross's sadness that he never got to know his own father. It is Ross's sadness that his father never got to know him. And no doubt, it finds its match in his father's sadness that he never passed down to Ross—as he did to Ross's brother, who followed in his footsteps and became a doctor—his own knowledge, his faith, his calling as a healer. In *Sherman's March*, for example, there is no sign that Ross knows what *Bright Leaves* enables us to know about his father. If Ross knew it then, he didn't then know how, or why, to express what he knew, or didn't know he knew it. So the knowledge of his father to be preserved and passed on in *Bright Leaves* is also self-knowledge, the filmmaker's knowledge of who he is.

This sequence ties together what seems to be the main storyline of *Bright Leaves*—Ross's pursuit of the truth about his great-grandfather—and the deeper concern, nestled within the film, with the filmmaker's achieving, and expressing, a new understanding, and appreciation, of his father.

In this spirit Ross seeks out some of his father's old patients, both black and white, whose conversations with the filmmaker add up to an eloquent composite portrait of a true physician.

Among the most moving of these scenes revolves around William Massey, on whom Ross's father performed surgery, and his wife, and with their middle-aged daughter, who tells Ross that the night before the surgery his father visited her father in the hospital. "My father is a praying person," she says. The two men prayed together." When Ross says that he had never heard this story, she replies, "Daddy didn't tell you? And your father didn't?" "No." "Well," she says, with a knowing smile, "sometimes daddies don't talk about things like that. But my dad did." She adds that this was a reason her parents called Ross's father every Christmas morning to sing "Silent Night" for him. This comment sets up one of the cleverest, yet most touching, little passages in the film. Ross cuts from the daughter to her elderly parents, framed frontally, sitting on their front porch, singing "Silent Night" to the camera. This is followed by a cut to Ross's father, in his house, his wife holding a telephone to his ear as he listens, smiling, to the Masseys singing on the other end of the line.

Ross's father was one of those daddies who didn't talk about things like this, yet he is a worthier figure for Adrian to emulate than the Gary Cooper character in *Bright Leaf*, whose main attraction for Ross—apart from the fact that he is incarnated by a star of the magnitude of Gary Cooper—is his status as a noble, if conflicted, failure—a figure whose role in *Bright Leaves* is comparable, in many respects, to that of General Sherman in *Sherman's March*. Tying these two figures together seems almost obligatory when, at the conclusion of the Patricia Neal interview, there is a dissolve to the sequence in *Bright Leaf* in which Cooper, after Patricia Neal leaves him, cries out in anguish that he wants to watch it burn as his house is consumed by flames, *Gone with the Wind*-style, as the image fades out.

Ross's identification with the Cooper character—the noble, proud yet conflicted rebel who fails—is intertwined with the reflections, so important to all his films, on the South. As *Bright Leaves* moves in the direction of reconciliation and forgiveness, Ross's temptation to identify with his great-grandfather's losing cause—to keep on fighting the Civil War, in effect—recedes, as his father increasingly moves into the foreground.

The interview with Patricia Neal, Gary Cooper's co-star in *Bright Leaf*, marks another significant moment in this trajectory. Earlier, Ross had asked her how it felt to act with Cooper in *Bright Leaf*, and she had said, with a bare hint of emotion, that it was well known that he was the love of her life, adding, "I was with him for about five years and that was the end of that. I got married and had children, and, you know . . ." Now Ross tests out on Miss Neal his theory that there are "secret documentaries nestled in every Hollywood movie." He asks her how it makes her feel, watching a film like *Bright Leaf*, that she is seeing herself as she was so many years ago. Does it help her to remember things about her life then? Firmly, yet, as always, graciously, she says, "No, I don't even think that way." Of course, Patricia Neal is not denying that there *is* a "secret documentary" nestled in *Bright Leaf*, that she *could* view the film as a memento of her passionate affair with Gary Cooper. But she has no use for thinking that way. She has moved on.

The filmmaker, too, has moved on. Jokingly, he symbolically lays to rest his old self, the self addicted to melodrama, in the shot of the vaulted ceiling of the cathedral-like Duke University chapel, viewed from below—as if from the point of view of Washington Duke and his son James, who had the chapel built to house his father's remains and whose body is now lying beside his father's. They seem, as Ross puts it, "to be resting in peace," although they lived their whole lives without understanding each other.

This chapel represents another of the film's metaphors for itself, I take it, one which acknowledges, for all its irony, that *Bright Leaves* is no less concerned than *Time Indefinite* or *Six O'Clock News* with the question of God. *Bright Leaves* is a kind of chapel, built without hands, in the words of "That Old Gospel Ship," one of the great old gospel songs that are integrated in the film, in which conflicts are laid to rest.

From Patricia Neal's enigmatic smile, at once angelic and mischievous, there is a decidedly strange cut to a shot—it echoes the opening shot of the sequence—of the view through her hotel room window. In this shot, devoid of human figures, we see a cluster of black bags of garbage on the roof of the building across the street, the plastic blowing in the wind, the entire view mottled with shifting shadows, as Ross says in voice-over, "The interview was over. Patricia Neal has to go to her next appointment."

This shot is so striking, so strange, that it seems to demand, even as it resists, interpretation. What is the point, the secret fiction, nestled within its photographic recording of reality? Well, metaphorically, what is the trash in these bags, ready for reaping by the grim garbage collector? Is it Ross, whom Miss Neal has just dismissed to move on to her "next appointment"? his pet theory? Patricia Neal herself (who, sadly, died not long after her appearance in this film but not without a glorious swan song in Robert Altman's *Cookie's Fortune*)? Or is the shot's secret point one that has nothing to do with what is in these bags but in the way the wind blows the black plastic, the way unseen, moving clouds create shifting effects of light and shadow? For this shot always makes me think of the shot in *Six O'Clock News*—another view through a hotel room window—that accompanies, or motivates, Ross's question as to whether it is really possible that God is hiding in *these* shadows.

In any case, it is this strange shot—whether we think of it as of garbage bags or of shifting patterns of light and shadow—that dissolves into the charged image of Gary Cooper watching with grim satisfaction as flames consume his house. And surprisingly, or perhaps not so surprisingly, after this image of fire fades out, the image that fades in is one of ashes being scooped from a trash receptacle into a black garbage bag. This shot, which introduces an impromptu interview with the cleaning woman—I want to call her a charwoman—whose job is to empty the trash receptacles and ashtrays in and around Ross's motel, thus serves to link together, in a surrealistic chain of associations, the Patricia Neal sequence, the fire that burns down Cooper's house, and piles of cigarette

ashes. After the cleaning woman departs the scene, Ross holds on a beautifully composed shot of the parking lot in front of the hotel, with garbage cans placed at regular intervals segmenting the frame.

"I allow myself an intermission of sorts from the theatrical complexities of *Bright Leaf*," Ross says in voice-over, segueing to one of the film's most extraordinary sequences. "I spend the next day just filming around my motel." There is a cut to a shot of a covered garbage receptacle, with the black plastic lining sticking out around the edges, blowing in the wind and providing the shot with its only movement. "For me, filming can be an almost narcotic experience. . . . Come to think of it, it's not unlike smoking cigarettes. When I look through a viewfinder, time seems to stop. A kind of timelessness is momentarily achieved."

Ross's words echo his earlier line, "The thing I most remember about smoking was how it made me feel both that time had stopped and that time would go on forever. Smoking made me feel sort of momentarily immortal." It is an idea crucial to the film that there is a connection between filming and smoking. They are both addictive, and their appeal is the same. They make one feel that time has stopped, that life will go on forever. And yet smoking kills. Does filming, too, exact a cost? To whom?

As Ross is describing the almost narcotic experience of filming, there is a shot of the back window of a car, then a shot of fluffy clouds in a bright blue sky. There seems to have been no reason for Ross to have taken these shots. Thus they serve as illustrations of Ross's testimony that, like smoking, filming itself is pleasurable.

As we view these shots, do we feel the timelessness Ross says that he feels when he looks through the viewfinder? If so, do the shots enable us to imagine what he was feeling when he filmed them? Or does time seem to stop for us, too? Is it Ross's calm or our own that we feel? I phrase the question in this way to bring out the deep connection between this moment and one of the two greatest passages in *Six O'Clock News*, the one in which Ross films a man named Salvador in his modest home in South Los Angeles. Salvador, grievously injured when an earthquake caused a parking garage to collapse on top of him, has largely recovered from his wounds. A man of faith, he sits there in silence, totally absorbed in a Christian comic book. Ross, knowing they have nothing more to say to each other, does not try to engage Salvador in conversation but films in silence. The resulting shots—of Salvador; of the pages of the comic book that hold him in thrall but have no such hold on Ross or, presumably, on us; of various objects in the room, again of no particular interest; finally, a close-up of a faucet, slowly dripping—illustrate Ross's testimony, in voice-over, that a strange calm has come over him. He wonders whether this is Salvador's calm. Is this the serenity that comes from faith in God? Does this calm tie the two men together or seal their separation, their aloneness? Is this transcendence or the emptiness of utter boredom?

But back to *Bright Leaves*, where at this moment there is a cut to Ross, looking through the viewfinder of his camera, which seems to be out of doors, on a tripod, and aimed right at us—as if we, not he, were the camera's subject. (It delights me that my reading of this passage, and others in the film, resonates so harmoniously with Marian Keane's in this volume.)

"Just filming around here," he says in voice-over. "Playing with exposure, depth of field and mirrors and trying to see how many special effects can be created without the use of special effects." While he speaks these lines, the image keeps changing as he opens and closes the diaphragm, pulls focus, and zooms in and out, ultimately revealing that Ross and his camera, in fact, are not on the street but inside his hotel room, shooting into a mirror.

In relation to the space of this shot, we thought we knew where we stood. Now we recognize that the shot has been turned inside out spatially. And when Ross adds, "I don't even notice the large rat that is about to slip by in the background," and a moment later such a rat scuttles across the frame, we recognize that temporally, too, the shot is bewildering. Ross's narration, as always, is in the present tense. But his words here highlight, instead of eliding, the gap between the time of shooting and the time of speaking. The "present," as his words invoke it, is—was—already the past. And he spoke—speaks—to us in the present, a time which, for him, is the future. Is this what it means for filming to stop time—that past and present and future endlessly reflect and indeed become each other?

Part of the appeal of smoking, Ross had earlier suggested, is the intimacy smokers share as they breathe the same air, the smoke in their breaths mingling. Ross, in his voice-over, is forever sharing intimacies with us, sharing with us his thoughts and feelings. When, in the midst of taking this shot, he looks up at the camera, that is, at his own reflection in the mirror, Ross is alone in his hotel room, of course. Yet his voice-over confides in us what he is—was—imagining at this moment, namely, Adrian—some time in the future, when Ross is no longer around—looking at what Ross has filmed, that is, looking at what he is now filming—his own mirror image. But if Ross, as he is filming, is imagining the viewer who will one day be looking at this to be *Adrian*, can he really be speaking *to us*? To whom is he confiding this? To whom are his words really addressed? To Adrian? To himself? To us? To no one?

There is now a cut to Adrian, who looks into the camera before pulling his gaze away with a smile. "I can almost feel him looking back at me," Ross says, "from some distant point in the future, through these images and reflections." Adrian is quite literally looking back at Ross,

who is behind the camera. But Adrian is not "looking back" from the future. He is "looking ahead," from out of the past, the time, years earlier, when this shot was taken.

Ross says that he can "almost feel" Adrian looking back at him "through these images and reflections." At what moment does he "almost feel" this? The moment he is invoking is one in which he is viewing this shot, as we are, not the moment when he filmed the shot. So this line marks a significant shift. Ross is no longer speaking about what he was imagining when he was looking through the viewfinder. By "these images and reflections" Ross can only mean this sequence itself. In other words, the experience Ross is now invoking pertains to the time of his speaking of these words, not the time of his taking of these shots. His words testify to his sense of the uncanny power of these "images and reflections" as they are used in *Bright Leaves*. It is through these "images and reflections," as they appear in the finished film, that Adrian in the future will be able to "look back" at him, Ross "almost feels" as he writes, and speaks, these words.

Ross's words here articulate his aspiration for *Bright Leaves*. He wishes for these "images and reflections" to be a medium through which he can make himself known to Adrian—and to us. And in the opposite direction, he wishes these "images and reflections" to be a medium through which he can envision the kind of person Adrian will one day become, the kind of person that we, too, should aspire to becoming.

Staying with Adrian, the camera observes, in a series of shots, his at first fumbling but ultimately successful attempts to tie his shoelaces, as Ross says, in voice-over, "Apparently, Adrian was just learning to tie his shoes, and apparently I just wanted to preserve the moment." His shoes now tied, Adrian picks up two big pieces of rope and begins tying their ends together. "I guess he was at the stage where he was learning to tie all kinds of knots," Ross comments, and then a downward tilt of the camera reveals that the other end of one of these ropes is tied to Ross's leg. The last shot of Adrian shows him grinning at the camera as he unties the knot that momentarily bound him to his father.

Ross says in voice-over, "I didn't film this for any particular reason. It was just a little scene, a little moment, fading forth from then to now." He may have had no particular reason for filming Adrian "learning to tie all kinds of knots," but he has reasons for inserting this little scene here. Among these reasons is its highlighting of the image, and concept, of tying knots, and its associating of these images—jokingly, to be sure—with the ties that bind father and son. Tying knots is a recurring figure that I take it to be yet another of the film's metaphors for itself, for its own making (shades of Hitchcock's *Rope*!).

I have in mind, for example, the shots of Ross's brother, the future doctor, and their father, who was teaching him how to tie sutures. Ross had already used these shots in *Backyard*, a short film he made before *Sherman's March*, so their appearance here also serves to bind together Ross's individual films, or to reveal how closely they are bound to each other.

Perhaps the most important instance of this recurring figure in *Bright Leaves* takes us to the film's ending, and to the ending of this essay, in a way that, if you can forgive me for saying this, ties up loose strings.

After the Tobacco Festival—from now on to be called the Farmers' Day Festival—that provides *Bright Leaves* with a uniquely upbeat finale that celebrates the reality of change (even as it acknowledges that the more things change, the more they stay the same), there is a little coda that begins with a static shot of a ship tied up in the Wilmington harbor as Ross says, in voice-over, "So, for over 200 years ships have sailed from Wilmington, North Carolina, with shipments of American tobacco." There is a cut to a dreamy shot—taken just after sunset, a pale full moon hovers overhead—of a ship—presumably the same ship, loaded with tobacco, but we can just as well imagine it to be a slave ship—that has embarked on its journey, surrounded in the frame by the blue of the water and the blue tinged with pink of the sky.

"They've sailed down the river and out to sea," Ross's narration continues, as the ship glides slowly and silently across the frame, "destined for countries where people have always appreciated bright leaf tobacco and aren't concerned with the fact that it may slowly be killing them. A money manager in Hong Kong, a waitress in Marseilles, a travel agent in New Delhi, pause from their day's work, light up an American cigarette, and inhale. Time stops momentarily. A dreamy calm envelops them, and they smile, as if having been taken to a mysterious, faraway place."

The fixity of the camera, combined with the absence of people, links this dreamy shot with the shots that were used to illustrate the narcotic-like pleasure of filming. Ross speaks words that likewise tie together several main strands of the film. "Time stops momentarily. A dreamy calm envelops them, and they smile, as if having been taken to a mysterious, faraway place." (In a fine cut of *Bright Leaves*, this dreamy shot was absent from the film's ending. In its place were two static shots: first, a shot of the ship's masts and cables framed against the sky, second, a shot of a thick rope, tied around a stanchion, that secures the ship to its mooring. These shots had the advantage of tying together, symbolically, all the film's images of ropes and knots. However, they had the disadvantage of being distinctly "undreamy.")

When Ross is looking through the viewfinder at such moments, time seems to stop, he has told us, and he sometimes imagines Adrian, in the future, looking at what he is shooting, what he has shot. So it is yet another of the film's magical moments when there is a cut to an intimate shot of Adrian's hand, cupping a tiny fish in a pool of water, the sound of waves locating this scene as happening at the beach and linking it with Adrian's initial entrance.

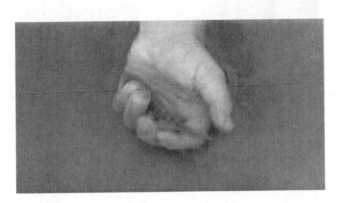

In this shot, Adrian isn't looking back at his father, but presenting something for his father to film. Off-screen, we hear Adrian say something like "You can do like this, because it can die." The camera tilts up, capturing the intent expression on Adrian's face, the boy's evident concern for the fish's life, then tilts back down as Adrian gently opens his hand to let the fish swim out of it, then moves his hand to pick it up again. This image uncannily invokes—but as it were, undoes—the frightful image at the heart of *Time Indefinite* that Jim Lane discusses in his essay for this volume. I want to say it lifts that image's curse of a fish out of water gasping for breath moments before a little boy stamps the life out of it.

A cut to a longer shot, from a different angle, enables us to see the shoreline in the background and reveals that the fish was trapped in a pool cut off by the receding tide. When Adrian stoops down to pick up the fish, this is no longer a gesture addressed to the camera. And as Adrian runs toward the edge of the ocean, accidentally drops the fish, picks it back up, and finally, reaches the shore, the camera stays behind. Finally the image fades out.

Adrian is at once "tying a knot," forging a bond with the fish, and letting it go, forging a bond *by* letting it go, by preserving its life, keeping it from dying. Ross, filming Adrian, is at once "tying a knot," strengthening his bond with his son, and letting Adrian go, embracing his son's freedom, blessing him on his way. This is expressed by the camera's remaining behind, so that, visually, Adrian recedes further into the distance until he is finally enveloped in the dreamy calm of the shot.

In this calm, we feel the withdrawal of the world, a withdrawal from the world, a kind of death. "O death, where is thy sting?" we may well wonder as the hauntingly beautiful gospel song "The Old Ship of Zion" fades up on the sound track, the image fades to black, and the final credits begin, enlivened by the song's words of comfort ("As I step on board, I'll be leaving / all my troubles and trials behind. / I'll be safe with Jesus the captain / sailing out on the old ship of Zion.").

When tobacco is smoked, only ashes remain. Used as they are in *Bright Leaves*, the shots Ross films, even when he films them for no apparent reason, become something rich and strange. This shot records a moment of reality, but in it reality is also transcended. We smile, having been taken to a mysterious, faraway place. *Bright Leaves* does more than make this transcendent place seem real. The film makes it real. Its images and reflections are "bright leaves" that do not slowly kill us, but help us appreciate life, help bring life back to us, help bring us back to life, help keep us from dying.

In the Rhu interview, Ross confirms my sense that in making *Bright Leaves* he aspired to make a film that heals, rather than kills. Rhu refers to Ross's essay about Walker Percy's novel *The Last Gentleman*, in which Ross connects filmmaking with his father's medical vocation through the concept of autopsy. Ross replies, "The present that is captured on film is, I guess, the corpse of the present" (Rhu 2004, 10). But he adds—noting that this is a thought he had never had before—that in filming "you're performing not only an act of observation of something that's expired, you're also trying to bring it back to life again. . . . That's very much at the heart of . . . my experience . . . of making these documentary films. Shooting large amounts of footage, assembling it in an editing room years later, and then trying to restore some version of the life that you feel is due to it, that you feel relates to how you experienced it at that time. It's a little . . . like medicine. In some metaphorical way, you are trying to revive the patient, to bring the patient back to life."

I would add only that the patient in need of revival is less the past, the world on film, than the present. Physicians do not raise the dead, after all; they heal the living. To bring life back to the living at times requires freeing the ghosts of the past—including the ghosts of our own dead selves—to rest in peace. That requires acknowledging the dead, achieving a new perspective on the past. Filming can hardly accomplish this, but perhaps composing a film like *Bright Leaves* can. That is Ross McElwee's faith.

"I make films in the present tense," Ross tells Rhu. "They capitalize upon the spontaneity of the moment. It's not scripted. It's not rehearsed. This isn't 'Take Three.' It's the one and only time it happened. You either get it or you don't" (Rhu 2004, 8). Or in the words of the gospel song, "Get on board the old ship of Zion. It will never pass this way again."

Here on earth, Vlada should be smiling. *Bright Leaves* has kept faith with the art of cinema. In heaven, Ross's father should also be smiling. His son has become a "praying man" after all. And he has taken up his father's calling.

PART 3

Jean Rouch:
The Filmmaker as Provacateur

9

PAUL STOLLER

Jean Rouch and the Power of the Between

J EAN ROUCH'S GREATEST CONTRIBUTION to the human sciences and to the cinema was to create a body of work in which the limits of the ethnographic are the limits of the imagination. In Jean Rouch's universe ethnographers participated fully in the lives of their others. Dreams became films; films became dreams. Feeling was fused with thought and action. Fusing poetry and science, Jean Rouch showed us the path of wise ancestors and guided us into a wondrous world where we not only encounter others, but also encounter ourselves. In this essay, I attempt to demonstrate how Jean Rouch's more than sixty years of experience in West Africa planted him firmly in the "between," a space in which he developed his creative vision, a vision that provides a felicitous example for doing ethnography in the complex and chaotic social worlds that constitute twenty-first century social life.

Songhay people from Niger, who are the subjects of most of Jean Rouch's films, confront the complexities of social life with patience. They like to wait, as they say, for their paths to emerge. The culture of the academy, one that influences all of us who work as scholars, is one that expects results—not a long wait for a path to emerge. This cultural tendency makes the specter of describing—let alone understanding—the complex forms of social life a formidable challenge. The work of Jean

125

Rouch, I shall attempt to demonstrate, provides a model of how to get to the space of the imagination, how to confront complex social formations with innovative verve.

The greatest issues of Rouch's time—war, colonialism, and racism—fired his imagination. They inspired him to seek new ways to understand and represent the complex forms of his social world—new ways to sweeten life in the world. No matter the challenge he faced, Rouch was unafraid to take risks, to try something new, or to bear the consequences of his choices. When he found himself, as was often the case, on an intellectual, artistic or cultural crossroads Rouch would often choose the less-traveled path and say: "Pourquoi pas?" Why not try something different? This playfully deep creativity met the challenges of the complex social forms he attempted to describe and understand.

Consider how Rouch confronted the philosophical imponderables of the Dogon people. The late Germaine Dieterlen once called the Dogon, who live along the Bandiagara cliffs in northeastern Mali, the philosophers of West Africa. Indeed, if you read the transcriptions of Dogon songs and sayings, it becomes evident that they have long pondered the mysteries of life and death. But it is through the *Sigui* ceremonies, held every sixty years, that the Dogon dramatize their most profound thoughts about the imponderables of life and the nature of death. Although anthropologists like Marcel Griaule had written authoritatively about the *Sigui*, no anthropologist had ever witnessed a *Sigui* ceremony. Given the prospect of a new sequence of *Sigui* ceremonies that would begin in 1967, how should anthropologists approach this complex ceremony? Rouch thought that film, rather than a more "acceptable" textual evocation, might be the medium to probe the deep philosophical mysteries of the ceremonies.

Overcoming a variety of obstacles, Jean Rouch and Germaine Dieterlen filmed the entire sequence of *Sigui* ceremonies between 1967 and 1973. In 1967 Rouch, Dieterlen, Gilbert Rouget (an ethnomusicologist), and Guindo Ibrahim (a sound technician), traveled to Yougou to film the first of the seven yearly ceremonies. Shaded by a giant baobab tree, the *Sigui* initiates, all men naked to the waist, danced in a serpentine procession. Rouch wrote:

> I will always remember this sequenced shot of several minutes, where I discovered the Tai square overrun little by little by a serpentine line of men, classed strictly by age ranks, all dressed in indigo cotton trousers, bare-chested, wearing on their necks and ears and arms their wives' or sisters' adornments, their heads covered by white embroidered bonnets . . . carrying in their right hand a fly whisk, and in their left hand the *dunno*, the T-shaped chair, and singing

to the rhythm of the drums: "The *Sigui* takes off on the wings of the wind." (Rouch 1979, 23–24)

Like the *Sigui*, Rouch and camera took off on "the wings of the wind" and flew for seven years.

Prior to the film, Dogon specialists had a particularistic view of the *Sigui*. They knew how to stage the *Sigui* ceremonies celebrated in their own villages. Using the filmed images of the entire ceremonial sequence, which included symbolically distinct footage from seven villages along the Bandiagara cliffs, Rouch and Dieterlen could interpret the *Sigui* from a broader perspective. From this vantage, they discovered that the *Sigui* was fundamentally about life, death, and rebirth. During the first three years of the cycle, the ceremonies, performed in Yougou, Tyougou, and Bongo, evoked the whys and wherefores of death-in-the-world. The final four ceremonies, performed in Amani, Ideyli, Yami, and Songo, evoked themes of life-in-the-world. The sixty years between ceremonial cycles represented the sixty-year life span of the first human being, Diounou Serou. The *Sigui*, in fact, is the seven-year celebration of Diounou Serou's immortal reincarnation as a great serpent. The serpent, symbolized by the serpentine line of dancers described above, flies on the wings of wind. The *Sigui* takes off in Yougou. After a seven-year journey that winds like a snake through the major Dogon villages, the *Sigui* returns from Songo to the place of his death and rebirth, Yougou where, after another 60 years, the cycle will repeat itself and the world will be reborn—in 2027. Rouch's confrontation with the power of Dogon culture compelled him to use film as a powerful tool to uncover the complex central themes of how the Dogon make sense of the mysterious cycles of life and death (Stoller 1992, 174–98).

Rouch was also one of the first anthropologists to confront the complex issues of power and race. He did so by making provocatively imaginative films, films of what he called "ethno-fiction." These included *Jaguar*, *Les maîtres fous*, *Moi, un noir* and *La pyramide humaine*, *Chronique d'un été*, and the wonderfully humorous *Petit à Petit*.[1] In all of these films, Rouch collaborated significantly with African friends and colleagues. Through this active collaboration, which involved all aspects of shooting and production, Rouch used the camera to participate fully in the lives of the people he filmed as well as to provoke them and, eventually, his audiences into imagining new dimensions of sociocultural experience. Many of the films of this period cut to the flesh and blood of European colonialism, compelling us to reflect on our latent racism, our repressed sexuality, and the taken-for-granted assumptions of our intellectual heritage. They also highlight the significance of substantive collaboration, a research tactic that Rouch called *anthropologie partagée*, "shared anthropology," in the construction of scholarly knowledge. Through these provocative films, Jean Rouch unveiled how relations of power shape our dreams, thoughts, and actions (Stoller 1997, 119–35).

Much has been written about the disciplinary vicissitudes of visual anthropology in the social sciences. My comments here are not intended to add to the ongoing—some would say never-ending—debate. Instead, I would like to explore how the late Jean Rouch, scientist and human- ist, anthropologist and filmmaker, ethnographer and artist, confronted powerful images in an attempt to understand the African realities—of the Songhay and Dogon—that challenged his sensibilities. For Rouch the question that pushed him to the productive outer limits of social science and film practice was: How do you come to terms with knowledge not yet known to us? In this chapter I attempt to explore how Jean Rouch's deep experience in West Africa, which made him a sojourner of the be- tween, and which, in turn, compelled him to invent radically new ways of representing social life.

Rouch and Songhay Sorcery

Jean Rouch conducted most of his ethnographic work among the Songhay- speaking peoples of the republics of Niger and Mali. From 1942 when he first traveled to Niger as a young civil engineer building roads until his tragic death on a Nigerien road in 2004, Jean Rouch was intensely interested in the practices of Songhay sorcerers. Rouch learned a great deal about Songhay sorcery from one of its greatest practitioners, Mossi Bana who lived in Wanzerbé, which is known in Songhay as the village of sorcerers. We know from Rouch's monumental ethnography *La religion et la magie songhaï* that the Songhay sorcerer, called a *sohanci*, possesses a number of capacities that challenge our taken-for-granted assumptions (see Rouch 1989). The *sohanci's* extensive knowledge of healing plants, some of which have, as yet, no scientific classification, is not surprising. There are, however, two domains of the *sohanci's* practice that defy our scientifically contoured beliefs: astral projection, the ability to displace oneself to distant places and domains, and the presence of the *sisiri*, the magic chain that a select few of *sohanci* carry in their stomachs. When Rouch first learned about the putative existence of the *sisiri*, he, like most of us, asked, How can it be? How can a person carry a small metal chain in his stomach or intestine without dying from metallic poisoning? And yet, Rouch observed *sohanci* dances in Wanzerbé during which dancers at the climax of their trances brought up their chains of power. In one of his early works, *Les magiciens de Wanzerbé*, in fact, Rouch captures on film a *sohanci* dancer producing his *sisiri*. Rouch used film to document the unthinkable (see Rouch 1948–49).

When Rouch screened *Les magiciens* to a group of physicians, they proposed to test the hypothesis that a person could carry a metal chain in her or his stomach. Believing that chain production was simply a matter of sleight of hand, they asked if they could accompany Rouch to Wanzerbé with a portable X-ray machine. They wanted to X-ray the *sohanci* dancers to see if they *really* carried chains in their stomachs. Rouch agreed, and a few months later, he and two French physicians traveled to Wanzerbé with a generator and a portable X-ray machine. At dusk after a long trip, the trio of Europeans sat down on canvas director's chairs and poured themselves a whiskey to celebrate the end of a long day. Just then, the homeward-bound senior *sohanci* of Wanzerbé walked in front of them. In a flash, one of the physicians fell from his chair. Violent convulsions rocked his body. The second physician tried to minister to his colleague—without success. Rouch suggested they abandon the experiment and return immediately to Niger's capital, Niamey, where the convulsing physician could be evacuated back to France. Bantering gibberish, the crazed physician finally made it back to Paris. As soon as he found himself on French soil, the symptoms disappeared. He never returned to Niger, and no one ever again proposed to X-ray a *sohanci*. Rouch never offered an explanation—at least to me—of this stream of events. Through the film *Les magiciens de Wanzerbé* and this story, he did suggest that *sohanci* possess knowledge "not yet known to us." In so doing, he challenged us to stretch the boundaries of our imaginations (see Rouch 1993).

The Songhay *sohanci* is also said to have the capacity to let the wind carry him to distant places. Like their ancestor, the Songhay King Sonni Ali Ber, these practitioners claim that they can transform themselves into vultures, the familiar of Sonni Ali Ber and his descendants, and fly off to faraway lands. In doing so, they tend bring back some form of evidence to prove the "truth" of their trip. My teacher of things Songhay, the late Adamu Jenitongo of Tillaberi, Niger, claimed that he had traveled to a house I used to own in Washington D.C. How could he have done so? As far as I knew, he had traveled a bit in Burkina Faso as a young man, but had never been to Europe or North America. Even so, he gave me an uncannily accurate description of my living room—the color and patterns of two Turkish carpets, the shape and texture of my coffee table, the presence of African art objects on top of a bookshelf, the color, shape, and arrangements of furniture. It was as if he had just visited my home.

This kind of displacement would be, to say the least, difficult to document, but Rouch, who never let genre limit the expansiveness of his artistic expression, eventually attempted to recreate the magical space of astral projection. He did so in the latter part of his fanciful film, *Madame l'Eau*.[2] Using the poetic tone of surrealist poet Paul Eluard and the seductive music of a three-string lute, Rouch's camera follows his actor and friend Tallou Mouzourane as he goes to a seaside dune in Holland with a donkey, recites an incantation, and is whisked up in a swirling, howling wind that carries him from Europe to Africa and finally to a dirt road in Niamey, Niger. Is this pure fantasy? Is it possible? Rouch, using the creative framework of ethno-fiction, characteristically leaves it to us to ponder these existential questions as we reflect about what is and what is "not yet known" to us.

Rouch and Songhay Spirit Possession

The bulk of Jean Rouch's corpus of more than 120 films is focused on Songhay spirit possession. Rouch witnessed his first spirit-possession ceremony in 1942 in the Songhay village of Gangell. From that moment until his death in 2004 Rouch used his camera to seek a better understanding of how people "see" and "talk" with the Songhay spirits. He also used the camera, as in his film *Horendi*, to ponder the delicate relationship in a spirit-possession ceremony among music, musicians, and dancers. Most famously he also produced films like *Les maîtres fous* to document a set of spirit powers that made mediums impervious to fire, poison, and pain.[3]

Songhay people believe that a human being consists of three elements: flesh (*ga*), life force (*hundi*), and the double (*bia*). Flesh, of course, is our material being—the body. The life force is placed in the heart at birth and dissipates at the moment of death. The double is our immaterial aspect. We see it as a reflection of ourselves in the surface of water or in a mirror. The double marks the individuality of our being; it sets the tone of our personalities, our likes and dislikes, the quality of our expression. It is our being in the world. Human being is anchored by flesh. The spirit, by contrast, exists as pure *bia*, a shadow or reflection without a body. When spirit possession musicians play their special songs and when the *sorko*, or praise-singer to the spirits, recites the "old words" of his special praise-poems, spirits are drawn to the bodies of their mediums. At the right moment, the spirit displaces the double of his medium and takes over her or his body. Because the double encompasses personal traits, when a spirit double displaces a human double, the body of the medium is transformed. The medium's expression changes as does her or his bearing. In possession of what it usually lacks, the spirit uses the body of the medium to demonstrate its other-worldly power. So situated, the spirit dances, demands sacrifices in its honor, and gives advice, often in the form of warnings, to the members of the audience.[4]

It is perhaps unthinkable for us to admit the existence of sprits that can take over the bodies of mediums. For many people, spirit possession is little more than theater. Scholars often suggest that spirit possession is brought on by hallucinogenic drugs or through self-hypnosis. Rouch knew that spirit possession could not be explained away so simply. Accordingly, many of Jean Rouch's unedited films are studies of the onset of spirit possession—careful examinations of physical and emotional transformation. In these films, the camera attempts to "see" what the musicians, mediums, and spirit priests perceive during a ceremony. How can they "sense" the invisible presence of spirits?

This "sense" of the absence-presence of spirits is wonderfully evoked in Rouch's *Les tambours d'avant: Tourou et Bitti* (1971). At the beginning of this short one-take film, Rouch says: "to enter into his film is to plunge into the real." Here Rouch, like a Songhay spirit, is transformed into the camera that is between Africa and Europe, between the world of the spirits and the world of rationality. Similarly situated in the between, we see what Rouch sees. We approach the village of Simiri, famous in Niger for its spirit-possession troupe. Continuing, we come upon the compound of Sido Zima, the spirit priest of Simiri. We pass a *kraal* in which several sheep are tethered to small wooden posts. Perched on Rouch's shoulder, we approach the dance grounds. Rouch-the-camera focuses on an old man dressed in a billowing indigo cape—Sambo Albeda. Having danced for more than four hours in the hot sun, Sambo, a medium to the Black Spirits, spirits that control the land, is tired. Despite the best efforts of the musicians and the spirit priest, the spirit has refused to displace Sambo's double. Will the ceremony be a complete failure?

Rouch now approaches the musicians who are playing the drums of yore, the Tourou and Bitti. The Tourou is fashioned from a large gourd over which is stretched sheepskin. The Bitti is cylindrical. The ends of the drum are also covered by stretched sheepskin. Unlike the gourd drums that are more typically played during Songhay spirit-possession ceremonies, these are struck with the hand. We see the musicians playing their drums of yore. We hear the drum rhythms and the high pitched whine of the monochord violin. Can the musicians "see" the invisible spirit seeking out its medium? Sambo Albeda resumes his spirited dancing.

Suddenly the music stops. The violinist "senses" that the spirits are close. No longer Sambo Albeda, the old dancer is now Kuré, the hyena. Kuré wants meat. Kuré dances. He is hungry.

Daylight is fading, but Kuré's presence compels old Tusinye Wasi to dance. Soon she is possessed by Hadjo, the Fulan slave who is one of the Black spirits, which represent the earliest inhabitants of Songhay.

The film goes on to record a conference between the spirits and spirit priests. The spirits want meat. The spirit priest wants a good harvest, for these spirits "control" pests like locust and birds that can easily destroy a crop of millet or sorghum, the staples of the Songhay diet. The spirit priest douses the spirits with a perfume that these spirits covet. It is almost dusk and Rouch moves away from the action so that the camera sees what the children of Simiri are seeing. The sun sets on Simiri and Rouch's film.

In *Tourou et Bitti* Rouch—and his camera—take us into another domain of experience not yet known to us. In this work Rouch grants us access to a world full of imponderables. He never attempts to explain how a "spirit" might displace a person's immaterial being. He never offers a theoretical explanation of how a violinist or a drummer could "see" an invisible presence. Instead, he provides images that defy simple explanation, images that trigger our imaginations (Stoller 1992).

Jean Rouch's most famous—and most controversial—film, *Les maîtres fous* (1955), is also about Songhay sprit possession. Scholars have long discussed the importance of this film in the history of film. Anthropologists have noted the importance of *Les maîtres fous* in the development of both ethnographic method and visual anthropology. Some scholars have suggested that the film underscores processes of cultural resistance; others argue that the film demonstrates the power of what Walter Benjamin called the mimetic faculty.[5] In this chapter, I will not add to this substantial debate. Rather, I'd like to demonstrate how this film, like *Tourou et Bitti* and *Les magiciens de Wanzerbé*, documents the unthinkable.

Les maîtres fous is a thirty-minute film that describes the yearly ceremony of Hauka spirits in what was the colonial Gold Coast. The participants are all men from Niger who traveled to the Gold Coast to find jobs in places like Accra and Kumasi. As Rouch explains in *La religion et la magie songhaï*, the Hauka, which in the Hausa language means "crazy" or "mad," are the most recent of Songhay deities. The first example of Hauka spirit possession occurred in 1925.

It all began during a dance of girls and boys. During the dance a Soudye woman, Zibo, who was married to a Timbuktu sheriff, began to be possessed by a spirit. They asked her who it was. It said: "I am Gomno Malia" [governor of the Red Seas]. The people said they did not know this spirit. Then others came and took the bodies of some of the young boys. They too spoke their names, and the people did not know them. The spirits said: "We are the Hauka, the guests of Dongo." This occurred at Chikal, very close to Filingue. A few days later, all the boys and girls of Filingue had been possessed by the Hauka (Rouch 1989, 80).

During the colonial period in Niger, this Hauka mimicry proved to be intolerable to the local French authorities. In fact, Major Croccichia, the commandant of Niamey, arrested the Hauka and confined them for three days. Upon their release, they staged another ceremony, whereupon Croccichia had them arrested again. In the Hauka, the French "discovered the presence of an open dissidence, a society, the members of which openly the social, political, and religious order" (Fugelstad 1975, 203–16). Eventually, many of the Hauka mediums left Niger for the colonial Gold Coast, where the movement flourished between 1935 and 1943. By the time that Rouch filmed *Les maîtres fous* in 1953–54, the Hauka movement was well established in the Gold Coast.

In many ways the Hauka mimicked European colonial culture in West Africa. As previously mentioned, such mimicry, which references themes of colonial domination, social oppression, and cultural resistance, has attracted the attention of film scholars, anthropologists, and African studies specialists. As someone long critical of French colonial politics, Rouch also thought it important to document the Hauka phenomenon. And yet, this literature, including my own early writing about the Hauka, has neglected to focus on the power of images depicting events "not yet known to us." Rouch shows us Hauka deities thrusting their hands into a boiling vat of dog meat stew without ill effect. We watch as the Hauka, in the bodies of their mediums, expose themselves to fire without burning their flesh. This defiance of physical forces underscores the Hauka's power in the world, a power to change the order of things and perhaps make life a bit sweeter. How can this occur? Is it possible?

In his documentation of Songhay spirit possession, Rouch projects a set of powerful images upon his viewers. Offering little in the way of "rational" explanation, he challenges his viewers to come to grips with what they are seeing. Indeed, *Les maîtres fous*, like many of Rouch's other films about Songhay spirit possession and sorcery, documents the existence of the incredible, the unthinkable. These unexplained "colonial" images trigger our imaginations and challenge us to decolonize our thinking and decolonize our being (Stoller 1992 and 1995). Confrontation with the inexplicable, the incredible and the uncanny also, I would argue, compelled Rouch to take representational risks in his works. Just as his exposure to the wonders of African world-making brought Rouch into unthinkable intellectual arenas, so his experience in Africa triggered his imagination to create new forms of ethnographic representation. Why did he feel to need to take disciplinary risks? How could he find the will, amid much disciplinary criticism, to push forward?

Rouch and the Power of the Between

During a televised interview in 1980, Robert Gardner, the highly regarded and highly provocative documentary filmmaker, posed this question to Jean Rouch: "Are you an anthropologist or are you a filmmaker?" "Well," Rouch smiled, "anthropologists think I'm a filmmaker and filmmakers think I am an anthropologist." He smiled at Gardner and said nothing further. For Rouch, that boundary-defining question was beside the point. Just as the Songhay sorcerer lives in a space between the village and bush, between the world of social life and the world of the spirits, just as the cancer patient in remission lives in a space between health and illness, so Rouch lived between France and West Africa, between ethnography and fiction, between anthropology and film—a liminal figure par excellence. Long exposure to the imageric power of things African—"not yet known to us"—compelled Rouch to understand the creative power of the "between." If Rouch's creativity is representative—and I think that it is—then embracing the "betweenness" of being-in-the-world may well be a path, to borrow from the anthropologist Michael Jackson, to a representational clearing.

The between is a central concept in Moroccan mystical thinking. In his thoughtful and elegantly argued book, *Imaginative Horizons*, Vincent Crapanzano describes how Moulay Abedsalem, his Moroccan friend and mentor, thought of the between. For Moulay Abedsalem, the between is *barzakh*, and *barzakh* . . .

> is what lies between things—between edges, borders, and events. He likened it to the silence between words and dreams. "The dream is between waking life and sleep," he said, using the expression "little death" for sleep to emphasize, I believe, the absence (*ghaib*) he, like other Moroccans, associated with sleep and dreaming." (Crapanzano 2004, 57)

The notion of the between has deep roots in Sufi thought. It is a central tenet in the philosophy of the Andalusian Sufi, Ibn al-'Arabi (1165–1240). Al-Arabi says that the between is:

> Something that separates . . . two other things, while never going to one side . . . , as for example, the line that separates shadow from sun light. God says, "he let forth the two seas that meet together, between them a barzakh they do not overpass," (Koran 55:19); in other words one sea does not mix with the other. . . . Any two ad-

jacent things are in need of *barzakh* which is neither one nor the other but which possesses the power . . . of both. The *barzakh* is something that separates a known from an unknown, an existent from a non-existent, a negated from an affirmed, an intelligible from a non-intelligible. (Ibid., 57–58)

For many of us, the nebulous contours of the between become spaces of ambiguity that can generate fear and anxiety, as when the cancer patient attempts to negotiate the indeterminate space between health and illness. And yet, the liminal can also be illuminating.

The liminal has often been likened to the dream. . . . It suggests imaginative possibilities that are not necessarily available to us in everyday life. Through paradox, ambiguity, contradiction, bizarre, exaggerated, and at times grotesque symbols—masks, costumes, and figurines—and the evocation of transcendent realities, mystery and supernatural powers, the liminal offers us a view of the world to which we are normally blinded by the usual structures of social and cultural life. (Geertz 1983)

The liminal, then, can be a space of creative imagination, of provocative linkages, of *barzakh*, of personal empowerment. When anthropologists, filmmakers, or writers mix these elements into a narrative, their stories not only evoke the things most deeply human but do so in ways that underscore the existential multiplicities of social life in a complex world.

Artists and scholars, especially anthropologists, are always between things—between "being-there," as the late Clifford Geertz put it, and "being-here," between two or more languages, between two or more cultural traditions, between two or more apprehensions of reality (Crapanzano 2004, 64). Like Jean Rouch, anthropologists are the sojourners of the between. We go there and absorb a different language, culture and way of being and return here, where we can never fully resume the lives we had previously led.

Living between things can have several existential repercussions. It can simultaneously pull us in two directions so that, in the end, to quote a Songhay ritual incantation, "We don't know our front side from our back side." This state usually leads to indecision, confusion, and lethargy. The between can also carry us into the ether of what Jean-Paul Sartre famously called "bad faith," a systematic and continuous denial of who we are. If, however, we find a way to draw strengths from both sides of the between and breathe in the creative air of indeterminacy, as Jean

Rouch did during his sixty years in West Africa, we can find ourselves in a space of enormous potential growth, a space of power and creativity. For me, that is the power of the between, the power of anthropology. From the indeterminacy of the between, I am convinced, Jean Rouch found the will to take intellectual risks that steered his work in new creative directions that, in turn, enabled him to focus on the tale he wanted to recount.

As Rouch's example implies, the dynamics of the between propels us toward the story. Beyond the theoretical flavor of the day, is there not always, as Rouch like to say, a story to tell? The great contemporary novelist Tim O'Brien, like Jean Rouch, understood this central truth of the human condition. "Stories are for those late hours in the night when you can't remember how you got from where you were to where you are. Stories are for eternity, when memory is erased, when there is nothing to remember except the story" (O'Brien 1990, 38).

Whatever form they take, stories are indeed for an eternity. Like the stories of Jean Rouch, they wind their way through our villages and in their telling and retelling, they link the past, present, and future. To tell these stories is to take off, as the Dogon people like to say, on the wings of the wind, a wind that carries us ever closer to the elusive end of wisdom. In the end it is the texture of the story that marks our contribution to the world. In the end, it is the contour of our stories, as Jean Rouch knew well, that etch our traces in the world.

Notes

A version of this paper was presented at a retrospective and symposium held at the University of Miami to mark the occasion of the filmmaker's death. Papers from the symposium were published, as part of the *Transatlantique* series, in *Jean Rouch: A Celebration of Life and Film*, ed. William Rothman (Fasano, Italy: Schena Editore, 2007). This paper is included in the present volume by permission of Schena Editore.

1. These works are considered films of what Rouch called "ethno-fiction," the first cases in which Rouch played with genre to confront the complexities of colonialism and racism. See Rouch 1953–54, *Les maîtres fous* (Films de la Pléiade); 1957, *Moi, un noir* (Films de la Pléiade); 1958–59, *La pyramide humaine*, released in 1961 (Films de la Pléiade); 1960, *Chronique d'un été* in collaboration with Edgar Morin (Films de la Pléiade); 1969, *Petit à Petit* (Comité de Film Ethnographique [CFE]).

2. See *The Cinematic Griot*, op. cit., 105–17. Rouch recounted these stories to me during a daylong interview in Paris on March 7, 1990.

3. See Jean Rouch *Horendi* (Paris: CFE, 1972). See also, *The Cinematic Griot*, 145–61, and Paul Stoller, *Embodying Colonial Memories: Spirit Possession, Power and the Hauka in West Africa* (New York: Routledge, 1995).

4. See Rouch 1989. See also Paul Stoller, *Fusion of the Worlds: An Ethnography of Possession among the Songhay of Niger* (Chicago: University of Chicago Press, 1989).

5. There is a rich literature on *Les maîtres fous*. See Michael Taussig, *Mimesis and Alterity, a Particular History of the Senses* (New York: Routledge, 1993) for the discussions of embodied memory. In the same vein, see Stoller 1997. For an extensive reanalysis of *Les maîtres fous*, see Henley (2006). For historical and political analysis of *Les maîtres fous*, see, among many works, Nicole Echard, 1992, "Cults de possession et hangmen social: L'exemple du bori hausa de l'Ader et du Kurfey (Niger). *Archives des Sciences Sociales de Religion* 79(2):87–101; and Finn Fugelstad, *A History of Niger (1850–1960)* (Cambridge: Cambridge University Press, 1983).

10

DANIEL MORGAN

The Pause of the World

J EAN ROUCH'S CAREER ENCOMPASSED two distinct disciplines, filmmaking and ethnography. More often than not, he tried to bring them together, to see how ethnographic study could inform his filmmaking and how filmmaking could be used to expand and deepen the practice of ethnography. Much of this had to do with Rouch's development of what he called "shared ethnography," in which he screened the films he was making for the people who were in them, incorporating their comments—and sometimes their voices—into the final version.

It's not my intention here to deal with questions about Rouch's contribution to ethnography.[1] Instead, I want to look at the details of the films themselves, since their formal construction has a tendency to get lost amid speculation about their larger significance. In particular, I will focus on a worry or anxiety that persists throughout Rouch's ethnographic films, one that has to do with the difficulty of involving a (primarily) Western audience in a world with which it is unfamiliar. I will try to show that these films exhibit a felt need to bridge a gap between dissimilar worlds. It is an anxiety that is not just present as a thematic trope or motif. Rather, it is within the basic formal construction of the films that Rouch negotiates and works through the difficulty of bridging the gap between the audience of his films and the worlds his films show.

A range of strategies for dealing with this anxiety can be found across Rouch's work. An early example involves one of his first attempts at ethnographic filmmaking, *Bataille sur le grand fleuve* (Battle on the Great River, 1952). In presenting a hippopotamus hunt on screen, Rouch decided to accompany it with a hunters' song: "Following the old traditions of Westerns, at the most dramatic moment of the hunt, I had added a music track." But the fishermen told him that his decision was wrong: " 'the hippopotamus underwater has very good ears, and if you play music, he'll escape!' Since then, I have almost totally suppressed musical accompaniment, except where it is part of the action."[2] This episode is certainly an instance of Rouch's commitment to a shared ethnography; in light of comments made by his subjects, he modifies his practice to make it accord with the terms of the world he presents. At the same time, the episode also evinces an anxiety about the viewers of *Bataille sur le grand fleuve*. He describes his initial desire to add music to the hunt as an attempt to bring his film within the contours of a familiar cinematic genre—he singles out the genre of the Western here—an act that would place the world of the hunters within a recognizable context for the film's audience. Based on the hunters' remarks, Rouch recognizes the confusion this presentation entailed. But the very fact of his desire to use music in the first place indicates a worry that the gap between the audience and the world shown on film is too great to be surmounted on its own. (That he describes his later work as "suppressing" such a use of music suggests that this desire never entirely left him.[3])

I don't think there is anything like a linear progression over the course of Rouch's career, a set of discoveries he makes that leads him to a full resolution of this worry or anxiety. If anything, a tendency to use related motifs across multiple films, precisely at the moment when such worries surface, suggests that he never finds a solution that satisfies him once and for all. Rather than survey the different techniques Rouch employs to negotiate this tension, I'm going to focus instead on elucidating a particular formal strategy that crops up several times in his work of the late 1960s and early 1970s. Films such as *Jaguar* (1957–1967), *The Drums of Yore: Tourou and Bitti* (1971), and *Funeral of Bongo: The Old Anaï (1848–1971)* (1972) deploy a set of related formal and thematic techniques in an attempt to have the world of the film serve as a bridge for the audience to enter a world with which it is unfamiliar.

Oddly enough, the formal strategy that is of interest here does not first emerge in Rouch's ethnographic films. Instead, he first articulates it as a formal experiment in the *cinéma-vérité* film he made with Edgar Morin, *Chronique d'un été* (Chronicle of a Summer, 1961). There, Rouch discovers something about the possibilities of cinematic form and conventions, a discovery that, in his later ethnographic films, he will employ to work through the worry over his audience.

The moment in *Chronicle of a Summer* where this experiment takes place occurs toward the end of the sequence set in Saint-Tropez. It is a sequence that comes late in the film, when the collection of individuals Rouch and Morin have assembled leave Paris to go (or are asked to go) on holiday. Two of them, Landry and Catherine, have been talking about life in Saint-Tropez—more specifically, they have been talking about Sophie's life as a model—while walking around the beachfront. Later, in a conversation on a rooftop, Morin asks Sophie for her opinion on the matter, and Rouch prods her to talk about how well she knows the city. What follows is a lengthy monologue, delivered in voice-over, about life in a resort town, about the glamour of the people who journey there for vacation (and to be seen), and about whether one gets bored in Saint-Tropez. During this, we see Sophie walk through a café, then go down to the beach on a wooden path, and finally—in a shot from above—sit down on the edge of a pier that extends out over the water. Sophie finishes her speech, saying, "Personally, I'm not bored in Saint-Tropez. . . . So there," as we see her toss her hair, then lean back to lie down on the pier.

Rouch[1] now cuts to a new shot. He shows a tree, shot from below, its trunk extending upwards from the bottom of the frame. The tree's branches spread out to fill the image, filtering the sunlight that comes in from the top left; its leaves are buffeted by a stiff wind, the sound of which can be heard—indeed, the sound of wind was first audible in the preceding shot of Sophie. After a brief pause, the camera starts to tilt down and pan to the right, moving across the tree until it reveals a house nestled in the near distance. Without cutting, Rouch positions the camera to frame the house underneath one of the low-hanging branches, holding the image for several seconds. The film then goes to a scene where Morin talks to his two daughters about his ambitions for the film, raising his recurrent question of whether life is happy or sad.

The shot of the tree works according to the rhetoric of (fictional) narrative cinema, in which the look of a character is manipulated to create a connection between shots. As Sophie lies back on the pier, the cut to the shot of the tree is done so that it feels as if the new shot were taken from the angle she would have were she looking up at it. In formal terms, Rouch uses a standard point-of-view construction to "suture" the shot of the tree into the narrative structure of the film.

The shot of the tree has two primary functions in the sequence. At its most basic level, the shot serves as a transition. Once Rouch gets us into the shot of the tree by way of Sophie's look, we are able to see the house in the distance, the presence of which will be the ostensible motivation for the subsequent cut to the conversation between Morin and his children (the assumption is that the conversation takes place in the house we see). The point-of-view structure placed around the shot of the tree thus allows us to move smoothly between scenes. More generally, the shot of the tree is part of the larger conceptual framework of point of view that the film explores. *Chronicle of a Summer* delves into the perspectives of various people on the world around them: their lives and loves, the political concerns of the time, and so on. It's a theme that's particularly prevalent in the sequence at Saint-Tropez, in which the vacation by the sea is explicitly described as constructed around a specific point of view. Over the first shot of the sequence, which shows Landry and Nadine playing in the water, Rouch says, "And that's how Landry has become the black explorer of France on vacation." The sequence will follow Landry's travels in Saint-Tropez, as he attends bullfights, remarks on the city, talks to Catherine and Sophie about the place of women at the beach, and even converses with Morin's children about the differences between his childhood and their lives growing up in France.[5] In this context, the use of a literal point-of-view construction suggests that Sophie's relaxation as she lies down to rest—the implication is that she gazes languidly at the tree buffeted by the wind—fits squarely within the sequence's conceptual framework, another example of the way people inhabit the seaside resort.

The work done by the shot of the tree, however, is deceptive in its apparent simplicity. A closer look at the way Rouch handles the point-of-view construction shows something more complicated at work. Within the formal conventions the shot appears to follow, Rouch articulates a set of radically different terms for relating to the world in and of the film.

It's precisely the smoothness of the transition that should give us pause. Rouch and Morin are fairly indifferent to such niceties elsewhere in *Chronicle of a Summer*, seeing no problem in abruptly switching scenes without so much as a token gesture toward continuity (formal or dramatic).[6] It's curious then that they take such care to create a coherent and apparently seamless transition here. In fact, as we look harder at this series of shots, the very logic of the transition begins to break down, and the point-of-view structure becomes recognizable as an illusion. This can be shown relatively easily. As the camera pans down from the tree, revealing the house in the background, it is clear that the shot could not have been taken from Sophie's position. Since she faces out to the water, a tilt of the camera to look inland would require her—by the logic of the sequence—to bend her head entirely backward. The rhetoric of her point-of-view in this scene thus implies a fiction that's impossible to sustain.

The creation of an illusory point of view, however, is not the end of the story. Rouch is not simply interested in using the rhetoric of cinema to reveal its inventive capabilities.[7] The way he lingers on the image of the trees blowing in the wind, and then slowly brings the camera down to show the beach house in the distance, shifts the shot's emphasis onto the nature of the world as it stands independent of Sophie's look. It becomes a shot about the tree, as an object worthy of contemplation in itself.

The shot of the tree changes the nature of the world shown by the film. As the coherence of the point-of-view structure breaks down, the shot of the tree begins to float apart from any narrative or discursive context. Rouch creates a break, or gap, in the flow of the film, a moment when its world is no longer moving forward in the way it had been. I want to describe this as the creation of a *pause* in the world, a moment where Rouch halts the rhythm of ordinary life. The effect of this pause is to produce a new kind of experience for the viewer, one that is not based on familiar forms of identification. We are outside the narrative frame to which we had become accustomed, introduced to a new sense of time—the capacity to extend a moment outwards and rest within it—that is articulated in the pause established by the shot of the tree.

The viewer is here presented with an interpretive ambiguity. If it's demonstrably false to say that the shot is from Sophie's point of view, it doesn't feel right to deny the power of its conventions on our reading of the scene. It's a tension that's not easily resolvable, in large part because it mirrors one of the basic concerns of *Chronicle of a Summer*. This is the question of what it means to study how people live in, perceive, and create the world around them. Morin, for example, describes the film as an investigation of

> not only the way of life (housing, work, leisure) but the style of life, the attitude people have toward themselves and toward others, their means of conceiving their most profound problems and the

solutions to those problems. . . . Several lines of questioning stand
out: the search for happiness; is one happy or unhappy; the question
of well-being and the question of love; equilibrium or lack thereof;
stability of instability; revolt or acceptance.[8]

It's at the basic level of how Rouch and Morin present the world in
which people live that the tension over point of view gains significance.
Most of the time, *Chronicle of a Summer* is interested in an individual's
subjective perspective on and engagement with the world: Marceline's
refusal to contemplate dating a black man, for example, or the African
immigrants' failure to understand the tattoo on her arm. Or in the overall
structure of the Saint-Tropez sequence, where the world is presented to
us through the explorations and perceptions of Landry. At other times,
however, a different way of presenting the world (of Paris in 1960) takes
over: This is a world whose meaning is independent of the perception
of its inhabitants.

If the shot of the tree evokes and makes explicit such ambiguity,
Chronicle of a Summer as a whole works to mitigate the tension it creates. First, Rouch places the pause in the world of the film—the source
of this formal and thematic tension—in the midst of a sequence showing a vacation by the Mediterranean. It's not the rhythm of Paris that's
interrupted, the driving force of urban life; the pause is set in a location
which itself constitutes an interruption to that life. Rouch thus situates a
new way of experiencing time in a world that is already predicated on a
mode of temporality akin to this "new" experience—and one that is easily
recognizable by an audience as belonging to a familiar world and pattern
of life. Second, Rouch and Morin provide surrogates for the audience
within the film. Shortly after the sequence at Saint-Tropez, they show
a discussion that took place among the participants of the film after a
screening of it, and then add a final scene of the two of them walking
and talking about its successes and failures. The placement of audiences
within the film, audiences that provide models for thinking about the
images and events that have just transpired on screen, effectively sidesteps
the question of how an audience crosses the gap between their world
and the potential disruptions to it that emerge within the world of the
film. Rouch and Morin provide an easy path for the audience to cross
over the divide.

Where *Chronicle of a Summer* establishes a set of formal resources
for creating a new relation to the world, several of Rouch's ethnographic
films make this formal strategy do more significant work. Because of the
centrality of the category of the self in Rouch's films and writings on
ethnographic subjects, the work done by the idea of a world in and of

his films, at both formal and thematic levels, has been minimized. To a certain extent, Rouch is responsible for this tendency. Writing on *Tourou and Bitti*, a film (and essay) that has come to stand in for his views on the role of the filmmaker,[9] Rouch emphasizes the importance of the concept of self to the cultures with which he works. He then extends his focus to the position of the filmmaker himself:

> If the notion of *personne*—the self, person—is effectively one of the key religious factors involved in trance, possession dance, magic, and sorcery, it appears that it would be dishonest to leave the matter there, since the "self" of the observer who attends to these phenomena equally merits critical attention.[10]

From there, Rouch describes the various participants involved in ritual possession dances, trying to map out the "concepts of the 'self' among the Songhay-Zarma," before returning at the end of the essay to the role of the filmmaker. He describes how "the filmmaker can throw himself into a ritual, integrating himself with it," and then claims that, in *Tourou and Bitti*, "For the Songhay-Zarma . . . my 'self' is altered in front of their eyes in the same way as is the 'self' of the possession dancers: it is the 'film-trance' [*ciné-trance*] of the one filming the 'real trance' of the other."[11] On the basis of such remarks, Paul Stoller describes Rouch's status in the film as the newly created being of "Rouch-the-camera," a self able to act within the contours of possession rituals. "Had someone else been filming the sequence that day in Simiri," Stoller writes, "I am certain the mediums would not have been possessed. Such is the power of Rouch's persona in Songhay" (Stoller 1992, 170).

The problem with Rouch's argument here is that it belies an anxiety to which his films otherwise testify. The formal features of Rouch's ethnographic films—features of the kind we saw in *Chronicle of a Summer*—suggest that his understanding of the self (of the possessed dancers, for example, or the possessed filmmaker) in fact depends on a more general account of a world. His role as a filmmaker, and the capacity of his camera to produce the effects it does, depends not just on his own perception of the world but on a delineation of that world and the possibilities for action within it—that such things as possession are possible at all—prior to his presence there. We can find Rouch acknowledging this dependence in various places. He writes, for example,

> I learned with the Dogon that the essential character in all these adventures is not God, representing order, but the foe of God, the Pale Fox, representing disorder. So I have a tendency, when

I'm filming, to consider the landscape . . . as precisely the work of God, and the presence of my camera as an intolerable disorder. It's this intolerable disorder that becomes a creative object. (Rouch 2003, 154)

And elsewhere he speaks of his films as exemplifying what would be "the Songhay theory of the person of the filmmaker," thereby articulating a world in which he—insofar as he is able to become "Rouch-the-camera"—will be able to play a role (ibid., 185).

I do not want to deny the importance of the category of the self in Rouch's writings and films. But I do think that the prominence he gives it has obscured some of the deeper tensions in his work. There is in fact an interplay between the role of the self and the development of the idea of a world, an interplay that emerges precisely over the question of how (Western) viewers can inhabit worlds alien to them. Such a tension motivates—sometimes explicitly, sometimes implicitly—Rouch's repeated emphasis on the ability of his presence to lead viewers into the worlds he shows. Thus, responding to an interviewer's sense of the immediacy of the viewer's immersion in his films, Rouch agrees with this assessment, saying by way of explanation, "I was, behind the lens of my camera, the first viewer of my film. So if I got bored during filming, the viewers to whom I might show the film would be equally bored. I was *the* viewer, so my improvisation was that of a viewer" (ibid., 150). Rouch suggests that, at the time of filming, he is simultaneously a viewer of the film being made, and that this position guides his actions. The idea of the viewer as filmmaker is peculiar, if underdeveloped—Rouch (unfortunately) does not pursue it further—but it emerges out of another argument he is making at the same time. By setting himself up as the "first viewer" of his films, Rouch tries to establish the claim that his place and the viewer's are essentially interchangeable. It's an argument that promises a quick fix to the actual distance of the viewer from the world the film shows. Rouch seems to be saying that, if he is able to gain access to the world of the Songhay or Dogon, then by identifying with him (and his gaze through the camera), the (Western) viewer can pass over the gap between worlds.

That the worlds Rouch's films show are alien, and that they therefore require bridges to aid the audience in entering them, comes through in a late film, *Funeral at Bongo: The Old Anaï (1848–1971)* (1972). *Anaï* chronicles the rituals that follow and commemorate the death of Anaï Dolo, a Dogon elder who died at the age of 122. The film begins, after several introductory shots of a village and the surrounding landscape, with Anaï sitting in the door of his hut, unable to see or move but still a central part of the community. Rouch says, "Six months after the shoot-ing of these very frames"—there is a cut to a close-up of a cluster of tall yellow stalks of grass blowing in the wind—"Anaï Dolo died." As he says this, the camera slowly begins to pull back and refocus so that the whole landscape comes into view: A small patch of grass is growing up between several rocks located next to each other on a flat, rocky surface, the plains receding into the distance in the background.

The shot lasts for almost twenty seconds, the wind audibly continu-ing to ruffle the stalks, before Rouch cuts to a shot of the same patch of grass from a position that appears to be 180 degrees from the previous shot. He holds this shot for only a few seconds before cutting to a final close-up of the grass. This time the shot begins in darkness, the stalks of grass illuminated by light, suggesting that the shot is taken at night. Rouch's voice-over returns: "His corpse was buried in the cave of the dead." It seems at first, given the darkness in the frame, as though we are in that very cave. But then the camera pulls back, and it turns out that we are still outside: the time of day is close to evening—the sky is dark, but there is still some light in it—and the dark background is in fact the face of a rock in shadow behind the grass.

As with the false point-of-view shot from *Chronicle of a Summer*, this sequence of shots is motivated by events within the film. Having just learned that Anaï has died in the time between when the footage of him was shot and when the rest of the film was made, the shots of the grass are placed within the time and space of mourning. But how? What role do they play? Rouch says that Anaï's body was buried in the "cave of the dead," but what we see doesn't look like it could be that. We assume that the shots have to do with Anaï's death, and a commemoration of it, but there is nothing within the film to tell us their function. And Rouch, who is elsewhere careful about labeling what the images show, isn't more specific here. Perhaps a better way to think about the shots of the grass is to treat them as functioning at a metaphoric level, as a transition from the recollection of Anaï to the commemoration of his death. (The rest of the film, after all, deals with his funeral.) Yet the sequence is nonetheless detached from this narrative. The way the grass is filmed suggests a kind of self-contained nature to the sequence. We get several views of the patch of grass in the rocks, taken from different angles, but each shot is detached from any framing context, showing only the immediate surroundings (or the far, distant plain). The sequence floats free of its context in a world.

My sense is that what the shots show is to a certain extent less important than the fact of the shots themselves, their temporal duration, and their placement into this particular moment of the film. The shots create a pause before the celebrations begin, and they do so precisely at a moment of transition in the world of the film. The film's opening shots were explicitly set in Rouch's world, the world of an outsider: Rouch says that *he* filmed Anaï Dolo sitting in front of his compound, that Anaï Dolo died when *he* was away, and that now *he* is back to film the funeral celebrations. Throughout the rest of the film, however, Rouch is within the Dogon world, speaking about the events and people the film shows; his status as an outsider to the culture recedes into the background.[12]

The pause that the shots of the grass create, then, is structurally the juncture between these two worlds. But it is also a bridge between them, as Rouch manipulates time to provide a means for the viewer to enter the world of the Dogon. As with the shot of the tree in *Chronicle of a Summer*, the shots of the grass here bring the world to a pause by interrupting the flow of the film. The effect of this is to bring the viewer into a different temporal relation to the world of the film, a relation outside the linear narrative unfolding of the funeral celebrations. It is a temporality that Rouch explicitly associates with the Dogon, and with the world of Africa more generally. Rouch will frequently speak of his belief that the modern, Western civilization needs to learn the values he associates with the Songhay and the Dogon: a sense of community, a closeness to the land, and, most importantly, a sense of time disconnected from the imperative of historical change. In an interview, Rouch notes that

> in France, if a car is stuck or there is a flat tire, there is a catastrophe. In Africa, however, it's a joy because you stay there. A person will say, "Good, we are stuck. Now we can stay a few days and meet people whom we never met before and will never meet

again." . . . At first I would be furious, but I learned the African way, and now I don't mind such things. I don't even wear a watch. That's the kind of perspective I tried to capture in [*Cocorico, Monsieur Poulet*, 1974].[13]

Another interview, this time about *Anaï*, exhibits a similar argument, as Rouch speaks approvingly of the Dogon belief that Anaï has not left the world once and for all but has been transformed—a belief his interviewer describes as the movement from "human time to mythical time" (Rouch 2003, 176).

The work of the shots of the grass in *Anaï* is to tie the unfolding of this new model of time to the recognizable and familiar activity of mourning. Rouch's evocation of the death and burial of Anaï, before and during the shots of the grass, suggests that he means these shots to set out, within the film, a moment in which Anaï's death can be mourned. The world of the film slows down, giving us the space in which to mourn, an activity that constitutes a break in the normal routines of life. By associating mourning with a temporality he marks as belonging to the Dogon (or, more generally, to a non-Western) world, Rouch is able to ease his viewers into an unfamiliar and alien world. In mourning, we come to inhabit the world as the Dogon do; we are introduced to the space of mourning with them. Were it not for the formal (and thematic) bridge Rouch provides, the world of the Dogon might have held us at a distance.

Rouch ends the sequence by emphasizing that a transition to a new world has taken place. After the third shot of the grass amid the rocks, and before he turns to the funeral rites themselves, Rouch inserts a last shot. Over the final image of the grass, he says, "And, as tradition would have it, a big tree in the family field"—there is a cut to show a tree, barren of leaves, lying on the ground—"fell by itself." The camera then tracks to the right, following the length of the tree to its end.

The placement of this shot, coming at the end of the series of shots that stand in for the mourning of Anaï's death, marks the world the film is about to enter. By telling us that the tree fell of its own accord and then explicitly connecting this fact to the dictates of tradition, Rouch makes it clear that the world of the Dogon, as he presents it, is not just about their beliefs. It is a genuine world in which physical phenomena ally with cultural practice. The world the film is about to enter—the world into which the viewer is being taken—is radically different from the one in which it began.

The way the transition in *Anaï* works suggests something more general about how Rouch deals with the anxiety about crossing the boundary between worlds. That a boundary is there, he takes as a given; but he also believes that his films can cross it, and that viewers, because his films are able to serve as bridges into new worlds, can have their passage eased. We can see the interplay between the film's world and the world the film presents in the opening moments of *Jaguar* (1957–67), a film that follows three travelers as they go from Niger to Ghana and back again. *Jaguar* begins with a shot of the sky, a few clouds intruding into the pale blue. Over this image, a voice (not Rouch's) says, "Madame, we are going to tell you a story." Another voice asks, "Which story?" and the first voice responds by describing the journey of the travelers to Ghana, the "Gold Coast," in order to seek fortune and wealth. These voices, so far unlocated within the world of the film, set out its terms: This is going to be a story, one of Rouch's "ethno-fictions," and it deals with issues of migration within Africa. (This is not, the opening voice-over implies, a world known to its addressee; that's why the story has to be told.) As the voice-over begins, the camera starts to move. Tilting down and away from the sky, it uncovers the top of a bare tree in the middle distance, and then brings the rest of the tree into view—a tree devoid of leaves, its branches twisting and rising up towards the sky. The effect of the image/sound juxtaposition here is to mark the tree as indicative of the move into the story: "Madame, we are *going* to tell you a story." It is the gateway to the world to which the travelers belong.

Rouch develops the motif of the tree in the subsequent shots. The initial shot of the tree is held for about ten seconds, while the narrator sets out the promise of money in Ghana. There is then a break in the speech and a cut to a closer shot of the tree, one of its branches extending from the bottom middle of the frame toward the upper left-hand corner; a second, smaller branch to its right reaches straight up. The opening credits now begin, with the name of the producer superimposed in the top right corner of the frame, followed by the title, "Jaguar," written in large letters across the center, and then "un film de Jean Rouch" back in the upper right. A cut leads to a shot of dry grass blowing gently in a breeze, over which the rest of the credits appear, and then the film itself begins with a cut away from the grass to show the flat plains, bare trees dotting the dry earth. The voice-over returns, introducing us to the names of the travelers and announcing the beginning of their voyage.

The tree in the opening of *Jaguar* thus marks the intersection of two worlds. The first has to do with the world the narrator spells out, namely, the world of Africa (and the journey from Niger to Ghana) in which the characters live and dream. As in *Anaï*, the isolated tree, separated from the surrounding countryside, is given the role of indicating a movement into a distinctly non-European world. At the same time, by virtue of the title and credits placed over it, the tree is made to stand in for the world of the film, the world of *Jaguar* itself. Taken together, we can say that entering the world of the film, the "story" of the three travelers, thus counts as simultaneously entering the world through which they travel.

Such a combination of worlds is central to the operation of what's sometimes taken to be the paradigmatic instance of Rouch's ethnographic work: *The Drums of Yore: Tourou and Bitti*. The importance of this film is largely derived from a particular stylistic device it contains, one that Rouch would later describe as a discovery that opened up new possibilities for his work. This is the "sequence shot," in which the camera is mounted on Rouch's shoulder as he walks among and encounters people in an extended, unbroken take. Rouch writes, "For me then, the only way to film is to walk with the camera, taking it where it is most effective and improvising another type of ballet with it, trying to make it as alive as the people it is filming" (Rouch 2003, 38–39). Steven Feld argues that the sequence shot draws attention to Rouch's presence in the creation of the film. The technique is used "not to break down and explicate events [as in classical cutting] but to show how the familiar observer [that is, Rouch] perceives and interacts with them and authors a subjectively experiential account of them the moment he films."[14]

The overall events in *Tourou and Bitti* are fairly straightforward: the film shows the ritual of possession, the way spirits inhabit or "mount" the dancers, with Rouch's commentary providing explanations. It is the form of the film, and the way it transforms the events that take place, that is so striking. In a single, ten-minute shot, Rouch provokes—and then records—the possession of the dancers. The film begins as Rouch enters the village of Simiri, where a ceremony is underway to summon spirits to end a drought; nothing had happened for the first three days of the ceremony, but as he walks into the village square and begins to film the musicians, possession finally occurs. Rouch then proceeds to record the interaction between the dancer and the drummers, circling the clearing in the middle of the village as more people (and more spirits) join the dance. (He also shows the children of the village watching their parents, learning how the ritual takes shape and what its purpose might be.) As the shot nears its end, Rouch notes that the sacrifices are about to begin, and then remarks, "I should have gone on filming, but I wanted to make a movie, return to the start of my story, and I pulled back slowly to see what the schoolchildren saw: A small village square in the setting sun where, in a secret ceremony, men and gods spoke of coming harvests." As these words are spoken in voice-over, Rouch draws back from the village square, back in the direction from which he originally entered, and tilts the camera up to reveal the sun.

The common way of understanding the film comes from Rouch himself. In "On the Vicissitudes of the Self," Rouch claimed that the effect of the virtuosic sequence shot placed him in a kind of *ciné-trance*, and that the state of mind he was in as he wandered through the village was sufficient to induce the spirits—hitherto absent from the ceremony—to arrive. They recognized in him a familiar being, a self who was already possessed, which meant that it was safe for them to finally emerge into the village. Rouch writes,

Looking back at this film now, I think that the shooting itself was
what unlatched and sped up the possession process. And I would
not be surprised if upon showing the film to the priests of Simiri,
I learned that it was my own ciné-trance that played the role of
catalyst that night. (Rouch 2003, 101)

Rather than an observer looking at and examining the ceremony, Rouch
becomes the central participant in the ritual itself. In a sense, he transforms
the idea of a participant-observer: the very act of observing, of making a
film that records the ceremony, constitutes a full participation in it.

Such an account of *Tourou and Bitti*, however accurate it might be,
is not quite the whole story. The first thing to note is that the film is
not, strictly speaking, made up of one shot. In addition to the central,
ten-minute take that shows the possession ceremony, another shot opens
the film. It is a shot that has generally been ignored by critics, and it
goes unremarked on by Rouch in his writings and interviews about the
film, but it is important for how *Tourou and Bitti* works. The opening
shot sets out the conditions—both within and for the film—that allow
the transformations of the self that Rouch describes to occur.

Tourou and Bitti, then, begins not inside the village but with a shot
of the branches of a tree. Framed against the bright blue of the sky, the
branches are rendered almost in silhouette, their leaves ruffled by wind.
The film's credits appear at the bottom of the frame, and the camera tilts
down to bring the ground into view. Beneath the overhanging branches
swaying in the wind, several buildings can be seen in the distance, an
open field intervening between them and the camera. The grass is yellow and sparse, with several trees standing in isolation. The camera,
apparently mounted on Rouch's shoulder, begins to move forward toward
the houses, bouncing with the rhythm of his steps. As he walks, Rouch
begins to speak in voice-over:

"LES TAMBOURS D'AVANT"
(TOUROU et BITTI)

On March 11, 1971, after three years of famine, the people of
Samiri in the Zermiganda of Niger staged a possession dance to ask
the forest spirits to guard future crops against locusts. On March
15, Daoudo Sorko, son of the Zima, Daoudo Zima, asked us to
watch the fourth day of the ritual, when they played the antique
drums, Tourou and Bitti. By late afternoon, no dancer was yet
possessed, but my sound man, Moussa Hemidou, and I behind
the camera nonetheless opted for a 10-minute sequence to obtain
a real-time film document of these ancient drums that will soon
be silent forever. So, this film becomes an initial experiment into
an ethnography of the first-person.

This narration clearly doesn't belong to the world of the film, spoken
instead after its completion. At the same time, it is recorded so that certain
moments in the voice-over are synchronized with significant movements
by the camera. As Rouch starts to talk about "the people of Samiri," for
example, the camera leaves the shelter of the tree—we can see the last
branch pass out of the top of the frame—and begins to approach the
village. And over the final lines of the voice-over, relating how the drums
"will soon be silent forever," Rouch tilts the camera downward to look
at the dry ground in front of his feet. The screen goes black, and we
see the final title of the prelude—"un film de Jean Rouch"—before the
central part of the film begins with an image of the sun.

Rouch's voice-over introduces us to the world of the village, a world
in which possession is a genuine way of responding to and influencing
the natural world (rain, drought, insects). As in *Anaï*, the world in question involves the alignment of physical forces and cultural practices. At
the same time, the opening shot and voice-over foregrounds the activity
of filmmaking, the fact that we are watching a mediated encounter with
the events about to take place in the village. Rouch describes how he
was invited to make the film ("Daoudo Sorko . . . asked us to watch the
fourth day of the ritual"), and then specifically tells us the kind of film
it will be ("I . . . opted for a 10-minute sequence to obtain a real-time
film document of these ancient drums that will soon be silent forever").
More explicitly than in *Anaï* and *Jaguar*, Rouch here places the world
of the film directly within a world that is not his own. "Entering a film
means diving into reality," he says as the primary sequence shot begins,
moving from one world to another.[15] And the reality he enters is one
that encompasses and allows for possession rituals.

The function of the opening shot in *Tourou and Bitti* is to declare,
for the viewers of the film, Rouch's need to inhabit the world of the
Songhay in order to make a film about them. The viewers need to know,

the shot suggests, that this identification of worlds is what enables the successful work of the film. The placement of the film within the world of the Songhay creates the conditions necessary for Rouch's own *ciné-trance*, and thus the conditions necessary for that trance to affect the world of the Songhay. If it's true that, without the presence of the camera, the possession would not have happened, it's also true that, outside the world of the Songhay, Rouch's activity would not have counted as a *ciné-trance*, and he would not have been able to articulate what he would later describe as the "Songhay theory of the filmmaker." The ten-minute shot would have done no work. It would have been mere virtuosity, and viewers would have been left far outside a world they might otherwise have been able to explore—a world that, Rouch hoped, they might even have been able to understand.

Notes

1. For two examples of works that take up this part of Rouch's project, see Stoller (1992) and Taussig (1993, 236–49).

2. Jean Rouch with Enrico Fulchignoni, "Ciné-Anthropology" (Rouch 2003, 157); cf. Jean Rouch, "The Camera and Man" (Rouch 2003, 42).

3. A similar concern with a Western viewer can be found in Rouch's remarks on the screening of *Les maîtres fous* (1955); see Rouch (2003, 163).

4. I take it that it is Rouch, and not Morin, who edits this sequence. Morin suggests as much in his comments on the film, although he does claim credit for initiating the general discussion about Saint-Tropez from which Sophie's comments are taken. See "*Chronicle of a Summer*: A Film Book by Jean Rouch and Edgar Morin" (Rouch 2003, 255, 243).

5. The use of Landry as an explorer of France foreshadows the more systematic explorations of Paris that Damouré Zika undertakes in *Petit à Petit*.

6. One example of this comes earlier in the film, at the end of a conversation between Jean-Pierre and Marceline. Marceline is talking of her sense of failure at the dissolution of their relationship, connecting it to her general and pervasive sense of being beaten down by the world, when there is a sudden cut to a new scene. Over a shot of a table surrounded by dinner guests, located in an obviously different location, Rouch announces, "We've reached the point where the film, which up to here has been enclosed in a relatively personal and individual universe, opens up onto the situation of this summer in 1960." Morin then immediately turns the conversation to the Algerian War. It's not that the scenes are entirely unrelated to one another. Jean-Pierre and Marceline identify political disillusionment as one of the main reasons for the tensions between them, and the Algerian War is certainly an example of a situation where such questions would emerge. But the moment of transition itself is strikingly abrupt: we had just been in the midst of an extended and emotionally fraught shot of Marceline—a shot in which we saw (for the first time) the numbers tattooed on

her arm from a concentration camp—and then Rouch and Morin simply declare that the film is switching course. And so it does.

7. Elsewhere, this is certainly an interest of his. William Rothman has noticed a prominent example toward the end of *Chronicle of a Summer*, in the discussion of the film in a screening room. There, Rouch joins together shots of Marilou and Jean-Pierre so that they appear to be looking at one another, thereby implying the existence of some sort of relation between them, and that—this through a further shot—Marceline knows (or imagines) this. Over the cuts between these shots, we hear a woman remark of the film they've just seen: "What's not true? Cameras can't lie." Rothman argues that, "by conspicuously synchronizing the series of shots with the words 'Cameras can't lie' (an effect of simultaneity created in the editing room, it might be noted), *Chronicle* brackets this ostensible assertion, suggests that it may be a 'lie' " (Rothman 1997, 72). This brief sequence amounts to Rouch's declaration of a fact about the conventions of (Hollywood-style) editing: that "they are capable of lying, perhaps incapable of not lying" (ibid., 72).

8. Edgar Morin, "Chronicle of a Film" (Rouch 2003, 232–33).

9. This has to do in large part with the excellent and celebrated reading of the film by Paul Stoller, who draws heavily on Rouch's discussion of his own practices (Stoller 1992, 161–73).

10. Jean Rouch, "On the Vicissitudes of the Self: The Possessed Dancer, the Magician, the Sorcerer, the Filmmaker, and the Ethnographer" (Rouch 2003, 87)

11. Ibid., 99; cf. Stoller 1992, 169.

12. One of the techniques Rouch uses for this purposes is to assume the voice of his subjects. Rather than report what Anaï, for example, says, he speaks the words as if he were himself within the conversation.

13. Jean Rouch with Dan Georgakas, Udayan Gupta, and Judy Janda, "The Politics of Visual Anthropology" (Rouch 2003, 223–24). Rouch's sense of a shift in the experience of time as he moves away from the Western world is not entirely surprising. Claude Lévi-Strauss found something similar in his trips to South America, noting how the trip across the ocean detached him from the historical events going on in Europe, from the sense that there was history at all.

14. Quoted in Stoller 1992, 163n1.

15. Elsewhere, Rouch describes his own practice by saying, "My position is: you have to believe in the beliefs of the other." He says this in Manthia Diawara's film, *Rouch in Reverse* (1995), discussing *Les maîtres fous*.

11

ALAN CHOLODENKO

Jean Rouch's *Les maîtres fous*

Documentary of Seduction,
Seduction of Documentary

Les maîtres fous is nothing less than a challenge to our way of thinking.

—Paul Stoller (1992, 158)

True knowledge is knowledge of exactly what we can never understand in the other.

—Jean Baudrillard (1993a, 148).

Cinema is the art of ghosts.

—Jacques Derrida[1]

I N WHAT FOLLOWS, I WILL ARGUE THAT Jean Rouch's provocative filmmaking practice, which he dubbed *cinéma vérité*, can be understood, in Derridean terms, to deconstruct and disseminate the documentary and ethnographic film. Further, that Rouch's films, in Baudrillardian terms, seduce the documentary and ethnographic projects, documenting their impossibility, the impossibility of science (in this case anthropology, ethnography, and also psychology), documenting that the only truth is that there is no truth. This is the ironic, delirious, cruel, seductive "truth" of *cinéma vérité*—the "truth" of illusion. Or as William Rothman eloquently writes of the French director Jean Renoir's worldview: " 'Reality' is illusion, 'illusion' is real, and to suppose otherwise is 'the grand illusion' " (Rothman 1997, 64).

In consequence, there is in the work of Rouch, Derrida, and Baudrillard—as there is in the "direct cinema" of Frederick Wiseman, I have argued elsewhere (Cholodenko 1987 and 2004b)—a certain madness, a certain delirium, a certain *folie*. The films of both Wiseman and Rouch are in their own ways *follies*. Indeed, Wiseman's first film, *Titicut Follies* (1967), is profoundly linked, not least etymologically, to Rouch's earlier *Les maîtres fous*. And insofar as the present essay follows on from their work, it is inescapably marked by that folly, is unavoidably speculative, partaking of Baudrillard's own description of his speculations on "illusion" as "real"—"theory-fiction." But my story is already getting ahead of itself—and me.

Les maîtres fous, Rouch's ethnographic "science-fiction," like *Titicut Follies*, Wiseman's documentary "reality-fiction," takes deconstruction's hybrid form. Just as Wiseman's film is at the same time *both* reality and fiction and *neither* reality nor fiction, Rouch's film is *both* science and fiction and *neither* science nor fiction. Also taking such a hybrid form, we might note, is the *ciné-trance*, as Rouch describes it, of the *cinéma vérité* filmmaker mutated by the act of filming into at the same time *both* a human being and a medium of the camera and *neither* a human being nor a medium of the camera. So, too, is Rouch's stated goal of transforming the ethnographic film, reanimating it as an ethnography shared by the filmmaker and the filmed subject. Wiseman and Rouch propose, even as their work demonstrates, that all documentary film, all ethnographic film, takes this hybrid form.

Mick Eaton, in his essay on Rouch, "The Production of Cinematic Reality," implicitly establishes a relation between Rouch and Derrida when he writes that from Rouch's provocative acts of filming "a different kind of cinema emerges, conceived of as neither documentary truth, for the participants are always performing, taking on roles, nor theatrical fiction, for the role they adopt is conceived of as more real than the real" (Eaton 1979, 51–52).

Even as Eaton's neither-nor phrasing figures deconstruction's hybrid form, he cues a shift to a relation between Rouch and Baudrillard, as he does when he describes Rouch's conception of *cinéma vérité* as "cinema-provocation," quoting Rouch's famous line, "Not to film life as it is, but life as it is provoked" (Ibid., 51). Arguably the most provocative of contemporary French thinkers, Baudrillard is the thinker who made provocation his vocation with his "theory-fiction."

For Eaton, quoting the filmmaker's own words, Rouch's provocative acts of filming reveal a new truth, "which is not the 'truth' of the pro-filmic event [not cinema truth], but the 'truth' of cinema itself—'cinema is the creation of a new reality' " (Ibid., 52). Carrying us beyond deconstruction's hybrid form, Eaton's "more real than the real" designates for me what Baudrillard calls the hyperreal. The hyperreal is the "new reality" that *cinéma vérité* creates or, better, animates. Not the surreal, the hyperreal, characteristic of the post–World War II world, what Baudrillard calls his third order of simulacra, the order of the ecstatic, of hypertelia, the pushing of things to their extreme limits where, "more x than x," they at once fulfill and annihilate themselves, becoming virtual.[2]

A play of roles such as Eaton describes is to be found in *Les maîtres fous*, a 1954 film Rouch was invited by mediums of the Hauka cult of the Songhay people to make of their annual ritual. It is a film built of an apparent opposition between what Rouch's voice-over calls crucially "the bedlam" of life in Accra and the pursuit of peace, of surcease from that bedlam, on the part of members of the cult through the rituals, including trance, that they perform in the bush, to which the majority of the film is given over. There we see not only initiation and penitential purification rituals but possession ceremonies, where mediums enter a trance and are possessed by and exchange with their spirit doubles, the Hauka, "the new Gods," "the gods of the city, the gods of technology, the gods of power," who enact the colonial oppressors of the Hauka past (French) and present (British). We watch these specters mimic the roles, military ceremonials and protocols, and roundtable conferences of those "masters," parodying and aping them to the limit, a cruel, violent performance made all the more telling by a cutaway to actual shots of the British Governor and the parade of troops at the opening of the Colonial Assembly in Accra to show us what is being mimicked before the film returns to such mocking.

Not only do we witness shocking, disturbing images of shaking limbs, spastic movements, contorted bodies, and foaming mouths of the Hauka, the Hauka demonstrate that they are more powerful than their oppressors by applying fire to themselves without being burned, thrusting their hands in boiling water without being scalded, and violating the taboo against killing and eating a dog. The Hauka even drink blood gushing from the slit throat of the dog, that horror for us capped by the sight of the dog's warm blood running from the mouth to the chin of the spirit Samkaki. Then the next day we see the cult members back at work in Accra, seeming much the better for the experience, ostensibly happy, no longer diseased but at ease, with Rouch's voice-over, accompanying shots of the General's staff digging a trench in front of, appropriately, a mental hospital (the words in English!), speculating, theorizing: "Comparing these smiles with the contortions of yesterday, one really wonders whether these men of Africa have found a panacea against mental disorders. One wonders whether they may have found a way to absorb our inimical society."

For Michael Taussig, *Les maîtres fous* is a film of "mimicking mimicking mimicking" (Taussig 1993, 97). The Hauka spirit-doubles (the mimetic double of the material human entity, which together form a couple (Ibid.), through conscious playacting and, at the same time, bodily possession operating at a nonconscious level, mimic the Europeans. They at once assume "the identity of the European" and stand "clearly and irrevocably eye-bulgingly apart from it," exemplifying and performing "actors acting." Taussig sums it up by saying, "What's being mimicked is mimicry itself—within its colonial shell" (Ibid., 241).

For Paul Stoller, the Hauka imitate their colonizers and their institutions as a way to tap into the power of the Europeans and reroute their force, becoming stronger than their "masters" (Stoller 1995, 122–24, 195–96).

I would put it thus: The Hauka absorb from their opposite a power they in turn double. What *Les maîtres fous* shows us is the very process of Baudrillard's hypertelia (Baudrillard 1990a, 9), "more x than x." Through their ecstatic, hypertelic performance, the Hauka become at once hyper Europeans—more European than Europeans—and at the same time hyper "primitives"—more "primitive" than "primitives." Such hyper Europeans are the pure and empty form of Europeans, their implosion, their end, even as the hyper "primitives" would meet their end if their power did not allow them the means to turn this simulative process to their advantage.

Moreover, the ecstatic, hypertelic performance of the Hauka is what the film not only shows but *performs*. Inscribing the Hauka in its title (in the Hausa language, "Hauka" means "master of the wind, master of madness"[3]), the film *Les maîtres fous* ("the mad masters") is isomorphic with its subject—a "mad," nutty, ecstatic hyperethnographic "science-fiction," an ethnography pushed to its extreme limits, at once more science than science and more fiction than fiction. Hyperethnography—the pure and empty form of ethnography—at once performs and documents the implosion, the end, of ethnography.

Consider Rouch's voice-over. In classic ethnographic films as in classic documentaries, the voice-over exerts its authority over what is imaged, the latter tending to read as illustration of the former. In the print I saw of *Les maîtres fous*, the voice-over is in English, spoken by Rouch, and presents itself as omniscient (except for its last words, "One really wonders . . . One wonders . . ."), as expert on its subject (the Hauka sect), and endeavors to be as knowing and precise as possible in describing the details of the Hauka ceremony that is imaged. Yet not only does Rouch's French accent blur many of the English words, demonstrating an inevitable problem of translation of one language into another, such a demonstration occurs simultaneously in another register. What is imaged of the ritual is at once so familiar—more familiar than familiar—and so unfamiliar—more unfamiliar than unfamiliar—that it turns on the voice-over, establishing not the coincidence of verbal description and referent the voice-over assumes it has secured, but rather the unbridgeable gulf between them, the gulf between the cultures that form the frame of the film. So while Rouch's words and tone claim a familiarity with what they describe, their effect at the same time is to establish a remoteness that radically undermines that claim, turning our sense of the voice-over from denotative to connotative, from prose to poetry, from documentary to fiction, reinforced of course by the explicit subjective speculation that ends the film (Rouch's "One really wonders . . . One wonders . . ."). What is highlighted thereby is not only the lack of authority the voice-over wields over what is imaged but also the superior power of the imaged over the imager. The Hauka are seen at once to conform to the words spoken and to exceed, absorb, and annul them, remaining veiled, lost in translation. So the film leaves the viewer not with a sense of knowing its subject, as in classic ethnography, but rather of not knowing it, at best of knowing only that one does not and cannot know it.

In "The Borders of Our Lives" (Cholodenko 2004b), I argued that Wiseman's documentaries, his "reality-fictions," are hyperdocumentaries or postdocumentaries that document (not the Derridean suspension but) the Baudrillardian collapse of the opposition between "reality" and "fiction," hence the collapse of documentary "as such," that filmic mode "presumed to be where fantasy and fiction end, where one can gain a purchase on the real (and its correlates: the true, the meaningful, etc.)." Rouch's hyperethnographic films, his "ethno science-fictions," fall prey to the same fatality. They are postethnographic films (and, I should note, subsumable within hyperdocumentary).

But *Les maîtres fous* is still more.

In his essay on cinema, *The Evil Demon of Images*, Baudrillard offers this definition of Seduction: "To begin to resemble the other, to take on their appearance, is to seduce them, since it is to make them enter the realm of metamorphosis despite themselves" (Baudrillard 1987, 15). We might call this the Zelig effect, thinking of the protean Woody

Allen character who takes on the qualities of everyone he encounters. We can now also call it the Hauka effect. The Hauka exemplify and perform Seduction, including the Seduction of ethnography and the ethnographic film, but in the form of the mimetic violence of defiance and parody. Insofar as the Hauka model their performance on Western models, in observing the Hauka the West does not see the Other; it sees only itself, or itself done violence to. The Hauka effect is thus fatal to attempts at analysis and interpretation, including my own treatment of the voice-over. The seductive effect is the same as that of Zelig, who for Baudrillard anticipates and "leads astray all possible interpretations" (Ibid., 16).

Seduction is for Baudrillard the world's elementary dynamic. It is a game of challenge—the very term Stoller uses to characterize *Les maîtres fous* in our epigraph—an outbidding, of duel, defiance, and leading astray, of reversibility. It is the hallmark of the world of metamorphosis and myth, illusion, game, and play, the rule and the dual, ritual, magic, dance, and theater, form and artifice, the immaterial, that Baudrillard calls his first order of simulacra. And, crucially, Seduction and his first order of simulacra bear privileged relation for Baudrillard to the "primitive" world, which itself privileges metamorphosis and myth, ritual, magic, and theater. Baudrillard has in a number of texts addressed "primitive" cultures, Other to the West, that refuse to be assimilated by the West and that the West has not been able to assimilate. Taking my cue from those texts, I would say this of the Hauka: Mobilizing their powers of simulation and Seduction, they seduce their colonizers and the knowledges, discourses, sciences, technologies, institutions—Western culture "as such"—that the colonizers impose on them, including those brought to bear to interpret and explain them (preeminently anthropology, ethnography, and psychology, including ethnographic film, including this very film *Les maîtres fous*). The Hauka turn them all into pure projections that they reflect back on the projectors, so that the projectors see only themselves. Or as one of the film's titles declares, but insufficiently so for me, of the game played (including *by* the film): "ce jeu violent n'est que le reflet de notre civilisation" (this violent game is only the reflection of our civilization). That it is a game is itself significant, for that is what Seduction is.

The Hauka effect this reversion by means of the rituals they perform, through imitating their colonizers better than the colonizers imitate themselves. The Hauka "outmad" their "mad 'masters,'" and in so doing become more mad than mad and more master than master, become "masters" of their "masters," making their "masters" enter the realm of metamorphosis despite themselves, at the same time preserving, by means of this game, their own distance, their own "Radical Exoticism," an Otherness in no way reducible to simple difference, a foreignness irredeemable, irrecuperable, irreconcilable—that of the Other "as such," a superior figure in Baudrillard's universe.

As I was reviewing Baudrillard's chapter "Irreconcilability" in *The Transparency of Evil* in researching this essay, I was astonished to discover, or rediscover (how could I know which?), these words: "From this point of view there is not much difference between Japan and Brazil, or between either of them and Jean Rouch's "manic priests": all are cannibals in the sense that they offer a lethal hospitality to values that are not and never will be theirs" (Baudrillard 1993a, 143).

Puzzled by the translation "manic priests," I turned to the French text, where I found these words: "les primitifs occidentalisés des Maîtres-Fous de Jean Rouch" (i.e., the occidentalized primitives of Jean Rouch's *Maîtres fous*.) (Baudrillard 1990b, 147). Baudrillard had explicitly written about *this* film, including the Hauka in his list of nations, cultures, and cults singularly exemplifying radical Otherness!

What Baudrillard's words imply for me is that the Hauka, diverting and evading their Western colonizers, offer them a "lethal hospitality," taking hostage, miming, aping, absorbing (as Rouch's narration proposes when he says, "One wonders whether they may have found a way to absorb our inimical society"), devouring, assimilating, integrating, incorporating their guest/enemy and its powers within their ritual, ceremonial, cyclical order. At the same time, they neutralize or annul what our civilization has imposed on them, turning their hostage to their own advantage. Thus the Hauka preserve their own singularity, their Baudrillardian hyperreality, at the same time strangely turning into Baudrillard's first order of ritual and ceremonial, the order that bears a privileged relation to the "primitive" world—a world to which the Hauka, the "new gods," never not belonged (a point to which I shall return).

Stoller insightfully links Rouch with Antonin Artaud (Stoller 1992 and 1995), declaring the brutal, "cruel" images of *Les maîtres fous* "the cinematic equivalent of Artaud's Theater of Cruelty" (Stoller 1995, 6 and 196–98; see also Stoller 1992, 53). Stoller argues that spirit-possession rituals are the kind of pretheatrical rituals that inspired Artaud's Theater of Cruelty, a theater demonstrating, as Artaud wrote, "the much more terrible and necessary cruelty which things can exercise against us" (qtd. in Stoller 1992, 52).

I would elaborate upon this connection by suggesting that Rouch shares the "logic of delirium," and the "fatal strategies," that I explore in my essay linking Artaud and Baudrillard, "The Logic of Delirium, or the Fatal Strategies of Antonin Artaud and Jean Baudrillard" (Cholodenko

2000). In my view, Stoller miscasts Artaud by seeing him solely as "Artaud the Reconcilable," as I put it, and associating him with the Principle of Good, the search for reconciliation, cure, salvation, the realization of his authentic self and the materializing of this world. My "Artaud the Irreconcilable," by contrast, is to be associated with the Principle of Evil, with the impossibility of such a realizing, with the impossibility of materializing this world—with Seduction, Illusion, Radical Exoticism, the endlessness of the agonistics of Artaud's dualist, doubled nature. And in the duel between Good and Evil, it is Evil—a word he uses interchangeably with the word "cruelty"—that is the superior power for Artaud. It is cruelty that can reanimate both theater and life and restore the lost continuity between them—theater as "true illusion," whose only value is "its excruciating, magical relation to reality and danger." This "truth of illusion," this delirious cruel truth, this truth of delirium, is a truth Artaud and Baudrillard share with Rouch (and, I might add, with the cinema of Wiseman).

In reference to Artaud, Baudrillard posits the savage power of the pure sign, its cruel capacity to erupt in a reality to which it at the same time bears a fundamental antagonism, operating against and irreconcilable with it, as it is irreconcilable to and for the subject. In such a light, reality is the effect of the sign, whose power he associates not only with Artaud's notion of cruelty but with "primitive" culture, with "sacrifice as a scene of murderous illusion," with what for Artaud is true theater and its sacred charge: to reveal evil in the world, a theater at once of blood, violence, paroxysm, invective, and ecstasy and of implacable rigor and necessity.

Theater as "true illusion" is for me, as for Stoller, what the Hauka perform in *Les maîtres fous* (see Ibid., 161). It is a theater of abjection, of revulsion, akin to what Baudrillard writes of Buto and its "fierce energy," its "twisted, electric . . . bodies . . . always in a state of mental electrocution, as Artaud would say" (Baudrillard 1990a, 133). This delirium, this frenzy, of the whole ceremony at the high priest Mounkaiba's compound is set up precisely as a piece of mise-en-scène in what feels like a stage space, its center that of the sacrificial altar, around which sacred space are enacted the performances of the Hauka Gomno, the Governor-General; General Malia; Major Mugu; Kapral Gardi; Samkaki, the Truck Driver; Madame Lokotoro; Madame Salmà, and so on, who often make what feel like stage entrances. And to add to the theatricality, the film's concluding section, back in Accra the day after the ceremony, introduces those whom we saw possessed now back in their daily roles. It is a kind of "curtain call" recalling films like *Citizen Kane*, which end with the cast of characters. The ending of *Les maîtres fous* enhances the theatricality, illusion and magic of the ritual, and of the film itself, insofar as it again brings us no closer to knowing these people (despite Rouch's genial words "the Lieutenant is a pickpocket," "the General in real life is just a Private," etc.), but augments once more our irreducible distance from them, the secret they keep from us.

Like Wiseman's films, *Les maîtres fous* is, as Stoller says, "long on images and short on explanations" (Stoller 1992, 153) and requires that the viewer, assaulted by these provocative images (and sounds, too), engage in making the meaning of the work. Yet this is an impossible task, given that this film is, as Stoller puts it, "nothing less than a challenge to our way of thinking" in that these images "document the scientifically unthinkable" (Ibid., 158). What is shown is a shock to our "cozy epistemological presuppositions," Stoller declares. He proposes that Rouch's goal is "to transform his viewers," "to challenge their cultural assumptions," having the Western audience "confront its ethnocentrism, its repressed racism, its latent primitivism," to begin "individual decolonization," "the decolonization of a person's thinking, the decolonization of a person's 'self'" (Stoller 1995, 197).

Stoller sees this process operating at the service of meaning, truth, and reality and at the behest of "therapeutic ends" (Ibid.), i.e., salvation, cure, and individual, social, and political betterment. Yet above and beyond this confrontation with the inexplicable, and the concomitant realization that the Hauka know things we Westerners do not, there is, for me, at the same time a process of Seduction of the viewer, and the director too, each being led astray from the world of meaning, truth, and reality and toward the world of illusion. Indeed, the film has its own quirky corroboration of this, for we hear the voice-over declare of the Hauka watching the Governor's ceremony: "Amid the crowd there are Hauka dancers looking for their model. And if the order is different here from there, the protocol remains the same." The Hauka—the "new gods"—turn themselves into what they were never not, even as they exemplify what Baudrillard calls the "primitive double." Baudrillard writes:

> The double, like the dead man (the dead man is the double of the living, the double is the familiar living figure of the dead), is a *partner* with whom the primitive has a personal and concrete relationship, sometimes happy, sometimes not, a certain type of visible exchange (word, gesture and ritual) with an invisible part of himself.... The primitive has a non-alienated dual-relation with his double. He really can trade, as we are forever forbidden to do, *with his shadow* (the real shadow, not a metaphor), as with some

original, living thing, in order to converse, protect and conciliate this tutelary or hostile shadow. (Baudrillard 1993b, 141)

This shadow is a figure of exchange, with a "full part to play," "autonomous," "like a living being, capable of responding and exchanging" (Ibid.). For Baudrillard, the exchanges of Hauka spirit and medium we witness in *Les maîtres fous* are typical of "primitive" cultures, a form of what he terms "symbolic reversibility" whose only Western equivalent would be the antique world of myth where gods and men metamorphosed into each other (Baudrillard 1988, 59, 78–80).

While Baudrillard uses the terms "spirit" and "shadow" to name this "primitive" double, he also marks it with the term "specter" (Baudrillard 1993b, 140), noting that "the primitive double generally passes for the crude prefiguration of the soul and consciousness," but offers a counter to all psychologized or ontologized forms of the specter (soul, spirit, mind). The life of this double, this specter, is *lifedeath*, or as Baudrillard says, "the double is the familiar living figure of the dead" (Ibid., 141).

But, as Baudrillard points out, "primitive" culture *includes* death and the dead within itself, whereas at the very core of the "rationality" of Western culture "is an exclusion that precedes every other, more radical than the exclusion of madmen, children, or inferior races, an exclusion preceding all these and serving as their model: the exclusion of the dead and of death" (Ibid., 126).

Since the exclusion of death can only animate its rebound, in that effect we find what Freud calls "the return of the repressed," an uncanny return of the specter that takes the form of the haunting double, a figure not of continuity with the living, like the "primitive" double, but of discontinuity with and repression of it, prefiguring the subject's own death—a specter that Freud will come to ally with what he calls our animistic fears of the return of the dead, the anthropological form of Freud's uncanny.

In Baudrillard's view, Freud falsely projects that Western fear onto the "primitive" and the primitive double in order to recuperate it for Westerners as our "archaic traces," exemplifying Freud's overvaluation of his own mental processes, "along with our whole psychologistic culture . . . [t]he jurisdiction of the psychological discourse over all symbolic practices" (Ibid., 143). What this suggests is that a Western viewer would tend to project Freud's model onto *Les maîtres fous* and thereby be shocked by the return of that which the West has radically excluded, the Radical Other of the West in the form of the Hauka themselves—"primitive" culture modeled on and modeling itself after, hyperconforming to, the West's own model exclusion, death, for which the Hauka stand as exemplary figure of the uncanny.

In other words, the Hauka spell death to the West's modeling of them, including its modeling of "primitive" culture in terms of anthropology, psychology, and psychoanalysis, and all Western disciplines based on them (including anthropological and psychoanalytical film studies and film theory). The Hauka not only mimic and mock our Western modelings, they absorb, perfect, and annihilate them, even as they reverse them through Seduction, turning them into our projections.

Put differently, for Baudrillard the primitive specter belongs to a radically Other order, one superior and anterior to the Western one (see Gane 2000, 14). This means that all Western models of the "Hauka," of the "primitive," or indeed of *Les maîtres fous* itself must come up against not only their limit but their reversal, even as the Hauka effect, like the Zelig effect, "leads astray all possible interpretations," including mine. All this, again, makes my reading inevitably speculative, inevitably "theory-fiction."

Baudrillard came to replace the terms "symbolic reversibility" and "death" with the term "Seduction" to describe the process of reversion, of reversibility (what the Greeks called *peripeteia*), that is for him the fundamental process of world. But he continued to insist on the superiority of the rituals of "primitive" cultures, insofar as they have no notion of the reality of the world but rather relate to the world through myth as radical illusion and exemplify his fundamental rule: Seduction.

The radical Otherness of the "primitive" produces an ironical effect upon Western culture that Baudrillard associates with the pure Object. In fact, in his recent, most astonishing articulation of this ironical process, he links the radical Other with the object as quantum mechanics defines it. Never has science postulated, he declares,

> even as science fiction, that things discover us at the same time that we discover them, according to an inexorable reversibility. We always thought that things were passively waiting to be discovered. . . . But it is not so. At the moment when the subject discovers the object—whether it is an "Indian" or a virus—the object makes a reversible, but never innocent, discovery of the subject. More—it is actually a sort of invention of the subject by the invented object. . . . It is as if we had torn the object from its opaque and inoffensive stillness, from its indifference, from the deep secret where it was asleep. Today the object wakes up and reacts, determined to keep its secret alive. This duel engaged in by the subject and the object means the loss of the subject's hegemonic position: the object becomes the horizon of the subject's disappearance. (Baudrillard 2000, 76–77; see also 54)

This revenge of the object on the subject, on all knowledge, including scientific knowledge, is what *Les Maîtres fous* presents and performs for us—not only the disturbance of the observed by the observer but the simultaneous, at least equal, disturbance of the observer by the observed (see Cholodenko 2005, 7n31). For Rouch: "The fundamental problem in all social science is that the facts are always distorted by the presence of the person who asks questions. You distort the answer simply by posing a question" (Rouch 2003, 219–20). In saying that *cinéma vérité* "has nothing to do with normal reality" (Eaton 1979, 50), Rouch opens the door not only to surrealism (the usual frame of reference, including his) but to Baudrillardian hyperrealism, to Seduction, to the object of quantum mechanics, to quantum reality (Cholodenko 2006), even as *Les maîtres fous*, as ethnographic "science fiction," does what Baudrillard says science fiction has never done: It shows us that things discover us at the same time as we discover them according to an inexorable reversibility, even as it performs that process for us.

More occidentalized than occidentalized, the lethally hospitable and hospitably lethal Hauka push occidentalization to its limits, to its pure and empty form, and ironize it, making it turn on itself, showing that its opposite was always already immanent in it. They thereby preserve their opacity, inscrutability, singularity—their secret, that of the "pure Object." The Hauka not only hyperrealize the Westerner, turning themselves into "more Westerner than the Westerner," they also make the Westerner metamorphose into Hauka. Westerners see ourselves become Hauka in this inverse mirror of madness, violence and savagery they hold up to us, a mirror that shows they were always already immanent in us.

Rothman relates what Rouch's films teach us:

> Rouch's profound insight, gleaned from his investigation of the way the Songhay understand these matters, is that filming and being filmed are akin to phenomena of possession, that filmmakers as well as the people they are filming are capable of becoming possessed, or, at least, capable of undergoing a metamorphosis so profound as to be meaningfully compared to possession. In truth, this insight is capable of illuminating a wide range of films, perhaps all films. (Rothman 1997, 92)

For me, this insight *is* capable of illuminating all films insofar as all films are forms of *animation*, reanimating not only those imaged but those doing the imaging, as well as those viewing those images.[4] With this qualification: films are at the same time forms of Seduction, which spells death to all forms of possession, including identity and self-identity. Meaning to lead astray (from the Latin *seducere*), Seduction privileges dispossession, dissemination, irresolution, indeterminacy, irreconcilability, loss, disappearance, and death. Leading them astray, reanimating them, metamorphosing them—this is what we see the Hauka do to those who would possess them, even as they reanimate, metamorphose, themselves, ostensibly restoring themselves to health through a process in which they do not adapt to Western culture but adapt Western culture to them. They do not simply get Western culture "out of their system," they get it *into* their system, assimilate it, and in that way get it *out* of their system.

That Rouch as maker, as director, is dispossessed at the same time as he is possessed is a point he himself makes in speaking of the metamorphosis, the reanimation, that the *ciné-trance* effects for him. He is seduced, led astray. As for the subjects, these Hauka mediums are not only possessed and possessing, they are, as mediums, as in-betweeners, at the same time dispossessed and dispossessing, seduced and seducing, reanimated and reanimating, like that other medium, film—a kindred spectral medium in the service of revenge, likewise by "mad masters," by evil spirits, by "primal animistic forces." These specters mark ethnographic and documentary film, indeed all film, I have elsewhere argued[5]—as a form of animation. Like the protean Hauka, they mark film as protean, as *plasmatic*, Eisenstein's term for the essence of film as a form of animation, a form of animism (Eisenstein 1988, 21).[6]

Even as the Hauka turn *Les maîtres fous* into a pure projection of them, *Les maîtres fous* turns them into a pure projection of it. If film serves the revenge of the "mirror people," the revenge of the "mirror people" serves the revenge of film. Like the Hauka, film is lethally hospitable to what it images, to its maker, and to its spectators, reanimating them, seducing them, leading them astray, draining them of meaning, truth, reality. Its hyperreal shocks, thrills and chills, delights and frights—its attractions—turn spectatorship into spectership.

And film is lethal to itself. Here the sacrificial blood-drenched altar—void center of *Les maîtres fous*, the very dead point, blind spot, black hole of Seduction around which all in and of the film pivots—"comes to the fore," enframing all, turning all in and of the film back toward itself, what it never left nor never left it. The beginning of the film sets the stage for and performs this privileging of Seduction. It commences with white words against a black background, a preface that "warns us of the violence and cruelty of certain scenes but wants to make a complete participation in a ritual which is a particular solution to the problem of readaptation, and which shows indirectly how certain Africans represent to themselves our occidental civilization." Then, over black, we hear pipes, brass and drums, then a second or so later, the film fades into the image of the altar. A few seconds later, the words "Pierre Braunberger présente . . ." appear and then are wiped off the screen.

It is significant that these Western words are presented as white over a black background, that they are then wiped off the screen, that sounds start over black, and that the black fades into the altar as the very first image of the film. In a profound way, the altar is as one with the black that precedes it. It is upon them that are built the sounds of pipes, brass, and drums, with faint words "left, left, left" heard (an English marching band, it turns out, for it is the sound of the British Governor's own band at the parade of troops at the opening of the Colonial Assembly), and the film's opening titles in white letters and in French. This first shot of the altar, perfectly centered in the frame and circumscribed by almost indiscernible black fingers touching its rim, with a reddish-golden hue emanating from its center, reappears in the Hauka ritual sequence, now with Rouch's voice-over laid over it, when the penitents swear "If we do it again, we ask our Hauka to punish us with death."

    This sacred sacrificial altar, steeped in the blood of not only the dog but a chicken, is invested with such reanimating power over life and death, innocence and guilt, health and disease, that it serves as the film's symbol of the radical and superior alterity of the Hauka to the West. And the film's macrostructure is wedded to and performs that superior power, including the subtending by the altar of the Western sounds and graphemes at the beginning and of the voice-over through the film and its subtle victory at the end in the nonwestern music that closes the film, recalling the music of the ritual, but here laid over a shot of Accra with the word "FIN."

This macrostructure is in service of and served by the film's problem/solution structure, first posed in the titles that preface the film and developed through the film's five "acts." The film is almost a classical five-part drama but with a collective protagonist, with a fourth-act *anagnorisis* (recognition), *peripeteia* (reversal), and climax resulting in a catharsis for the protagonist, the fifth act evidencing the "resolution" of "his" problem. Moreover, the altar's circular shape figures the circularity of the film's five-act structure, circular insofar as the word "bedlam" in the first act is remarked in the sign "mental hospital" in the fifth, where we see the Hauka's "General's staff" apparently cured of the ailments inflicted on them by Western civilization and hear Rouch's speculation about their cure.

Significantly, too, while the five acts are composed as alternating segments, cutting from city to suburb to city to bush (with brief parallel editing in the cut to the Governor's ceremony) to city, they are not set up in a relation of simple opposition. Rather their oscillation, framed by the altar at the head and the bush music at the tail of the film, suggests that Western civilization "as such" is built on a "primitive" culture whose violence and cruelty subtend and haunt the West, never not returning to and informing it. This is the "deepest" cultural meaning of *Les maîtres fous*, one inhering in so simple a moment as the travel to Mounkaiba's compound down the first paved road in Africa, now hopelessly overrun by grass.

In other words, the film is built on a set of ostensible polarities (city/bush, sickness/health, bedlam/sanity, civilization/savagery-cruelty-violence), which it not only deconstructs, inextricably coimplicating them, but hyperrealizes, pushing each to its limits in the game of Seduction played by those with superior powers in that regard, the Hauka exhibiting a "sickness" more healthy than healthy, a "bedlam" more sane than sane, "savagery, cruelty, and violence" more civilized than civilized, as well as, in the hyperguise of the Westerner, a "health" more sick than sick, a "sanity" more bedlam than bedlam, a "civilization" more savage, cruel and violent than savagery, cruelty, and violence. Likewise, the title preceding the film whose words refer to the "violence and cruelty of certain scenes" (which scenes it never names), and another just before the first sequence begins, repeating the word "violence," are made to turn on themselves.

It is telling that Rouch, narrating in English, uses the word "bedlam" to describe not the Hauka ceremony but rather the life of the city, "the adventure of African cities," places where "traffic never stops," "noise never stops," with "all these brass bands"—what we as Westerners watching the film take as anything but bedlam—and proposes that what we take to be bedlam—the Hauka ceremonies and rituals, the effort to handle the "rifles" and to march in the British way, to salute and otherwise acknowledge appropriately those of superior rank, the General's and Governor's insults to everyone, roundtable after roundtable trying to be constituted, everything seeming to take the greatest of efforts, even just keeping one's coordination, balance, and breathing, to say nothing of the Herculean efforts to achieve agreement on something as simple as deciding whether to eat the dog raw or cooked, etc.—is curative of the insanity of Western culture that has contaminated the Hauka. As a result, such bedlam, with its attendant violence, cruelty, and savagery, turns out to be their route to sanity and health and civilization, hence no bedlam at all, even as their needing to be cured of it turns upon us Westerners, suggesting that it is we who are insane and live in bedlam, with its violence, cruelty, and savagery, and need to be cured of it, but are unaware of our need.

That ostensible bedlam of the ritual, we might note, is enhanced insofar as Rouch's editing of the first part of the ritual, the nomination of a new member, seems designed to make that member morph into others across cuts, so we think we are seeing the same person but are not. It is further augmented by the horrific sounds on the sound track reinforcing the concatenation of abject images. The crucially nonsynch sound track (Mounkaiba alone is given a voice, but it is not lip-synched) assaults Western viewers with screams and words that sound to us like gibberish.

At the same time as an irreducible antagonism is shown between the West and the "primitive," the West becomes the special case, the reduced, conditional form, of the "primitive." White society and culture become the special case, the reduced, conditional form, of black tribal collectivity and ceremony, upon which the West and its whole culture of "real-izing," of materializing, of rationalizing, is built and at the same time founders in the face of the "primitive," which challenges that "real-izing," materializing and rationalizing, making it appear in order to make it disappear as illusion. The almost total absence of white persons in the film serves powerfully in this regard. While there are a few signs of the presence of whites, notably the boxes of White Horse Cellar whiskey being unloaded on the docks and the other English words that turn up in signs from time to time, the only time one actually sees white persons, rather than assumes one is seeing them, is at the Governor's parade, where from far above we see the white face of the Governor's wife, and in another extreme long shot a white man standing at the left frame next to someone with a camera on a tripod. So even the few whites who are seen are viewed in extreme long shot, as opposed to the close shots of so many blacks that foreground them and their story.

At the same time, and in a manner analogous to what the Hauka do to Western culture "as such," that altar of radical alterity, of Seduction, turns film back from its end to its origins, strangely returning it to what it never left nor never left it—the cinema of attractions, what used to be called "primitive cinema." In so doing, it not only reanimates film "as such" as never not "primitive"—never not Seductive—it situates at film's origin its originary Seduction. This is what *Les maîtres fous* singularly, uncannily, brings "home." In so doing, it posits the cinema of attractions—"primitive" cinema—as the condition at once of the possibility and impossibility of "classical" cinema, what Tom Gunning calls the "cinema of narrative integration," which is therefore never integrated.[7] The cinema of attractions—"primitive" cinema—is never not disseminating and seducing classical cinema, even as the quantum is never not disseminating and seducing classical physics.

While for Gunning the cinema of attractions returns in what he calls the "Spielberg-Lucas-Coppola cinema of effects" (Gunning 1986, 70), for me it returns already in *Les maîtres fous*, even as it tells and shows us that it is never not returning nor returned, even as Gilles Deleuze's time-image (of which Deleuze offers *Les maîtres fous* as an explicit example), as specter of the movement-image, is never not returning nor returned to the movement-image; as Derrida's hauntological is never not returning nor returned to the ontological[8]; and as Baudrillard's specter of Seduction is never not returning nor returned to the world of production, reproduction, representation, reality, simulation, as their reversion and death sentence. With its return of all the specters of the living dead, *Les maîtres fous* serves as exemplary performance and performer of all these reversions, standing as privileged example of the specter as *ur*-figure of the cinema of attractions.

Cinema and the Hauka: two protean, seductive, fatal mediums coiling around each other, at once symbiotic and radical antagonists, each exchanging with, reversing, and indetermining the other—film as Hauka, Hauka as film (as *cinematized*[9])—and at the same time dueling with the other, challenging the other to be more it than it, fatal to it as to itself, forming a pact, a knot, that will not be disentangled, deciphered, explained, or resolved, for which all idealistic colonial humanisms—including that of Rouch the Reconcilable—are no match, for they will be turned back on themselves. They will be seduced. For Seduction is the turn—the reversibility of anything and everything into its opposite.

Against those idealisms, like the doubled Artaud, the double of the reconcilable Rouch—Rouch the Irreconcilable, the radical "ethnologist" who would be, like cinema, more Hauka than Hauka! The seductive, fatal, cruel, provocative Rouch who shows us with *Les maîtres fous* that, as the Baudrillard epigraph to this chapter implies, not only is true knowledge the knowledge of the limits of knowledge, the only true knowledge is that there is no true knowledge.

Like Rouch, "the European who follows the spirits,"[10] who is seduced by the spirits and says to the viewer in turn, "Please Follow Me," *Les maîtres fous* is a seductive "ethnographic" film ritually initiated in, "possessed by," and serving the revenge of "the mirror people" on the efforts to master, possess, control, and know them (or anything, for that matter). Metamorphosing ethnography and anti-ethnography into radical "ethnography," *Les maîtres fous* reanimates "ethnographic" and "documentary" film, indeed, film "as such," as form of provocation, in the fatal sense of the term. Like the work of Baudrillard, it issues a challenge to reality, constituting a defiance, an outbidding, a leading astray—in a word, a Seduction—of it, summoning reality to appear the better to make it disappear in its apparition, demonstrating that reality is but the special case, the reduced, conditional form, of Illusion.[11]

As *Les maîtres fous* teaches us, not only is film "as such" a provoca-tion to the maker, the subject, the spectator, the analyst, the theorist, the world, to be more, they only exist insofar as they are provoked. Only reality as it is provoked is reality "as it is." And it is film's vocation to provoke. Which means that those who would endeavor to master film, to model the subject as its master and/or present themselves as film's master, would fall prey to the "mad illusion of mastery"—for me the third possible meaning of the term "*maîtres fous*."

In *Les maîtres fous*, as in the Baudrillardian universe, there can be but one sovereign, one master—Seduction. And it can never be pos-sessed, at least not by a human. Here the cutaway to the Governor's plumed hat and trooping of the colors inscribes far more for me than Taussig proposes when he writes, "What's being mimicked is mimicry itself—within its colonial shell."

To wit, the bird's-eye point of view (*à la The Birds* of Alfred Hitchcock, 1963)—let's call it the gods' or an omniscient point of view—declares the auteur of the film to be not human, nor only human: a specter.

And with these mad, knotty thoughts, these cruel, delirious log-ics—these follies—I will conclude this speculation.

Notes

A version of this paper was published in *Jean Rouch: A Celebration of Life and Film*, ed. William Rothman (Fasano, Italy: Schena Editore, 2007). It is included in the present volume with permission of Schena Editore.

1. Derrida says this in the film *Ghost Dance* (Ken McMullen, 1983).

2. To schematize, far too bluntly but I hope serviceably, Baudrillard's orders of simulacra are orders in the destiny of the world. The first order is that of Seduction—the world in its classical era, a world of enchantment, of metamorphosis and myth, of illusion and the immaterial, of rule and the dual, of ritual and ceremony, of magic, dance, and theater. The second order is that of reality and "real-izing," of production, reproduction, representation—the world of metaphor, of Christianity, of materialism, of law and the polar, of the dialectic and of contradiction. And the third order is that of hyperreality, virtuality—a cold, disenchanted world where the polarities sustaining meaning have imploded and the grand referentials of Western culture have been volatilized, a world of media and models, of obscenity, obesity and terrorism, of metastasis, of the cybernetic and the molecular, the codes of DNA and digitality, of television and the computer and their imageless screens of absorption where, fascinated, we see nothing. This is the desert of the real. See Baudrillard 1988 and 1993a.

3. Rouch states: "The title of this film, *Les maîtres fous* (The Mad Masters), is a play on words that translates both the word "Hauka" (master of the wind, master of madness) and at the same time the colonial situation where the masters (the Europeans) are crazy" (Feld 2003, 163). In *Titicut Follies* we observe an analogous operation, the personnel of the prison for the criminally insane, especially the psychiatrist, turned into the crazy ones, or rather, the crazier ones.

4. See Cholodenko 2004a as well as the introductions to Cholodenko 1991 and 2007.

5. Work starting with editing *The Illusion of Life*—the world's first book of scholarly essays theorizing animation, and theorizing it from "poststructuralist" and "postmodernist" perspectives—published in 1991. Key to my theorization of animation is the concept of the *animatic*, by which I mean not only the very logics, processes, performance, and performativity of animation, but the very "essence" of animation—the animation and animating of animation. The animatic—the singularity of animation—is anterior and superior to animation, subsumes animation, is its very condition of at once possibility and impossibility, at once the inanimation in and of animation and animation in and of inanimation. It is to animation as the hauntological is to the ontological for Derrida and Seduction is to production and simulation for Baudrillard. The animatic is that nonessence enabling and at the same time disenabling animation as essence, including Eisenstein's notion of plasmaticness as essence. The animatic makes every animation always already a reanimation. The animatic is not simply different but radically, irreducibly Other. See Cholodenko 2004a as well as the introductions to Cholodenko 1991 and 2007.

6. Insofar as the animatic at once enables and disenables essence, the ontological, all "real-izing," it has the most profound consequences for the theory and theorizing of ethnographic and documentary film—their metamorphosis, reanimation—the animating of a seductive, not merely productive, theory and theorizing of them, indeed of film "as such"—not merely as Eaton's "The Production of Cinematic Reality" but as its Seduction, what would be a provocative theory and theorizing, in the sense of the Latin *provocare*, to call forth, for me the calling forth of specters—the key event in and of *Les maîtres fous*—the return of the dead as living dead, the Hauka of the Songhay. Film as (such a) medium, hauntological, medium of the specter of Seduction—film "as" Hauka, *bia*, Homeric *psuchè* (with regard to *psuchè*, the Homeric *eidolon*, see Cholodenko 2005, 6), evil demon, simulacrum, simulating and seducing reality (and all its predicates) thereby, even as Seduction seduces simulation . . . Film as not only performer, performance, and performative, not only animator, animate(d), and animating, but animatic. (This includes delivering "a kind of electroshock," says Rouch, to a medium watching himself in trance in a film, making him go into trance again by that very sight (qtd. in Taussig 1993, 243). For his part, Stoller prefers the notion of an electric current that jolts, charges and recharges bodies (Stoller 1995, 198).

7. On Gunning, including his take on the subject of the mastery of cinema, see Cholodenko 1997, 82–83 n19 as well as Cholodenko 2004a.

8. For Derrida, ontology (beingness), the very ground of Western philosophy as a metaphysics of presence (fullness of being), is always already haunted by what it represses and must repress to *be* full, to be a presence. What ontology represses is the trace of the radical Other, which trace, though repressed, is never not returning to disenable that which it at the same time enables, that which is built upon it and its repression. For Derrida that trace of the radical Other upon which ontology is built is of the nature of hauntology; it is the specter that conjures ontology and makes of ontology a specter seeking to exorcise itself of what has at once enabled and disenabled it, for insofar as the ontological is never not haunted by the hauntological, the ontological can never be the fullness of presence it presents itself to be. As Derrida writes, "Presence is never present" (Derrida 1981, 303). What I call the "Cryptic Complex," which I have formulated in part after Derrida's notion of the hauntological, and which I have proposed, in my essay "The Crypt: The Haunted House of Cinema," as the *ur*-attraction/shock/ experience of cinema (even as the specter is *ur*-figure of cinema), is composed of the uncanny (as Freud characterizes it in his eponymous essay), the return of death as specter, endless mourning and melancholia and cryptic incorporation. The Cryptic Complex makes of cinema a crypt, a haunted house, as it does of all who experience it, making them the "haunt of a host of ghosts," ghosts never exorcised nor, on the other hand, assimilated, but rather incorporated in the crypt, including of the self, turning spectatorship into what I call spectership and making all theories of cinema based on ontology the special case, the reduced, conditional form, of hauntology. And making, as Derrida says, "every concept a concept of the specter and a specter of a concept" (Derrida 1994, 161). Derrida puts it this way of film: "Cinema is the art of ghosts." (See endnote 1.)

9. The cinema is "literally" inscribed in *Les maîtres fous* in the poster on "the Governor's Palace" advertising American movies, one of which is *The Set-Up* (Robert Wise, 1949). That title, like the poster, suggests that the performance is already what Rothman calls "theatrical" (nonspontaneous, noncandid), what I call "cinematized," not just as ritual—the Hauka's own or modeled on the British ceremonial of the trooping of the colors—but as inextricably coimplicated in cinema, including cinema as ritual.

10. A description of Rouch by one of Stoller's teachers in Wanzerbe, Niger, quoted in Stoller 1992, 6.

11. This is how I read Deleuze's words on the sense Rouch intended when he spoke of *cinéma vérité* (words the last part of which parallel Eaton's): "Thus the cinema can call itself *cinéma vérité*, all the more because it will have destroyed every model of the true so as to become creator and producer of truth: this will not be a cinema of truth but the truth of cinema" (Deleuze 1989, 151). "Destroyer," "creator"—"producer," too—are for me to be reread as "animator." For Deleuze, "no one has done so much to put the West to flight, to flee himself, to break with a cinema of ethnology and say *Moi, un noir*" as has Rouch (Ibid., 223).

12

MICHAEL LARAMEE

Petit à Petit and
The Lion Hunters

THE VALUE OF JEAN ROUCH'S FILMS is not fully acknowledged when they are studied only as works of science. Even Rouch's ostensibly "ethnographic" films—among them *Les maîtres fous* (1955), the short *Tourou and Bitti* (1971), *Funeral at Bongo: The Old Anaï (1848–1971)* (1972) and *Ambara Dana: To Enchant Death* (1974), all discussed in the present volume—should not, or cannot, simply be categorized as anthropology, shared or otherwise. Rouch was an auteur, a master of the art of cinema. His films are also collaborative endeavors that enriched the lives and understanding of all their participants. And Rouch, like Vertov, also made his films "to beget films" (Rothman 1997, 103).

Petit à Petit (1968–69)[1] and *The Lion Hunters* (*La chasse au lion à l'arc*, begun in 1957, completed in 1964) are two of Rouch's most remarkable and characteristic films that highlight different aspects of his work. Yet they have been accorded little serious critical attention, even by Rouch himself.

Petit à Petit

Petit à Petit (1968–69) is an inventive film that, among other things, calls into question and reverses the historical dynamic of anthropological practice by making Africans the investigators and Parisians the "Others"

179

under investigation. As Steven Feld summarizes the film, *Petit à Petit* is "a fable produced as a sequel to *Jaguar* (1957–67), which relates the curious and singular adventures of Damouré and Lam, two businessmen of contemporary Africa, in search of their role model" (Feld 2003, 365). Rouch describes the film himself as having "no theme: in reality Damouré came to Paris to do an internship with UNESCO. That was how we got to film Damouré in Paris" (Rouch 2003, 180). The spontaneity involved in the film's conception is further highlighted by Rouch:

> Here again we could not do a documentary. So we decided to do a sequel to *Jaguar*: the society of "Petit à Petit l'oiseau fait son bonnet," created in *Jaguar* by Damouré, Lam, and Illo, becomes important and sends its president, Damouré, to see how people live in multistory houses, because they want to build a skyscraper in Ayoyorou. That was our only starting point. (Rouch 2003, 180)

This spontaneity, however, in no way precludes artistic ambition, as the simple "starting point" Rouch speaks of engenders a film of tremendous insight into the nature of identity and selfhood in the colonial and postcolonial context. Essentially, the events in *Jaguar* led to the creation of the company Petit à Petit as an extension of the identities that Damouré, Lam, and Illo explore throughout both films. The fact that *Petit à Petit* can be referred to as a sequel to *Jaguar*, one in which the same central characters further their explorations of their own identities, reflects the fact that both films involve a process of self-discovery for Damouré, Lam, and Illo—the "real" flesh and blood "actors" who play, and are, themselves in these films.

Rouch, however, says little about *Petit à Petit* in his collection of essays, *Cine-Ethnography*. No doubt, this is at least in part because the film to which it is a sequel, *Jaguar*, his first "ethno-fiction," was a film that he believed "marked [him] permanently." As Rouch puts it, "All the films I do now are always *Jaguar*" (Rouch 2003, 164). Rouch's own privileging of *Jaguar* further marginalizes *Petit à Petit*, seeming to legitimize its critical neglect.

While it is undeniable that *Jaguar* wields a powerful influence on its sequel, *Petit à Petit* is anything but a carbon copy of the earlier film. Significantly, the two films have very different endings. *Jaguar* closes with its protagonists returning to their traditional village, putting their experiences of the modern world behind them. We might add that at the end of *Moi, un noir* (1958), the brilliant and powerful Rouch film that Jean-Luc Godard called "the greatest French film since the Liberation" (Godard 1986, 101) and Ousmane Sembène referred to as his favorite film about alienation, the traditional village life of their childhood is only a distant dream for the protagonists, who are resigned to the harshness of their lives in modern Abidjan and have only a vague hope that maybe the future will be better.[2] In *Petit à Petit*, by contrast, the protagonists' return to their village at the end of the film, but this is a step forward in their endeavor to *make* a better future for the village and for themselves.

It is surely no accident that *Petit à Petit*, a film with revolutionary content, was conceived in the period following the early films of the French New Wave (which *Jaguar* and *Moi, un noir* helped to beget) and the events of May 1968. The spirit of radical upheaval that exploded in May 1968, coexisting with the love for cinema among the younger generation that found expression in the French New Wave, was also affected by the Fifth Republic's failure to reform educational institutions. As Alan Williams notes, "The student rebellion which sparked the 'events of May 1968' was directed not only against the social stratification which the majority of young people saw as oppressive, but also against the new consumerism, which had heightened consciousness of the old order while promising so little of any real value to replace it" (Williams 1992, 387). Feld notes the connection of *Petit à Petit* to the events of May 1968 when he writes that, "In *Petit à Petit*, Rouch was responding directly to the changed political climate in France after May 1968, as well as the complexities of postcolonial African modernities and desires" (Feld 2003b, 10). In this sense, *Petit à Petit* responds to a situation in French history by including Africans as participants in a creative process, rather than excluding them by reducing them to objects of expoitation.

The aforementioned reversals of historical practices of anthropology that are central to *Petit à Petit's* narrative can also be viewed as revolutionary in the sense that the Africans have exchanged roles with the Europeans, deconstructing and complicating their historical relationship and placing Rouch's (and Damouré's, Lam's, and Illo's) ingenious film within the context of radical challenges in theory and practice, by Derrida among others, to outdated modes of thinking and approaches to life. Rouch provides space for Damouré, Lam, and Illo to investigate their own historical oppression and question these same values that have operated throughout African colonies and now must be confronted after independence, which for Niger was in 1960. Through this investigation, the film contributes to the quest for, and construction of, conflicting self-identities resulting from the inevitable clashes between "tradition" and "modernity" in postcolonial African nations.

Among the conflicting features in *Petit à Petit's* universe are Damouré's initial capitalist, money-driven, business-only attitude, as contrasted with his complete repudiation of those same values at the film's conclusion. Again, his return to his hut is not a retreat back to tribalism but rather a denial that capitalist values should be the guiding principle for society. Damouré's response—as well as Rouch's—to capitalist modes of thinking and ways of living is not passivity either. Damouré and Rouch are not simply refusing to participate in the capitalist world defined by this "new consumerism." Their response is *Petit à Petit*. The film *is* their rebellion, a point underscored when Damouré says, "The more I make love, the more I rebel, the more I rebel, the more I love it." If one acknowledges Rouch's intimate relationship with his films—and Damouré's intimate relationship with them as well—as one formed through love, then Damouré's remark is to be heard as equating making love with making films, and thus with rebellion. In other words, *Petit à Petit* is a rebellious challenge to authority made in response to the events of May 1968, but also with African protagonists. It is imperative to acknowledge the revolutionary implications of the film's innovative exploration of the conflicts of identify in postcolonial Niger.

Petit à Petit opens with an image of a man (Damouré) on horseback crossing the frame briskly from left to right. The scene is filmed in a single shot as the camera pans right, following him until the wind blows the hat off his head. When the figure is centered in the frame and closest to the camera, it becomes clear that an African man is sitting atop the horse.

The fact that he is not chasing anyone immediately makes viewers wonder what this man (and Rouch as well) is doing. When the following shot includes a herdsman, slow-moving cattle, and then a woman playing a flute, as the opening credits roll, a complete contrast is created through editing, the contrast becoming more obvious with the inclusion of men getting into a jeep.

Compared to riding a horse or walking, traveling by jeep is a technologically advanced method of transporting oneself. However, Rouch's presentation of the three different modes of transportation, not in any evolutionary order but simply as three different means of self-conveyance, does not privilege any one method over another. Different approaches to living can coexist. Nonetheless, the film also clearly suggests that this coexistence is inevitably burdened with problems that must be addressed in order to create an ideal society, whether in Damouré's Niger or in Rouch's France.

Damouré is introduced at a business meeting arranged in order to discuss the building he wants to construct with funding from the company (Petit à Petit). Damouré, as president of Petit à Petit, arranges a trip to Europe in order to investigate multistory buildings and the societies in which they exist. Damouré's idea is generally accepted by his peers, but Lam is somewhat reluctant, concerned that he will become "lazy" if the building and its cultural effects disturb his lifestyle. Lam says, "I live in the bush with my herds and Land Rover. A tall building'll make me lazy. I'd want to live in it instead of in the bush. That's why I don't want tall buildings. But take a look at France."

His comment reveals that Lam has integrated the Land Rover into his daily life as a bushman, complicating his stance against constructing a building in Niamey. Lam's disinclination is actually based on his notion that a Western lifestyle would overrun and agitate his life in the bush to the point at which he would choose the building over the bush. Lam seems to know that adopting multistory buildings into society will inescapably not only effect *where* he lives, but also *how* he lives; and he does not seem ready for either.

Despite Lam's hesitation, Damouré embarks on the mission, hoping he will reap valuable knowledge by observing Parisian lifestyles. The catchy theme song accompanying his travels to the airport suggests the casualness of Damouré's ambitions, but the film as a whole clearly challenges the morality of capitalism. The song's lyrics (Little by Little, I'll get my building, Little by Little, I'll be in France. I'd like to build a skyscraper more beautiful than the one in Niamey") specify the company's intention to acquire the means and knowledge to build the grandest building possible, with French skyscrapers as their model. By returning to the land of Niger's colonizers for further instruction on capitalist ventures, Damouré's journey places France, and more generally Europe, at the origin of their company's mode of thinking and conducting business. However, as the story progresses it becomes evident that the film does not simply view French or European lifestyles as commendable examples. Rather, it challenges and critiques European routines and customs. The first shots of France focus on the dark, dreary pavement on the rainy evening when the plane lands.

Fortunately for Rouch, the weather upon the plane's arrival enables the bleak images of the runway, and of Damouré exiting the aircraft on a dark night, to make a striking contrast to Niamey's bright sunshine when he first boarded the plane. Clearly, these initial images of France do not paint the country as a paradise, but Damouré's exhilaration during the cab ride from the airport reveals that he still expects to acquire significant insights by studying French culture. Damouré asks the driver many historical questions and receives more than satisfactory answers, provoking his exclamation, "Paris taxi drivers are like living dictionaries."

His initial amazement at the vastness of Paris, intensified during the cab ride, seems to have convinced Damouré that his mission will prove extremely profitable for his company. As Damouré pursues his investigation of the Parisians, however, he becomes increasingly critical of their customs and the city in general. Damouré equates their large staircases with mountains, and classifies the Seine as a "sadder" river than the Niger. He considers the air to be poor, except in the country where everyone travels on the weekends, causing traffic and eventually major development and thus suburbanization and the elimination of the countryside. In light of the abysmal weather, Damouré comments, "We use the sun as a guide back home, not here." He also mistakes French men for women, and women for men, and even regards French "cows [as] ugly," looking like "hippos [or] warthogs." Then, in one of the most memorable sequences, Damouré uses calipers, an instrument of traditional anthropology, to measure the skull sizes and body frames of passers-by. He even inspects some people's teeth.

This entire segment of the film is quite comical, as Rouch (and Damouré) no doubt intended, but there is seriousness underlying this ironic inversion of dehumanizing colonial-era anthropological procedures. These divergences from Damouré's way of thinking and living

that he discovers to be prevalent in Parisian culture testify to the implications of cultural differences, and also to the historical exploitation and oppression as a result of prejudices formed on account of those differences. The ability to critique such abominably degrading practices by granting Damouré space to reenact them facetiously is one of the radical features of *Petit à Petit*. Moreover, the fact that the film itself is a collaboration between Rouch, a Frenchman; Damouré, a Sorko fisherman; Lam, a Peul herdsman; and Illo, a fisherman suggests that cultural differences must not translate into cultural separation but instead into intercultural communication, learning, and acknowledgment (Rouch 2003, 179).

Damouré then surveys females and couples, criticizing the females' dress and the couples' willingness to kiss in public. He also makes notes about the impoliteness of people he approaches in the streets and the fact that children are friendlier than adults. However, the one fact that truly shocks his friends at home, to whom Damouré writes regularly about his observations, is that the chickens in France do not have their necks cut by a knife and instead are bled electronically.

This comment in Damouré's letter leads Lam to visit and attempt to bring him back to Niger. However, Lam's premonition that he would find himself tempted to adopt a more Western lifestyle becomes somewhat actualized as Damouré convinces him to stay and continue their business venture together. Instead of preventing Damouré from spending the company's money, Lam's visit essentially doubles Petit à Petit's expenditures. He takes Lam on a chairlift ride up a mountain. Watching the scenery change and writing his name in the snow, Lam is moved and undergoes something of a magical experience.

Lam cannot simply close his eyes to his unique experiences in France. He no longer resists Damouré's plans, as he did in Niger and immediately upon his arrival in Paris. It could be argued that while on top of the mountain, in response to his newfound curiosity as to what France has to offer, Lam embraces Damouré's maxim "It's good to find things out" as a personal philosophy. After being told the popular history of Christopher Columbus, Lam is intrigued, and even more so by the fact that America has larger buildings than Europe. He replies to Damouré by invoking the magic of the chairlift with the line, "We'll stop off in America via the ski lift." This line does not suggest that Lam actually believes the chairlift can take him to America, but that it did contribute to his own process of self-discovery and his consequent realization that he should value knowledge that can be gained in other countries and through contact with other cultures.

However, an affinity for France's snow-capped mountains does not translate into a love for everything about Parisian culture. As the partners explore the living conditions within large buildings, Damouré says, "It's unlivable, packed like sardines" and Lam asks, "People live in there?" Claiming that those buildings are "too big, too grand," they decide to seek another model. However, Damouré predicts that in the future Niger will also be overflowing with skyscrapers. Lam responds, "That's why Europeans who go to Africa visit the bush, because they've no room left. Not a forest to be seen," and looks all around, with nothing in view but concrete and steel. Damouré expects luxury to accompany multistory buildings but his dreams are yet to be fulfilled, and rather than discontinuing the mission the pair decide to buy a "one of a kind car," a Bugatti.

The partners then befriend several women. First, Safi (the acclaimed Senegalese director Safi Faye), a woman from Senegal living in France, and then Mariane, a French woman who eventually becomes the company's typist. They also encounter a hobo, Philippe, whom they

hire to return to Niger with them and work for the company in Africa. Their building does eventually get constructed, and the company becomes wealthier, but capitalism's inevitable inequalities and greed cause conflict among workers. First Mariane and Marie, a black secretary doing the

same work for less pay, exempify the fact that capitalism, in the form of the company Petit à Petit, has exploited the cheaper labor of Third-World citizens and further intensified cultural differences by privileging the work of one race over another. Rouch even films Mariane "locked in" at her desk while surrounded by large sticks on the beach.

The unequal pay and deplorable working conditions are denigrated by Mariane who exclaims, "It's the same here as in Paris, they exploit people." She later directly implicates her bosses with the remark, "The job at Petit à Petit is impossible. They are all thieves there." These statements indicate that Damouré has fulfilled his task of developing his society after the Parisian model, but that this model is based on shameful exploitation. The mode of thinking and way of living that Damouré and Lam observed in France are explicitly called into question. When Safi, Mariane, and Philipe decide to leave their jobs, their bosses, and Africa altogether, Damouré undergoes a transformation of principle and determines that capitalist societies are contemptible and disreputable models of living.

Damouré says, "We buy things cheap and sell 'em at a high price. That's capitalism. They said we're capitalists and we are." He continues to acknowledge many people's dissatisfaction with capitalist ideals and says, "The Petit à Petit company of schmucks is finished," and rhetorically asks, "Why build tall buildings (when) straw huts are better?" Clearly, Damouré thinks "Travel makes us see too many things" and is ultimately revolted by industrialized capitalist societies involved in what he dubs "the crazy race that never ends." Lam claims, "We've started a new civilization here . . . a modern one," a proclamation more representative of the real community Rouch, Damouré, Lam, and Illo create than the one formed within Petit à Petit. Nevertheless, the self-discoveries made as a result of investigating Parisians and adopting capitalist lifestyles lead to Damouré's self-realization that he should not model his way of living or mode of thinking on that of the French or on capitalism. This cinematic stance against an institutionalized economic and social philosophy is indicative of the radical post–New Wave spirit.

Rothman helps illuminate Petit à Petit's revolutionary nature:

> Rouch believes that our way of life must change, that our way of life cannot change unless we change, and that we cannot change unless our way of thinking changes. We must awaken to, awaken from, the horror to which we have condemned ourselves and our world. We must tear down the fences we have built, the fences we continue to build, to deny that nature exists within us as we exist within nature. (Rothman 1997, 101)

Petit à Petit is a call to awaken from the horrors of capitalism, colonialism, and historically oppressive anthropological practices. It advocates a reunion with nature, not as a "primitive" form of life but as a sophisticated lifestyle, a "modern civilization," to use Lam's words. It is clear that Petit à Petit is not only Rouch's rebellion, but Damouré's and Lam's rebellion as well. This coalition of filmmakers, of artists, of humans, is revolutionary in itself. It offers a valuable example of how we can tear down cultural fences in order to collaborate on a project that explores the conditions of the existence of those fences.

Although Petit à Petit has garnered little critical attention, Manthia Diawara, a significant African film scholar and artist, does acknowledge its influence in the opening moments of his film Rouch in Reverse when he says, in voice-over, "I feel like Damouré, who flew from Niger to Paris to explore French customs and culture in the film Petit à Petit," while we see the familiar image of Damouré boarding the plane.

Noting that he "always admired Rouch's work," Diawara points out
that Rouch intended his method of "shared anthropology" to give voice
to Africans who had been until then only the objects of investigation.
Diawara's project in *Rouch in Reverse* is to use Rouch as an informant
for his own investigation of France in order to "challenge" the notion
that France is a paradise, just as Damouré and Lam do in *Petit à Petit*.
Diawara refers to his methodology as "reverse anthropology." By following Rouch, studying his environment, and tapping into his knowledge
of French culture, Diawara constructs a film in which his camera goes
wherever Rouch takes it. In keeping with Rouch's stated aspiration to
make "films that beget films," *Petit à Petit* begets Manthia Diawara's
film, in effect. Indeed, *Rouch in Reverse* cannot completely be considered
Diawara's, as it is also Rouch's film (just as *Petit à Petit* is Damouré's
and Lam's film as well as Rouch's). In his voice-over, Diawara comments
that "Rouch is notorious for . . . setting his own agenda," adding, "I did
not want him to take over my film." However, from its very inception,
Rouch *does* "set his own agenda" for the film. Diawara's title—*Rouch in
Reverse*—reflects the fact that Rouch is no longer invisible behind the
camera but instead—as the object of study—is visible in front of it.
However, this reversal did not stop Rouch from "taking over" what is
ostensibly Diawara's film.

As Rothman has observed, "[W]hen Rouch screens his films to
Western audiences . . . it is his way of thinking and living, not theirs,
which becomes the object of their study" (Rothman 1997, 105). Diawara
extends such a study from Rouch's films to his daily life. But from its
very conception, Diawara's study of Rouch is itself profoundly influenced by Rouch's films. In *Rouch in Reverse*, to be sure, Diawara also
interviews people other than Rouch, the topics he discusses with these
people—Western images of Africa, education, war, racism, poverty, im-
migration—are usually motivated by, and return him to, Rouch's films
and way of life. Rouch irrefutably lies at the center of *Rouch in Reverse*.
Rouch's influence can be felt and seen whether he looks through the
camera or the camera looks at him and his "permanent childhood innocence," as Diawara puts it.

One of Diawara's most interesting sequences occurs in the Musée
de l'homme. As he is looking at African sculpture on display, he ponders
the "blood that trails the museum," and addresses a mask, "When will
you be free to come home?" Diawara asserts that "museums in the West
collect these objects and assign aesthetic and monetary values to them.
They deprive Africa of its inheritance and separate the ritual objects
from their true worshippers."

The Lion Hunters

Rouch's practice of "shared anthropology" did not "deprive Africans of their heritage," but rather encouraged them to participate in the preservation of their heritage. A film like *The Lion Hunters* is exemplary in this regard, since the idea for the film was suggested to Rouch by one of the hunters. "When I showed my first film to villagers in Niger, only about ten people in the audience had ever seen a film before, and yet they quickly discovered the flaw in my use of music during the hippopotamus hunt. And a man there said: 'You made a film about hippo hunting. Come to my place. I am a lion-hunter. Lion hunting is much better!' So that was the beginning of a new film (*The Lion Hunters*)" (Rouch 1995, 228). (Rouch also notes that it was at this screening that he first met Damouré and conceived the idea for *Jaguar*.)

In filming ancestral customs and collaborating with the participants to create a film, a work of art, Rouch's role may be likened to that of a cinematic griot, as Paul Stoller suggests. The first frames of *The Lion Hunters* testify to Rouch's purpose of informing the children about "the story of their fathers and their grandfathers."

This responsibility, entrusted to Rouch by the people of the Yatakala village, is taken very seriously by the filmmaker. He films the markings on the rocks left by past generations in an attempt to recreate the spirit of the land and its ancestors. Rouch's decisions as a filmmaker, though, largely depend on the instructions of the hunters engaged in their dangerous mission. He relies on their explanations of hunting practices that would mystify anyone not initiated into these rituals. One need only invoke the name of the hunting region, "The Land of Nowhere," to indicate that the area gets little attention and needs introduction. In the film, it is referred to as "the land of sand, the land of dust and haze."

Nonetheless, Rouch was able to capture amazing images of giraffes running beside their car in a classic contrast of nature and machine in which the giraffe effortlessly passes the automobile. The voice-over may call this the "Land of Nowhere," but clearly these signs of life indicate that this is a "somewhere."

Rouch elaborated on "The Land of Nowhere" in *Cine-Ethnographer*: "The film was made in a very specific place, which is at the exact boundary of three states: Niger, Upper Volta, and Mali. There are many lions there because it's so remote. . . . There are no boundaries, no border control, only a tree" (Rouch 2003, 195). Rouch also reveals that he wanted to acknowledge, in the voice-over, a sense of the adventurousness of the undertaking—his own as well as that of the hunters. In *The Lion Hunters*, Rouch does more than simply document an ancestral tradition. He also documents his own experiences and accounts for his role behind the camera and in the editing room.

> I wanted to express in the commentary the fact that we were included in this adventure, and that we put all our own fantasies into it, because we kidded around about these things, just joking. Maybe I was very ambitious, but my idea was to start from the beginning, to tell the story as they would tell it to their own boys, and it was to be the story of this particular hunting party in which Rouch was filming. (Rouch 2003, 196)

After several years and many failed hunts, which were assuredly full of self-discoveries despite their ultimate disappointments, Rouch and the hunters finally catch a young male lion and the audience is able to witness the rituals performed after the kill to appease the lion's soul. Tahirou Koro sprinkles powder on the lion's nose, ears, and anus so its soul will not drive the hunters crazy. This ceremonious practice, in which the hunters treat the lion with immense consideration, grants the audience some solace after watching the death of this magnificent creature.

After the second adult lion's death, however, Rouch uses the camera to make a profound statement concerning the power of cinema. After Tahirou expresses his respect for the lioness, begs it for forgiveness, and sprinkles its body with dust to help its invisible soul to liberate itself from its bodily imprisonment, the camera zooms into the animal's eye, as if to register the precise moment of the soul's liberation. The eye of the lioness, although now lifeless, remains fixed on the camera's own eye. Staring into this dead eye, like staring into the eye of the camera, reveals nothing except unfathomable blackness, for the lion's soul has departed.

Through this gesture of the camera, Rouch expresses himself directly to declare his respect for the soul of the dead lioness. The hunters, who know this lioness intimately, know that its soul is eternal and powerful. Rouch, who knows the camera intimately, knows that it has the power to capture souls, as it does in this shot—just as *The Lion Hunters* as a whole captures "Gawey Gawey," the "soul"—the adventurous spirit—of the heroic lion hunt whose story the film chronicles for the benefit of future generations, beginning with the children who reappear at the film's conclusion. And just as the film captures Jean Rouch's soul, his adventurous spirit, for the benefit of future generations, beginning with us.

Notes

1. The copy of *Petit à Petit* I have had the opportunity to study is the ninety-minute version that is available without English subtitles on a DVD released in 2005 by Editions Montparnasse. There also exists a 250-minute version divided in three parts: *Lettres persanes*, *Afrique sur Seine*, and *L'Imagination au pouvoir*.

2. Sembène makes this comment in the 1994 documentary *Sembène: The Making of African Cinema*, directed by Manthia Diawara and Ngugi wa Thiong'o.

13

WILLIAM ROTHMAN

Jean Rouch as Film Artist

Tourou and Bitti, The Old Anaï, Ambara Dama

I N HIS INDISPENSABLE BOOK *The Cinematic Griot*, Paul Stoller suggests that Jean Rouch understood his films to be of value insofar as they further the practice he called "shared anthropology." Inspired by Robert Flaherty's example, Rouch regularly screened his footage for the people he filmed, asked them questions about events he had captured with his camera, received answers that helped him film in ways that enabled him to ask new questions and receive new answers. In this way, filming furthered Rouch's pursuit of ethnographic knowledge. And from this knowledge sprang new films and, in turn, new knowledge. In screening his films to the people in them, Rouch's goal was also to share with them the knowledge the films engendered, to help these "ethnographic others"—the traditional *objects* of ethnographic study—to become *subjects* who shared in the observer's pursuit of ethnographic knowledge. And in screening his films to Western audiences, Stoller suggests, Rouch's primary goal was to win converts to his practice of shared anthropology. Insofar as Rouch, like Vertov, made films to beget films, his goal was to usher in a radically new practice of anthropology in which it makes all the difference that film, not writing, is primary. But can anthropology become cinema and still be anthropology?

It would be a serious mistake, I believe, simply to assume—on the basis of the fact that Rouch called his practice "shared anthropology," and without consulting the films themselves on the matter—that Rouch's work gives priority to science over art, to anthropology over cinema. For that would be to assume we already know what the difference *is* that film makes, and what *film* is that it makes such a difference. For Rouch, these were not questions already settled somewhere other than in his films. Within Rouch's films, what becomes of anthropology when it is transformed into cinema is a burning question. And what becomes of cinema when, as we might put it, it possesses, or is possessed by, anthropology is no less a burning question.

If Rouch has a legitimate claim to be included among the greatest masters of the art of cinema, as I believe he does, that claim in my judgment does not rest primarily on his celebrated films of the1950s and 1960s, for all their remarkable qualities and their powerful impact on other filmmakers. Ultimately, it rests on a number of his films of the 1970s—labeling them "ethnographic" or even "shared anthropology" fails to acknowledge their ambitiousness *as films*—that bring to fruition, and at the same time transcend, what Stoller calls the "one take/one sequence" method in which Rouch's camera is always restlessly moving and, within each sequence, he forgoes cutting from shot to shot. The series of films Rouch made about the spectacular *Sigui* ritual the Dogon perform every sixty years, for example, and the feature-length *Funeral at Bongo: The Old Anaï (1848–1971)* and *Ambara Dama: To Enchant Death*, among others, are great *films*, exemplary instances of the art of cinema. And the ten-minute *The Drums of Yore: Tourou and Bitti* (1971), a jewel-like miniature about a Songhay possession ritual, is a great film in its own right.

What do I mean by a great film? At a minimum, it must bear up under criticism of the sort that is invited and expected by serious works within the traditional arts. It must be a work in which, as Stanley Cavell puts it, "an audience's passionate interest, or disinterest, is rewarded with an articulation of the conditions of the interest that illuminates it and expands self-awareness" (Cavell 2005, 335). Part of the thrust of the readings that follow is that it is singularly challenging to put into words what it is that makes *Tourou and Bitti*, *Anaï*, or *Ambara Dama* great films—to find terms of criticism, words capable of carrying conviction, that illuminate our interest in such works.

It is partly for lack of such critical terms that, in writing about Rouch's work in *Documentary Film Classics*, I focused on *Chronicle of a Summer*, even though I suggested that *Anaï* and *Ambara Dama* were his artistic masterpieces. And the sequences of *Chronicle* I analyzed in detail were ones that were shot and edited in ways that emulate classic movies, rather than the memorable passages—Marceline walking through the Place de la Concorde, for one—that anticipate the "one take/one sequence" method of his later films. In the sequences I analyzed, it makes sense, as it does with Hitchcock sequences, say, to *interpret* every cut and every camera movement, to articulate its meanings and the authorial intentions that motivate it. In *Anaï* and *Ambara Dama*, or in *Tourou and Bitti*, for that matter, the camera moves incessantly, but those movements generally have no particular significance apart from binding the camera to Rouch's bodily presence. Insofar as he follows the "one take /one sequence" method, Rouch's camera's movements do not cohere into self-contained gestures that call for—or even allow—interpretation. (There are exceptions, but they prove the rule.) This method makes his films not only "documents" of the events he filmed but of his acts of filming as well.

And yet most of the time we do not have words even to *describe* the way Rouch's camera is moving. Nor do we have words—other than those he provides in his narration—to describe what we are viewing, to describe who is doing what, and in what way, within the world on film. Then what role is left for criticism? What can be said about films like *Tourou and Bitti*, *Anaï*, or *Ambara Dama*, about the conditions of our interest in them, that illuminates that interest, expands our self-awareness?

The Drums of Yore: Tourou and Bitti

Tourou and Bitti begins with a relatively brief shot, dominated by a tree silhouetted against the sky, taken from just outside the village that provides the film's setting. A title announces that this is "un film de JEAN ROUCH in the first person."[1] Then there is a cut to the single ten-minute sequence shot that constitutes the body of the film. What we view is everything the camera filmed, and what we hear—apart from Rouch's voice-over—is everything the microphone recorded. Rouch does not manipulate the footage; the world projected on the movie screen is reality captured by the camera with nothing added, subtracted, or altered. And yet, true to Rouch's theory and practice of *cinéma vérité*, it is not reality as it is, but reality as it is provoked by the act of filming, a reality that would not exist apart from the presence of the camera, that *Tourou and Bitti* "documents," revealing a new truth, a cinema truth: *cinéma vérité*.

Indeed, *Tourou and Bitti* serves as a textbook illustration of Rouch's oft-stated view that the camera is a catalyst that provokes people to reveal fictional or mythical parts of themselves which are, he never tired of asserting, the most real parts of themselves. We see this, for example, in the way the camera provokes the Songhay musicians to throw themselves into their performances with ever more flamboyant gestures, provokes schoolchildren to stare, and provokes invisible gods or spirits to possess human dancers.

Tourou and Bitti also serves as a textbook illustration of the view, which I presented in *Documentary Film Classics*, that it is the very presence of the camera, when it is doing its mysterious work, that provokes people into revealing themselves (Rothman 1997, 86–90). The fact that a film-maker need do nothing to "shake up" his subjects other than simply film them, I went on to argue, renders moot the distinction between *cinéma vérité*, as Rouch practiced it, and so-called direct cinema as practiced in the United States by the likes of Richard Leacock, D. A. Pennebaker, or the Maysles brothers.

Apart from the transition—Daniel Morgan's chapter in this volume alerts us to its importance—from the brief opening shot to the ten-minute take that transports filmmaker and viewer into the Songhay world, Rouch does not manipulate his footage in the editing room. Yet he does give shape to *Tourou and Bitti*. He gives it a beginning, middle, and end by his simple act of walking into the public square with his camera on his shoulder; shooting what takes place there, and then retracing his steps so that when his ten-minute magazine runs out he is back where he started. Viewing the film, it seems no mere coincidence that he closes this circle at the precise moment his film magazine runs out, or rather, it seems a coincidence Rouch was aiming for. After all, as he tells us in his voice-over, it was his intimation that he was soon going to run out of film that made him stop filming the conversation between villagers and gods taking place in the public square and start walking backward away from the square. The perfect simultaneity of his completing this trajectory and his camera's running out of film crowns Rouch's achievement in pulling off the virtuoso performance that at one level comprises the entirety of the film. This remarkable coincidence, coming on the heels of the equally remarkable coincidence—if it is a coincidence—that two dancers become possessed at the moment the camera attends to them, seems uncanny, as if Rouch's act of filming, as well as the events he is filming, are under the sway of supernatural forces, forces whose reality the film documents. (When Rouch screened and discussed *Tourou and Bitti*, he liked to underscore this suggestion by telling the story of his aborted attempt to repeat the experiment of filming a possession ritual in a single ten-minute take. This time, the possession happened immediately *after* he ran out of film. The lesson he drew from this, Rouch liked to tell Western audiences, was that it was unwise, even dangerous, to trifle with such powerful forces. He never tried the experiment again.[2]) In any case, *Tourou and Bitti* has a palpable air of mystery or magic about it. This air is enhanced by the way Rouch, in his narration, refers to the dancers, after they are possessed, not as their mortal human selves but as gods or spirits, as if he, personally, believed in the reality of the Songhay deities.

In any case, as this air of mystery reminds us, if *Tourou and Bitti* is shaped by Rouch's act of filming, it is also given shape by his narration. Essentially improvised, Rouch's narration presents itself rhetorically as his spontaneous response to the film, spoken to us as if he were in our presence, viewing what we are viewing as we are viewing it. But the narration, which is written in the past tense, also invokes an "original" scene in which Rouch, in the past, viewed through his camera's viewfinder the fabulous spectacle presently being projected by the magic of cinema on the screen before us. The man who silently filmed these events is the source of the voice now speaking to us. This is the mysterious reality Rouch's narration declares, both by his words and by the hushed, poetic quality of his voice, which bespeaks the sublimity of the ritual we are viewing, the ritual of our viewing, and the ritual of his own act of filming.

As is usually the case in his films, Rouch's narration for *Tourou and Bitti* performs a variety of functions. He explains enough about this Songhay possession ritual for us to understand up to a point—but not to the point of explaining it away, denying its mystery—what we are viewing. When people in the film speak—or gods for that matter—Rouch does not simply tell us what they are saying or simply translate their words; he speaks for them in their words—translated, of course—but in his own voice. He acts out their speeches, in effect, expressing their thoughts and feelings as if they were his own.

As is not usually the case, however, Rouch explicitly casts his narration for *Tourou and Bitti* in the first person. His words declare that he was present behind the camera when these events took place, that he was a participant, if a silent one, in the ritual he was filming. This is evident, for example, in the way he begins his narration:

> On March 11, 1971, after three years of famine, the people of Simiri, in the Zermaganda of Niger, staged a possession dance to ask the forest spirits to guard future crops against locusts. On March 16, Daoudo Sorko, son of the Zima, or priest, Daoudo Zido, asked us to watch the fourth day of ritual, when they played the antique drums, Tourou and Bitti. By late afternoon, no dancer was yet possessed, but my sound man, Moussa Hemidou, and I, on the camera, nevertheless opted for a 10-minute sequence to obtain a real-time

film document on these ancient drums that would soon be silent forever. So we made this experimental ethnographic film.

Rouch's words here not only refer to his presence behind the camera, they explicitly declare his purpose in being there, namely, to make an experimental ethnographic film, that is, the film we are viewing (a "real-time film document on these ancient drums that would soon be silent forever" consisting of a single ten-minute sequence shot). At this point, a title declares this to be a "first person film by Jean Rouch." The body of the film begins as Rouch's voice, on the soundtrack, speaks the words, "Entering into a film means diving into reality, being both present and invisible, as that afternoon at 4 o'clock when I followed Zima Daouda Zido, who met us at the edge of his village."

As will emerge in the course of the film, Rouch's characterization of his status when he is filming—"both present and invisible"—pointedly links him with the gods or spirits who are about to shed their invisibility by entering the bodies of dancers wishing to abandon themselves so that this might happen. Rouch "dives into reality," as he puts it, when he begins to walk with his camera into the Songhay village in which a possession ritual is underway. The narration continues: "We passed the corral of ritual sheep and goats to be sacrificed to the spirits robed in black, white, or red. We passed the shack where the spirits' horses are kept. In the square, before the orchestra, old Sambu Atabeido of Simiri was dancing."

At this point, the camera lingers on the dancer. Having said what needed to be said, Rouch's voice falls silent, as it will do several times in the film, enabling the spectacle animated by the "drums of yore" to weave its spell on us. Such extended stretches in which the world on film expresses itself directly, unmediated by Rouch's words and voice, are essential to the film's impact and its meaning. They are instrumental to the film's success in not only documenting a Songhay possession ritual but at the same time documenting the powers of cinema, which are no less mysterious than the powers of invisible spirits capable of taking possession of flesh-and-blood human beings.

In the second of these narrationless stretches, Rouch moves away from the dancer, who has been trying for four hours to become possessed, and toward the band. He hovers over the musicians who respond to the camera's attention by playing with increasingly flamboyant gestures, then begins moving back in the direction of the dancer. "Suddenly the orchestra stopped," Rouch says. When he adds, "I should have stopped filming," he makes clear that he took this silence as a sign—perhaps it was a sign—that the musicians were giving up hope that anyone would be possessed that day. But then, as Rouch tells us with mounting excitement in his voice, he sensed that something was about to happen. "I drew closer to the Bitti player, and I heard a cry: 'The meat! Kuré the hyena, here is the meat!' He was no longer Sambu Albeidu the Simiri farmer; he was Kuré, Kuré the hyena, spirit god of the Haousas."

Every time I view the film, I always have the impression that it is no mere coincidence that the possession takes place at the very moment the camera, by drawing close to the Bitti player, moves close to the dancer. I have a premonition that this is going to happen. Loading the deck, perhaps, Rouch provokes viewers to have such a premonition by informing us, in effect, that he moved so close to the dancer because he himself had such a premonition. In any case, it appears as if it is the very proximity of the camera that provokes the dancer to become entranced, to abandon himself so as to free the invisible spirit of Kuré to enter his body.

Of course, we would not find ourselves ready to sense that the possession was about to take place if we were not already under the spell cast by the "drums of yore" (as the dancer was; as Rouch, filming, was; as—Rouch would have it—Kuré was). For Rouch, as he was filming, the spell cast by the pulsing drums was inseparable from the spell cast by the world framed in his camera's viewfinder. For *Tourou and Bitti's* viewers—including Rouch himself, when he later recorded his narration—the spell cast by the drums cannot be separated from the spell cast by the world—visible yet absent—projected on the movie screen. In the world on film, the camera, itself invisible, has the power to provoke the invisible to reveal itself.

Despite the camera's proximity, at the instant the possession happens, the dancer's face is outside the frame, above its upper border; the camera's focus is on one of the drums.

Whenever I view the film, this, too, appears to be no mere coincidence. If *Tourou and Bitti* were a fiction film, such a framing, which renders the dancer's face invisible the moment the possession takes place, would clearly be intentional—perhaps a brilliant stroke, in fact. But we know—do we not?—that this is no fiction film we are viewing. There is no omniscient author, or god, behind the camera. It nonetheless appears to be no mere accident that the camera misses the moment the invisible spirit of Kuré enters the dancer's body. Is this, then, Kuré's doing—a declaration of the god's more than human powers? In any case, this framing has the effect of deferring Kuré's entrance, enhancing the dramatic impact when—thanks to the dancer's own movement and the camera's—the dancer's figure reappears in the frame and we see for ourselves the astonishing change in his demeanor.

Once again, Rouch's voice falls silent, allowing the spectacle to cast its own spell. Kuré, walking with a distinctive loping gait, strides over to the band and goads the musicians to play with even greater intensity. As the camera, approaching close, circles Kuré, we are at the same time accorded our first clear view of some of the children who have gathered to watch the dancing (and, no doubt, the filming).

After showing his film to the people in it, Rouch became convinced that it was his act of filming that precipitated the possession trance of the dancer. He was moved to write "On the Vicissitudes of the Self: The Possessed Dancer, the Magician, the Sorcerer, the Filmmaker and the Ethnographer" (Rouch 1978), an essay that attempted to explain how it was possible for the camera's presence to have this effect, not only on the dancer, but also on the invisible spirit Kuré. When the spell of the film wears off, we may well believe that this spirit is imaginary, not real, or even that the dancer was not really entranced at all but only acting. But then it still requires explanation how a camera can be so much as *imagined* to be capable of provoking a god into manifesting himself. What does this dancer believe Rouch's camera to be, that he understands its presence to be capable of provoking him to fall into a trance, to abandon himself, so as to enable, as he believes, an invisible spirit to possess his body?

When filming *Tourou and Bitti*, Rouch argues in "On the Vicissitudes of the Self," he, too, fell into a trance—a *ciné-trance* comparable to the trance that enabled the dancer to be possessed. "While shooting a ritual," Rouch wrote some years later, the filmmaker "discovers a complex and spontaneous set-up" (Rouch 2003, 8). To record it, he only has to "record reality," improvise his frames and movements.

> If, by chance, while shooting a . . . trance dance, I happen to accomplish such a performance, I can still remember the acute challenge of not wobbling, not missing focus nor exposure, in which case the whole sequence would have to be resumed, therefore be lost altogether. And when, tired out by such a tension, the soundman drops his microphone and I abandon my camera, we feel as if a tense crowd, musicians and even vulnerable gods who got hold of trembling dancers were all aware and stimulated by our venture. (Ibid., 8)

Rouch's growing commitment to the "one take/one sequence" method of filming, which reaches its apogee in *Tourou and Bitti*, confirms that his artistic roots, like those of Griaule, are in surrealism. Shooting in a trance, and not revising or correcting the improvised footage in post-production, makes Rouch's filming a kind of surrealist automatic writing that frees the resulting footage from the repressive mechanisms of the filmmaker's conscious mind, which was absorbed in merely technical details. And Rouch's narration, too, as we have said, is essentially improvised—his spontaneous response to his experience of viewing the film.

As Rouch describes it, in filming *Tourou and Bitti* he became so absorbed in pulling off his performance that he fell into such a *ciné-trance*. Walking into the village with the camera on his shoulder, he "dove into reality," as he puts it in the film's narration. At once "present and invisible," he became other than the person he ordinarily was. He became the being that Paul Stoller, in his eloquent account of the film, calls "Rouch-the-camera." Filming *Tourou and Bitti*, Rouch-the-camera walked among the villagers gathered for the ceremony, and also among invisible spirits who recognized him as belonging to their realm as well as to the realm of the visible. When the discouraged musicians stopped playing and yet Rouch-the-camera nonetheless drew close to one of the dancers, that dancer must have taken this as a sign that Kuré—invisible to ordinary human beings, the dancer believed, but not to Rouch-the-camera—was at last approaching.

According to Rouch's essay, the Songhay believe that when a dancer is possessed he or she is approached by an invisible spirit carrying the skin of a freshly slaughtered animal. The spirit wraps the skin around the dancer's head, at the same time capturing and protecting the "self" of the dancer, who is now in a deep trance, freeing the spirit to enter the dancer's body. When it is time to leave, the spirit lifts off the animal skin, liberating the displaced "self" of the dancer, who has no memory of any of this.

In his essay, Rouch suggests that a *ciné-trance* is comparable to such a possession trance, but he does not flesh out this picture. In *Documentary Film Classics* I sketch a way of doing so. The world viewed through the viewfinder of a movie camera, like the world projected on a movie screen, is a world of surfaces—the skin of the world. Thus when Rouch falls into a *ciné-trance*, his "self" can be captured, and protected, by quite literally being wrapped in the skin of the world. In this state, it is possible for the filmmaker's "self" to become displaced, his body to be possessed—and for him to remember none of this after he stops filming. Perhaps when filming *Tourou and Bitti*, Rouch *did* see the invisible spirit of Kuré in the viewfinder. If so, when he awakened from his trance, he had no memory of it.

When the dancer goes into his trance, he abandons his self, freeing his body to be possessed by Kuré's alien consciousness or spirit. Then what consciousness or spirit possesses Rouch when he becomes Rouch-the-camera? A camera is only a machine; it has, or is, no consciousness or spirit. Then who or what possessed Rouch when, for example, he moved from the drummers to the dancer? He tells us, in his narration, that he sensed that something was about to happen. But who or what made him sense this? Who or what made him respond to this premonition by moving the camera the way he did?

Then again, who or what *is* Rouch-the-camera? Perhaps a key is to be found in a profound observation by Stanley Cavell in *The World Viewed*. The fact that we speak of the person or object that a photograph is *of* as the *subject* of that photograph suggests both that he or she or it is what the photograph is about, what it studies, and—this is a further point Cavell makes in "What Becomes of Things on Film?"—that the object of this study—the world as it appears in the viewfinder, the world as it appears on film—participates actively in this study.[3] The photograph's "object" is also its subject. Thus when Rouch's "self" becomes "wrapped in the skin of the world" and he enters into a *ciné-trance*, the visible world—the objective world of people and things, the world in which gods like Kuré are invisible—reveals itself *to be* a subject, reveals itself *as* a subject; in the visible, the invisible is revealed, reveals itself. The camera's viewfinder becomes a kind of crystal ball in which the entranced filmmaker sees what to everyone else is invisible—the world as it is fated to appear on the movie screen. When Rouch enters a *ciné-trance*, then, he becomes possessed by the world framed by the viewfinder, a world in which the invisible reveals itself in the visible. In that world, Rouch himself is invisible. Thus for him to enter into a *ciné-trance*, his invisible self must be revealed, must reveal itself, in the visible. This means that, in the world framed by the viewfinder, hence in the world projected on the movie screen, Rouch's self must be revealed, must reveal itself, in the visible. (Rouch reveals himself in the world on film the way dreamers reveal themselves in their dreams.)

As *Tourou and Bitti* nears its close, Daoudo Sorko, hoping to persuade Kuré to help the village with its crops, is busy haggling with the god, whom he offers fresh meat. While this negotiation is going on, a second possession takes place, this time in full view of the camera. "She is no longer a Samiri woman," Rouch says. "She is Hadio, the captive Peule." (The Peule, a nomadic people dispersed across wide areas of West Africa, are traditionally herders who keep separate from the local farming populations.) He adds, "School children have come to see how their parents and grandparents dance," acknowledging the staring children who have become conspicuous in the background of this frame—no doubt, they're staring at the camera, as well as at the dancer-turned-god—and at the same time anticipating the film's ending.

As Daouda Sorko is sprinkling "Haousa perfumes on the gods and the band," Rouch, walking backward, begins pulling away from the public square, retracing his steps. "I should have gone on filming," he says, "but I wanted to make a movie, to return to the start of my story, and I pulled back slowly to see what the schoolchildren saw: A small village square in the setting sun where, in a secret ceremony, men and gods spoke of coming harvests." By this time, the camera is back where it started. As it tilts up from the earth to trees and the sky, the ten-minute magazine runs out.

Tourou and Bitti ends by completing a circle, and by symbolically bridging the realms of earth and sky, bodies and spirits, mortals and gods, visible and invisible. Rouch's closing words bring the scene down to earth ("a small village square in the setting sun"), which reminds us of the mysteriousness of what we have witnessed (a "secret ceremony" in which "men and gods spoke of coming harvests") in this world so different from our own.

Surely, when Rouch says that he should have continued shooting the gods and villagers but that he "wanted to make a movie"—a movie that ends by coming full circle—he is being ironic. We cannot believe that he regrets performing this experiment. His purpose in making this film was not, or not primarily, to advance scientific knowledge. He made this film as an artist, an artist committed to creating a work of cinematic poetry, a film with an aesthetically satisfying, and meaningful, shape or form.

Rouch gives the resulting film the title *The Drums of Yore: Tourou and Bitti* and, as we have seen, speaks of it as a "document" of the ancient drums. But if the drums are the film's subjects, what the film is about, what is it about them that it enables us to know? As we have seen, the power of these "drums of yore," as Rouch's film documents it, cannot be separated from the power of film, which *Tourou and Bitti* also documents. If the film is about the drums, it is also about itself, about film, about the entrancing power of the world on film. What makes the film an experiment is not simply its unconventional form as a single ten-minute sequence shot. It is an experiment that tests film's power to bridge the worlds of the visible and the invisible. It tests film's power to keep alive the voices of these ancient drums that, as Rouch's narration hauntingly puts it, "are soon to be silenced forever." And I cannot help but believe, now that Jean Rouch is no more, that *Tourou and Bitti* also tests the power of film to keep alive its author's voice, to keep Rouch's voice, too, from being silenced forever.

The film's ending invokes the point of view of children fascinated by the spectacle of a "secret ceremony" whose meaning escapes them. If one among them is driven to ask questions, there his initiation will begin. For in traditional African societies, "Knowledge is only transmitted to those who ask for it," as Rouch puts it in his narration for his great film *Ambara Dama*. By placing viewers in the position of these young children, Rouch is providing us with an opportunity to ask questions, too. Thanks to Rouch's narration, we know things the children do not know about the way their grandparents dance. But what of the camera's dance, the "secret ceremony" in which *Tourou and Bitti* originated? How can we make sure that its meaning does not escape us?

Funeral at Bongo: The Old Anaï (1848–1971)

As *Anaï* opens, an image of the sky fades in. The camera tilts down, framing a village in the plain below as the title of the film appears, then slowly zooms in on the village. Rouch's voice-over narration commences. "In Mali, overlooking the Plain of Bongo, there is a village called Bongo. Here, every sixty years, the Dogon of the Bandiagara Cliffs perform the *Sigui* ritual commemorating the death of every man's ancestor, Dyongou Serou, who died at the very beginning of the world."

There is a cut to what I take to be a shot from Rouch's six-part film document of the 1969 *Sigui* ritual—that is, a cut to the past from the present (which was already the past, of course, when he recorded his narration). As the sound of drums fades up, the camera zooms and pans until it frames, from a distance, a zigzag line of dancers. "To participate twice in a *Sigui* ritual means one is over sixty. Nevertheless, Anaï Dolo has attended three *Sigui* rituals in the village of Bongo." Just as Rouch is uttering Anaï's name, there is a cut to a shot that again shows the "present," although no internal evidence marks this transition. (In the world on film, no tangible sign separates present and past; all views are present, and all views are past.)

As the narration continues, the drumming slowly fades out, while the camera pans left past a great tree. "In 1849, he was in his mother's womb. In 1909, he ranked among the elders, all over sixty. In 1969, he was the dean and president of the Bongo *Sigui* ritual." Finally there is a cut to old Anaï Dolo sitting in his hut, with another man beside him. That man begins to speak. Rouch translates: "Anaï—he's over 120. He was born three *Siguis* ago." The man addresses a question to Anaï as the camera moves in to isolate the old man in the frame. "Anaï, how are you?" "What, me? I'm all right. Everyone is all right. I wish you a good trip."

As is Rouch's wont, when people in his films speak, he does not simply tell us what they are saying; nor does he simply translate their words. He speaks their words—translated of course—in his own voice, expressing their thoughts and feelings as if they were his own. Among major documentary filmmakers, Rouch is unique in making a general practice of acting out, in this manner, the utterances of the people he films. In truth, he had a remarkable gift for finding voices of his own— the voice he finds within himself for Anaï, for example, is remarkably sweet and gentle—that we can believe in as expressions of who those people are, an unerring ability to "channel" the people he films, to be possessed by them. There is a cut to a new shot as the other man rises, momentarily eclipsing Anaï in the frame, and exits, touching Anaï on the shoulder as he leaves. "Bless you on your way," Rouch says in his sweet, gentle "Anaï" voice. Alone now in the frame, Anaï sighs, touches his face, looks down, evidently turned inward.

This shot is held, inviting us to contemplate the blind old man's face, perhaps to wonder whether he is aware that he is being filmed. Rouch says, in a poetic voice infused with wonder and a touch of melancholy, "After sixty, for a Dogon, life starts anew. On his black chest, his white hairs are like the stars of the Milky Way. He is the very sky on earth. He is a full master of all knowledge."

Here, Rouch is no longer relaying to us what a "character" is saying. There is no one whose utterance he is acting out. And yet he is not simply speaking for himself either. Our impression is that the metaphors, if not the words, are particular to the Dogon. Throughout, Rouch's narration draws on his factual knowledge about Dogon society, much of it gleaned from the research of Marcel Griaule and Germaine Dieterlen, and on his knowledge of Dogon ways of conceptualizing their form of life, much of that knowledge likewise acquired from his mentors.

At one level, Rouch filmed Dogon rituals in order to vindicate Griaule's claim in his dissertation and in his popular book *Conversations with Ogotemmeli*—a claim that sparked controversy during Griaule's lifetime (and continues to do so long after his death) within the French anthropological establishment—that the Dogon had developed and sustained a society based on complicated but orderly conceptions, and on institutional and ritual systems, that constitute a philosophical system comparable in completeness and sophistication to that of the classical Greeks. As Griaule put it, "These people live by a cosmogony, a metaphysic, and a religion which put them on a par with the peoples of antiquity and which Christian theology might indeed study with profit" (Griaule 1971, 8). It is because Griaule's claim was true, Rouch believed, that filming Dogon rituals could further the quest for anthropological knowledge. By tapping into their knowledge, Rouch also believed, he could tap more deeply into the powers of film, hence further his own art and his own quest for self-knowledge.

Crucially, in his narration Rouch never separates his own ways of thinking from those of the Dogon. He does not say, for example, "The Dogon think of the old man as the very sky on earth." In *Anaï*, Rouch speaks in ways we might expect a Dogon, not a Frenchman, to speak. No doubt, Dieterlen helped Rouch to find appropriate words. They collaborated so closely in the making of *Anaï*, and *Ambara Dama* as well, that he graciously credited her as codirector. Yet it is always Rouch who speaks those words, and always Rouch who finds a voice of his own with which to speak them. And it is always Rouch behind the camera. Insofar as *Anaï* inscribes in its text the figure of its own author—that this is the case is central to my understanding of the film—that author is Rouch, not Dieterlen. But who is Jean Rouch, who in speaking such words finds his own voice? Who is he that he finds himself in his acts of filming?

Speaking words that express reverence for this "full master of all knowledge," Rouch seems personally moved. He may be acting, of course, but if it is an act, it is an act that reveals a deep truth about him. I cannot but believe that he *is* moved by the old man he is—was—filming, this man whose living image appears before us, projected on the movie screen. Rouch is—was—filled with wonder, by the awesome fact (he never seems to doubt that it *is* a fact) that this man was over 120 years old. But also, I cannot but believe, Rouch is moved by the respect, and the tenderness, that the Dogon show for their elders by speaking of them as "the very sky on earth." We sense the respect and tenderness that Rouch feels not only for Anaï, but also for the Dogon people this individual represents, a people whose language is so rich with poetry. (Rouch himself was about to turn sixty when he recorded this narration. Who in France would have been likely to speak of him—or anyone—as "the very sky on earth"?) And we are moved by Rouch's emotion as he speaks these words. And of course, we too are moved by Anaï himself, as Rouch's camera captured this elder.

In a more matter-of-fact tone, Rouch continues. "When his strength starts declining, he has to remain within the entrance of his house. He never goes out, but he takes an active part in the village life. Every leader has to greet him and keep him posted." Then the narration again becomes poetic. "The old man is back within his placenta in his mother's womb." For a moment, Rouch falls silent, as if inviting us ponder the mystery of this "full master of all knowledge," now a 122-year-old man so helpless that the Dogon envision him as back in his mother's womb—as if he were soon to be born into the world, not soon to die.

After this pregnant pause, Rouch breaks his silence. "Six months after the shooting of these very frames, Anaï Dolo . . ." There is a cut—again, it occurs just as Rouch is speaking Anaï's name—to a close-up of blades of grass dancing in the wind. ". . . Anaï Dolo died."

Although most of *Anaï's* screen time consists of a succession of improvised sequence shots whose unfolding was beyond Rouch's control when he filmed them, this shot is self-evidently set up. Apparently, Rouch took the shot, which conveys so eloquent a sense of isolation and loneliness, with the intention of placing it at this precise moment in the film—a moment that calls for a poetic way to mark Anaï's death. Cutting to this shot at this moment has the force of a gesture through which Rouch, the film's author, declares himself directly, declares himself to *be* the film's author.

Anaï was a revered member of his community, but all human beings die, as we are born, alone. Part of the poetry of the cut resides in its timing, the fact that it occurs during the pause that precedes the words that announce Anaï's death to us. From this cut alone, we know, even before Rouch's words tell us, that death has come to Anaï. But what makes it possible for us to know this? How can a simple cut declare a real death?

When he recorded these words, Rouch knew, but chose not to say, that Anaï had died in the interim. Anaï is already dead when his living image is projected on the movie screen. Rouch did not know, when he filmed Anaï, that the old man was fated to die so soon. And yet if Anaï were not already dead, we would not be viewing the film we are viewing. A film about Anaï's funeral makes his death necessary, after all. Expressively, the cut to the dancing grass not only announces Anaï's death, it registers it *as* necessary. It is almost as if, within the world on film, Rouch's filming of Anaï, combined with his gesture of placing "these very frames" precisely here, assents to Anaï's death, provokes death to possess him, causing him—or, we might say, freeing him—to die.

As the lonesome wailing of the wind fades up, the camera begins slowly zooming out and shifting focus, gradually making visible, and then bringing into focus, what was always already there behind the dancing grass—the vast plain that stretches to the distant horizon where sky meets earth. The camera continues refocusing and reframing until it

reveals the particular place where the grass is rooted. Then there is a cut to a new angle.

This refocusing, reframing, and cut constitutes a second authorial gesture, one that complicates the original cut. It implies a connection, first, between the blades of grass, which initially appeared poetically isolated, and the Dogon world as a whole, which it brings into focus. It also links the grass with the "cave of the dead," the particular place within that world where Anaï's body—but not his soul—is interred. The camera effects a shift of perspective that mirrors Anaï's passage from life to death, picturing it as the release of his soul from his body into the world—a world that the camera at the same time conjures into being, making it possible (as Daniel Morgan observes in his brilliant reading of the sequence) for the filmmaker and the viewer to enter it. Expressively, this shift of perspective represents Anaï's death; we might even say that the camera's gesture *enacts* his death. Again, it is as if Rouch, in filming "these very frames" and placing them precisely here, is acknowledging authorship of the film we are viewing—a film that declares Anaï's death to be a condition necessary for its own creation.

If a gesture of the camera—a cut, a shift of focus, a zoom—can make death necessary in the world on film, perhaps it is no wonder that Rouch was moved to develop his "one take/one sequence" method of filming, which freed him to forgo such gestures. And yet, faced with the challenge of filming Anaï's funeral in a way that acknowledged its true dimension, Rouch evidently felt the need to break with that method, as we see again in the passage that follows.

As Rouch speaks the words "In the house of Anaï, his great-grandson, on a calendar rope, counts the knots, counts the weeks that have passed since the death," there is a cut to him. The camera moves in on the knots as the great-grandson keeps counting, then tilts up to his face. Rouch's voice takes over. "34, 35, 36 . . . 36 weeks of five days each, which is six moons. The funeral may start!" Throughout this shot, the camera frames the great-grandson frontally. Clearly, he is counting for the benefit of the camera, although he seems to have been instructed not to meet its gaze. When his count reaches the magic figure of six months, he holds up the string of beads as if to make sure the camera gets a clear view of it.

This is another shot that Rouch obviously set up, this time with the great-grandson's complicity, with the intention of placing it precisely at this point in this film. The fact that after a certain point we only hear Rouch's voice, although the great-grandson keeps moving his lips, underscores our impression that it is really Rouch, the film's author,

who makes the announcement that the shot serves to set up; it is really Rouch who gives the go-ahead for the funeral to begin and thus effects the transition to the body of the film, which documents the main events of the days-long ceremony.

First, the tall masks that were last used in the 1969 *Sigui* ritual are brought out in honor of Anaï, who had been the chief of the Mask Society. Accompanying these images, Rouch's narration takes a mysterious turn. "The big mask is out. The tallest mask is out. A good man is dead. A good man is broken. Give mercy to this man. To the villagers, give mercy." Rouch's tone of voice and melodic cadence give these lines the quality of an incantation. Our impression is that he is quoting lines that were spoken, or chanted, as part of the funeral. But when and where were they said? By whom?

Next, Anaï's grandson recounts the 1895 battle in which the French colonialists defeated the Dogon and Anaï was seriously wounded. Rouch cuts back and forth between the scene of the telling and shots of the places referred to in the story, almost as if the camera can see into the past. (This is an editing strategy Rouch uses for a number of passages in *Anaï*.) Then the villagers reenact the battle.

This part of *Anaï* includes one of the long narrationless sequences that are among the glories of Rouch's films of this period. This mock battle is fabulously rousing. The spectacular natural setting of the Bandiagara cliffs, the exotic architecture that makes the human habitations seem as primeval as the cliffs themselves, the exotic clothes, the polyrhythmic music and the dancing combine to create an enchanting effect. Rouch, continuously improvising with his camera, is in the middle of all this action. Thus we, too, find ourselves in the thick of things. And yet, like Rouch, we also remain on the outside. As viewers, we have no role to play other than to take in this spectacle, as Rouch does from his place behind the camera.

Rouch does not say a word for over twelve minutes of screen time. He lets the spectacle speak for itself. Just as he finds no need to break the spell by speaking, I, too, find myself wishing to let the passage speak for itself. In any case, I simply don't have words to convey to those who haven't seen *Anaï* what it is like to experience this part of the film. The one point I do feel it is essential to make is that the ritual being filmed and Rouch's act of filming fuse when the family members playing the Dogon side of the battle repeatedly fire their flintlock rifles at the camera.

However sincere he was in making this film to share with the Dogon his quest for anthropological knowledge, Rouch is a Frenchman, after all. His people are implicated in the history of the Dogon, and this fact is not lost on them, or on him. But if their shooting at the camera acknowledges that Rouch is a Frenchman, not a Dogon, it also suggests something else. As I wrote in *Documentary Film Classics*,

A soul separated from its body is vulnerable, the Dogon believe, and also dangerous. However much it wanted to stay in the village that was its home, Anaï's soul had to be made to leave, even if it had to be frightened away. Shooting their rifles at the camera not only placed Rouch on the French side of the colonial war they were reenacting, it suggests that they associated the camera, or Rouch behind the camera, with the souls of the dead, as if Rouch, behind the camera, like Anaï, was a soul haunting a world in which he had no home, a soul longing to die his own death, yet reluctant to sever its ties with the living. (Rothman, 1997, 97)

In the film's second long narrationless sequence, Anaï's family make necessary preparations (washing away the impurities of death, distributing gifts, and so on). Throughout all the activities at Anaï's home, a mannequin of Anaï sits atop the roof. Anaï presides over his own funeral.

Overseeing the events Rouch is filming, Anaï becomes a kind of stand-in or double for the filmmaker behind the camera. This is one of the film's several strategies for bringing home the idea that Rouch, in the act of filming, is more like the invisible soul of a dead man than a living human being of flesh and blood.

"The impurities of death are washed off," Rouch says. "Now the soul of Anaï Dolo lies in the hands of the Nommu, the water spirit of the pond, keeper of all dead souls." There is a cut from the tassels of a blanket to the sky. A vulture soars overhead. As the camera follows the soaring vulture, the pulsing clicks of a castanet-like percussion instrument and a wailing horn fade in, accompanied a moment later by a Dogon elder's rhythmic chanting. "That very evening," Rouch says, "gathered on the public square, elders of Bongo say the *Tegué*. The *Tegué*: the great sayings of the Dogon. They tell about the adventure of the creation of the world. They tell about the animals of the bush. They tell about the history and the myths of the villages. They tell about the principal altars of the Dogon. And they tell about the saga of Anaï Dolo."

All this time, the camera has been following the vulture. Now there is a cut to a nighttime shot of the chanting elder. The shot is illuminated, as Rouch loved to explain to audiences, only by a pool of light cast by a flashlight strapped to his camera in the hope it would provide enough light to film. The way the shot is lit, with most of the frame in pitch black shadow, enhances the awesome sense that we have stumbled onto a scene so ancient, so primeval, that it is as if we were glimpsing the dawn of humanity.

With the clicking instrument in his hand, the elder is "throwing the Dogon sayings to the wind," as Rouch will later put it, the haunting cadence of his chant augmented by the steady, pulsing clicks. Speaking in a spellbinding, strangely soothing cadence that is itself almost a chant, Rouch begins translating the elder's words. He continues relaying the words of the *Tegué*, with the elder's chanting in the background, for a remarkable fifteen minutes of screen time.

Most of the lines Rouch intones are quite obscure to Westerners, to put it mildly, but he never interrupts the flow to explain their meaning.

In my experience, the obscurity adds to the mysteriousness of the scene, intensifying its enchanting power. And, as in many Bob Dylan songs, from the depths of obscurity certain lines unexpectedly leap out with poetic images that are startlingly clear and riveting. Certain other lines have a surprisingly playful quality. There is simply no way to convey a sense of the poetry of this language other than by quoting a section of it:

> I ask forgiveness.
> My mouth is too small.
> God has closed the door. Goodnight.
> Those who have laid the altar, goodnight.
> Those who have cut the willow thorns, goodnight.
> Those who have laid the foundation brick, goodnight.
> Those who have planted the central post, goodnight.
> Those who have laid the three kitchen stones, goodnight.
> Those who have held the calabash, goodnight.
> The night eaters are out.
> The day eaters are going in.
> They have had their day, goodnight.
> The first in the cave. The cave is full.
> We have had the day of the great father. Goodnight.
> God has closed the door.
> God of the east, goodnight.
> God of the west, goodnight.
> God of the north, goodnight.
> God, soft mother, goodnight.
> God has closed the door. Goodnight.
> God, who makes you die.
> God, who makes you live.
> The one on the road, he could see him within the bush.
> The one within the bush, he could see him on the road.
> The one who cries, he makes him laugh.
> The one who laughs, he makes him cry.
> God accuses the one who does not follow him: the fox.

The recital of the *Tegué* is a performance open to the public, not restricted to initiates. The chanting takes place in the public square. Nonetheless, the effect of the passage is claustrophobic. But it is only well into the passage, at the film's most astonishing moment—I dare say, it is one of the most astonishing moments in the history of cinema—that the theme of the recitation shifts to the diverse animals of the bush and there is a breathtaking cut from the elder chanting in the darkness to the inside

of a cave, where the camera pans the wall, which is studded with innumerable skulls of all sizes and shapes, presumably of the animals the
elder is invoking.

Monkey with the warm red hemorrhoid, his day has come,
    goodnight.
Small ostrich, faraway animal, his day has come, goodnight.
Crowned crane, who stands on one foot to shit.
She is the one who asks for the night. Her time has come,
    goodnight.
Very small ostrich, with his deep cry, his day has come,
    goodnight.
Running mare monkey, his day has come, goodnight.
Lazy monkey, his day has come, goodnight.
Male monkey, hanging, hanging and clinging, and who cries
    from nothing,
His day has come, goodnight.
Brother rhino, dark face, joyful heart. White moon, sad heart,
His day has come, goodnight.
Gazelle in the bush, smothered heart, running all the day,
Her day has come, goodnight.
Panther, who stretches and scratches. His day has come,
    goodnight.
Elephant, unwelcome stranger, ear like a shield, eye like the
    morning star,
Skull as big as a tomb, his day has come, goodnight.

Forget the elders, call the young.
Forget the young, call the elders.
Feet of millipedes, their shoes cannot be counted.
Take their share of the public square.
We have had the day, goodnight.

These sublime, awe-inspiring shots of skulls, combined with these chanted, poetic words (especially the haunting repetition, with variations, of the poignant refrain "Your day has come, goodnight"), engender an overwhelming intimation of, or yearning for, transcendence, and an all but palpable sense of mortality. All these skulls housed the minds of beings who have had their day. Before long, we, too, will have had our day. Bones will be all that is left of our mortal bodies when we depart on our long journey to the land of the dead.

Anaï blessed all who visited him, wishing them well on their journey. Every time Rouch intones the word "goodnight," he is giving his blessing, too, as the Dogon elder is. But from which side of the divide between the living and the dead is Rouch's voice coming to us? These shots reveal, or declare, the camera's connection with death, even as they bring home to us that every creature the camera films is—like Anaï, like Rouch, like us—mortal, fated to die. And yet at the same time the shots engender a palpable sense of immortality. Indeed, I can think of no other film passage that provokes viewers to feel so strongly that we are part of something greater than we can imagine; a sense that something of us will somehow go on after our bodies are dead and buried.

As the chant segues to an obscure litany of people and places in the Dogon world, Rouch's camera performs another startling gesture. Suddenly breaking out of its claustrophobic confinement, like Anaï's soul released from his body, the camera departs the cave. As if liberated from its connection with the filmmaker's own body, the film incorporates a series of views, each of a place invoked by the elder's recitation. With these cuts, *Anaï* taps fully into the power of montage, which Rouch had developed the "one take/one sequence" method precisely to forgo. (Early in the film, as we have seen, this montage was anticipated by the cut, a moment before Rouch's announcement of Anaï's death, from the old man in his hut to blades of grass dancing in the wind.)

This exhilarating passage is an explicit declaration of the power of film—a power film shares with the dances the Dogon incorporate into their rituals—to transcend the bounds of space and time. Film has the power to connect the visible and the invisible, the living Anaï and the soul of the dead Anaï, just as the dances at the heart of his funeral connect one man's life, the historical struggle of the Dogon people against their French colonizers, and the creation of the universe. For such power, film pays a price, as the passage acknowledges by linking the mystery of death, as meditated upon by the Dogon sayings, with the mystery of film, as *Anaï* meditates upon it.

The passage is also intensely personal. The words Rouch speaks and the voice with which he speaks them, I take it, give poetic expression to the feelings the inevitability of his own death arouses in him. The Dogon sayings at the same time illuminate the act of artistic creation that gives birth to the film we are viewing. For the words with which Rouch expresses his own feelings are literal translations of the words the elder is chanting, words that inscribe knowledge the Dogon hold sacred. In this passage Rouch also expresses himself cinematically in a succession of poetic images that match the chanted words in beauty and power. His gesture of breaking with the "one take/one sequence" discipline that binds the camera to the filmmaker's body engenders an overwhelming sense of liberation. Instantaneously transporting us from place to place, Rouch's editing aligns the camera, expressively, with the souls of the dead, released from their bodies, not with living creatures of flesh and blood.

Remarkably, as the recitation comes full circle ("For all the men of the south, my mouth is too small; for all the men of the north, my mouth is too small; I cannot count the feet of millipedes; their shoes cannot be counted; each of you, take your share of the public square; your day has come, goodnight"), there is a cut back to the elder and, again remarkably, back to the soaring vulture—as if it were only in a dream that the camera has moved at all, much less roamed to the far corners of the Dogon world.

Then, starting with a beautiful "magic hour" shot dominated by the great tree that appears again and again in the film, the camera once more ventures into the world, as the theme of the recitation finally turns to Anaï himself ("Old Anaï, you have bought the morning and sold back the evening. You have bought the evening and sold back the morning. You have entered the center of the market place. Old Anaï, your children who follow you, you their elder, they altogether, they who will never leave, may they follow the same brick path.").

Before returning for the last time to the chanting elder, the camera, in a series of shots, follows Anaï's great-great-grandson, viewed from a distance, as he follows a steeply climbing path that wends its way between towering rocks. (Rouch does not explain where this boy is going, or why.) "Old Anaï, if you find Kumakan, founding ancestor of our village, if you find your father's brother, if you find Ogumanya, if you find those who have left long ago, the men who are our grandfathers . . . you must fasten yourself to them, Old Anaï." Gently, the elder is reminding the soul of Anaï that he must not remain near the village, however he may long to do so. He must follow those who have already departed on the long path to Banga, the country of the dead.

Rouch's next words are perhaps the film's most touching. "Thank you Anaï, for faithfulness and forgiveness. We have nothing to ask of you. We don't reproach you for anything. Who can have such a gift of life, old Anaï? You have fed your friends. We have eaten and drunk with you. We don't have the mouth to thank you with. You, old Anaï, you are sleeping. May God give you a fresh bed." Suddenly, the camera has again returned to the chanting elder, as the long *Tegué* sequence draws to an incomparably satisfying close. "For you, Anaï, the rope has shrunk, the long rope that God gives to those who help him. Anaï, we will come to salute you every morning. Anaï, thank you."

Now that Anaï's family has washed away the impurity of death and Bongo elders have thrown to the wind the sayings of the old Anaï, nothing is left but closing the funeral on the public square. First, Anaï's grandsons consult the divination tables and learn that the time is propitious. Rouch has elsewhere summarized what follows:

> The following day, gunshots resound in the streets of the village, and the men gather and begin a long combat with rifle shots against death. The horn blowers call them to the western gate. The next day, on the terrace of the hunters' altar, another mannequin has been taken down. This mannequin represents the first ancestor, Dyongou Sérou, wrapped in *pey* cloth and lying on a bier made of horns, recalling the bier of antelope horns that was used in the burial of the first dead man. . . . On the public square, a cow has been sacrificed to recall the price that God demanded of men when he tricked them and introduced death into their world. The mannequin of Dyongou Sérou, carried on its bier, enters the public square and dances the dance of death. The men and women dance the dances of burial. The young men, armed with rifles, go up in the western mountains and fire off gunshots to chase death away. . . . One of the old men, a grandson of Anaï, takes up a bow and shoots at a target. In doing this, he is shooting the sun, shooting the fox, shooting to make life be reborn. After one last volley of shots, the warriors fight death throughout the village. Then, for the last time, they gather on the public square to sing courage, to sing life. (Rouch 2003, 371)

As the camera lingers on the villagers who are (in his beautiful phrase) "singing courage, singing life," Rouch reprises the tone and cadence of his rendition of the *Tegué*.

> Dogon men of Anaï, the day has come. Goodnight.
> Forget the elders, call the young.
> Forget the young, call the elders.
> Feet of millipedes, their shoes cannot be counted.
> Take your share of the public square.
> We have had the day. Goodnight.

The next morning, the camera tracks Anaï's great-great-grandson in a series of shots as the boy makes his way up the cliff and begins climbing up. (Rouch does not tell us this in his narration, but this child is the person who will be entrusted with the rituals that must accompany his dead great-great-grandfather up to the moment when he reaches the land of Banga.)

> Old Anaï, all good things to you. Son of a Dogon farmer, son of a skinny farmer with a skinny hand, the sun has put oil on your body. For you, Anaï, the rope has shrunk, the long rope that God gives to those who help him. The son of Anaï, the grandsons of Anaï, children of elephant, children of lion, they will come and salute you every morning. Anaï, God has created you, God has taken you back. Just go with him. Anaï, may God let you climb down easy stairs. . . . Anaï, may God show you the way to Banga. . . . Anaï, your children who follow you, you, their elder, and they, all of them, they will never leave you. Let them follow the same right way.

While Rouch is speaking these eloquent words, the camera continues, from an ever-increasing distance, to follow the progress of the great-great grandson. Finally, with the camera remaining fixed in place, the boy simply walks out of the frame and disappears from view.

The frame is thus poetically devoid of human figures when Rouch speaks the summary last words of the narration. "Anaï, thank you. Thank you for yesterday."

The final credits roll.

In making his great documentary *Night and Fog*, Alain Resnais, like Rouch, confronted the problem of how to convey the invisible in the visible. How was he to convey, in the medium of film, the reality of the past, the reality of the horror that was the true dimension of the Nazi death camps? The death camps, which were built by art and craft, were designed with fences around them to enable the outside world to deny the reality of what went on there. If art lies, and art kills, how can art tear down those fences?

In filming Anaï Dolo's funeral, Rouch confronted a comparable challenge. This is because his starting point was the understanding of Dogon rituals articulated by Marcel Griaule and Germaine Dieterlen. When the villagers in the public square perform the "dances of burial," they are dancing what, in the narration to *Ambara Dama*, Rouch (following his mentors) calls "the system of the world." The dances make visible, in color and motion, the "system" that finds expression in every facet of Dogon society and culture. These dances reenact the creation of the universe, the origin of death among human beings, the history of the Dogon people, and the life of one individual. In these dances, the invisible—dead souls, ancestors, gods—play essential roles, both as characters and as audience. How to convey this in the medium of film? How to create film images—how to recreate the world on film—so as to acknowledge the full dimension of a reality in which, in the Dogon philosophy, as Griaule and Dieterlen taught Rouch to understand it, there are no fences separating the visible and the invisible, the present and the past, the particular and the universal?

In the final shot of D. A. Pennebaker's *Monterey Pop*, I observed in *Documentary Film Classics*, the camera moves from clapping hands to clapping hands to clapping hands as if the whole world, with the camera within it, were joined in celebrating music, celebrating being human, celebrating life on earth, where everything changes.

In Pennebaker's film the "truth of cinema"—cinéma vérité—and the "truth of music" come together to affirm a shared dream of an America in which no fence separates the everyday from the festive. In reality, such an America remains a dream. But in the world on film, that dream is also a reality. And the world on film has a reality of its own; there is no fence separating it from the one existing world. For the dream to become real, all it would take is for America to stop denying reality. (Rothman 1997, 205)

As Al and Dave Maysles' *Gimme Shelter* was all too soon to bring home, however, the rock festival that *Monterey Pop* documents was unclouded by the killing at Altamont, the massacre at Kent State, the drug-related deaths of Janis Joplin and Jimi Hendrix. That is, the dream was unclouded by death. Dying, and killing, are inalienable elements of the reality that America keeps denying.

Thanks to the work of Griaule and Dieterlen, Rouch understood the Dogon to be a people whose form of life enables them to overcome the fear of dying and killing. Their rituals, too, are festivals. But rather than deny the reality of death, they commemorate the first man who died. If their dances in the public square render the whole system of the world visible in color and motion, within that system death is inextricably intertwined with life. In *Anaï*, no less than in *Monterey Pop*, the "truth of cinema" and the "truth of music" come together to affirm a shared dream of a world in which no fence separates the everyday from the festive. But in the Dogon world of *Anaï*, unlike the America of *Monterey Pop*, that dream *is* reality. For as we have said, in Rouch's understanding, it is the very "system" that is given expression by every facet of Dogon life that is on display in movement and color in the public square.

Of course, the ideal society *Anaï* envisions may itself be a dream, a myth or a fiction, as would be claimed by those anthropologists who have impugned Griaule's methodology. I have no standing to assess Griaule's scholarship. However, the scientific validity of Griaule's findings is a moot point as far as Rouch's film is concerned. For no filmmaker has understood better than he that the world on film always has an aspect of fiction, myth, or dream, for the world on film is always transformed or transfigured by the conditions of the medium of film itself. If Dogon society as *Anaï* envisions it is a fiction, it is a fiction that reveals deep truths. The world on film has its own reality, its own truth. As *Anaï* brings home more eloquently than any other film I know, nothing on earth is more real than film's mysterious power to bless us on our way.

Ambara Dama

In the *Dama* ritual that *Ambara Dama* (To Enchant Death) documents, masked dancers reenact the first death of a human being. They reenact, as well, the original performance of the *Dama* ritual itself, which was meant to empower the soul of the first dead man to follow the long path to the land of the dead. It was that first Dama, the Dogon believe, that led to the contagion that spread death so widely among human beings that it became a universal necessity, not a mere possibility, for all people.

At the heart of *Ambara Dama* is a passage in which Rouch, drawing the words of his narration from Marcel Griaule's texts, reflects on the experience of the beholders of the *Dama* ritual. He links it with the mythical role played by the original Dama in spreading the contagion of death, a role that hinges on the power of the dancer's mask to enchant the living as well as the dead. "Each mask is a myth," Rouch says.

> Each mask is a poem. If the mask charms the dead, it also charms the living. And the living are caught in their own trap. At the very moment they enchant the dead through their mask, they themselves are enchanted. The funeral choreography enchanted people of the mask society to the point where they bought the corpse and the right to perform the rituals. All this provoked the contagion of death, breaking such a taboo that it destroyed immortality.

All this time, the camera has been lingering on one of the mask dancers.

Displayed in museums, shorn of pulsing drumbeats, Dogon masks retain little if any of their power to enchant. But what becomes of the masks on film? In an extraordinary gesture, Rouch slows down the image (and also the sound track, bringing the music down an octave or two). By this use of slow motion, Rouch invites us to contemplate what we are seeing in light of the words he is speaking. But does he slow down the image in order to enhance the spectacle or in order to diminish it, to spare us its dangerous, potentially death-dealing, power?

At the end of *Ambara Dama*, the tall masks made for this *Dama* festival are brought back to their cave, where "their fatal charm" will only operate "against those who enter their forbidden doorstep." Rouch goes on:

> In five years, at the next Dama, these masks will be replaced by new ones. Formerly, old masks used to disintegrate in the caves. Today, the Dogon sell them to museums or amateurs who do not suspect that they spread death. But, obviously, a mask without music and dance . . . is nothing but a piece of wood. However, in caves where masks are resting, men have tried to recover a bit of their dangerous strength. On the walls, they have painted in red, white, and black, paintings which only initiated elders, like Ambara Dolo, can decipher. A rectangle—an antelope. A double cross—a Kanaga. A ladder—a storied house.

Interspersed with shots of the paintings are shots of a dignified-looking old man, evidently an initiated elder, contemplating them. Rouch does not say who this man is, or even refer to his presence.

I like to think that he is none other than the eponymous Ambara, one of the elders who died in the preceding five years and for the sake of whose souls this *Dama* was performed. Ambara Dolo had been one of Marcel Griaule's most trusted informants. (If this man is not Ambara, he serves as a stand-in for him.) Ambara's unannounced cameo here then corresponds to, but reverses, Anaï's appearance at the beginning of *Anaï*, declaring film's mysterious power to transcend or overcome the separation of present and past, visible and invisible, living and dead. Rouch's narration concludes:

> That picture book in stone is never read except by elders or sometimes by young shepherds looking for shelter. With charcoal, those youngsters add candid gravity to the old paintings, till the day when one of them, just like the Pale Fox of the myth, will ask an elder, What is this—Sun? Fire? Wonder? When the elder will answer, No. It is as fresh as water. . . . His initiation will start, because here knowledge is only transmitted to those who ask for it. Just like those who in the past have left in the red earth the mark of their fingers, Ambara Dolo is dead. But if his soul is now following the long way to Banga, the country of death, a part of his life strength is left here, in these very paintings, and they will transmit it to all the masks to come, to charm death.

In *Monterey Pop*, as I argue in *Documentary Film Classics*, Pennebaker's camera discovers a tangible sign of the true dimension of the world of the present in its closing shot of clapping hands. In *Night and Fog*, Resnais' camera discovers a tangible sign of the true dimension of the world of the past in an unbearably moving shot of the gas chamber ceiling, the stone scratched and clawed by the fingers of countless victims who knew they were trapped, knew their dream of dying their own death was being denied.[4] In that shot, Resnais also found a signifier of his own project as an artist. "In this image of marks painfully scraped in stone," I wrote, "Resnais is defining himself specifically as a filmmaker, defining his artistic project as one cut to the particular measure of the medium of film. For in every film image, the subject's 'mark' ('the unlived lines of his body') is 'scratched' by the subject's own flesh and blood (his 'wounded fingers')" (Rothman 1977, 85).

And in *Ambara Dama* Rouch discovers a tangible sign of the true dimension of the world of the Dogon—a world in which no fence separates the present from the past—in these paintings on the cave wall.

Rouch, too, is declaring his artistic project to be cut to the measure of the medium of film. To those Dogon who know how to read them, these paintings make visible (in color, if not in motion) the "system of the world," the world as a whole. On film, the images of these

paintings—like the images of the mask dancers; like all images on film, Cavell teaches us in *The World Viewed*—in their own way make visible the world as a whole.

Like those who painted those images on the cave wall (who "left in the red earth the mark of their fingers," Rouch says, his words uncannily echoing *Night and Fog's* narration), Ambara Dolo has departed "on the long path to the country of death." Yet "a part of his life strength is left here, in these very paintings," Rouch tells us, "and they will transmit it to all the masks to come."

For those painted images to transmit Ambara's life strength to future masks is for them to communicate to those masks the power to bless those who behold them. It is also to communicate their power to kill. And what of the images of these painted images on film? If Rouch's films have the power to enchant, they have the power to transmit "life strength." This means they have the power to bless us on our way. It also means they have the power to spread death.

When the Dogon perform the *Dama* ritual, they not only represent the contagion of death, they reenact it. In reenacting it, they enact it; they participate in the spreading of death. Thus they accept their own place in the very "system of the world" that makes death universal, a necessity, for human beings. In the ending of *Ambara Dama*, Rouch is acknowledging, as Resnais did in *Night and Fog*, the camera's implication—the filmmaker's *own* implication—in the reality that the film may appear merely to document—the reality that we must die.

When Rouch ends his narration in *Ambara Dama* by saying that here knowledge is only transmitted to those who ask for it, he is provoking his viewers—those among them who are questing for knowledge—to ask questions. When Rouch was alive, he loved to preside over screenings of his films so that viewers who were so moved could pose questions to him. Now that Rouch, like Anaï and Ambara, has departed on that long path to the land of the dead, we have only his films to pose our questions to. But if part of his life strength is left in these images projected on the movie screen, his films must retain some of his power not only to provoke questions, but also to answer them, as *Tourou and Bitti*, *Anaï*, and *Ambara Dama* have answered so many of mine.

May their images transmit my friend Jean's life strength to all films to come. (And to these words.)

Notes

This chapter is an expanded version of a paper presented at a retrospective and symposium that Kitty Morgan and I organized at the University of Miami to mark the occasion of the filmmaker's death. The proceedings of the symposium were published as part of the *Transatlantique* series: *Jean Rouch: A Celebration of Life and Film*, ed. William Rothman (Fasano, Italy: Schena Editore, 2007). My thanks to Giovanni Dotoli, coeditor of *Transatlantique*, for granting permission on behalf of Schena Editore for this essay to be included in the present volume.

1. All my quotes from *Tourou and Bitti* make use of the English subtitles incorporated in the VHS copy generously provided to me by Mme. Françoise Foucault (Rouch's longtime associate of the Comité du Film Ethnographique).

2. For the opportunity to participate in three of Rouch's incomparable summer seminars on his work, I am profoundly indebted to Kitty Morgan, who organized the seminars during three successive years at Tufts, Hampshire College, and Harvard. On the subject of Rouch and his films, I have learned most of what I know from conversations with Kitty.

3. Stanley Cavell, *The World Viewed: Reflections on the Ontology of Film* (Cambridge, Mass.: Harvard University Press, 1979), 28; "What Becomes of Things on Film?" in *Cavell on Film*, ed. William Rothman (Albany: State University of New York Press, 2005), 1–10.

4. The inclusion of a similar shot in the Nevers sequence of Resnais' *Hiroshima, mon amour* gives the lie to the claim, often repeated in critical appraisals of that film, that the woman's private suffering is trivial compared to the massive scale of the suffering caused by the bombing of Hiroshima.

Works Cited

Agee, James, and Walker Evans, 1960. *Let Us Now Praise Famous Men*. Boston: Houghton Mifflin.

Balasz, Bela, 1972. *Theory of Film: Character and Growth of a New Art*. New York: Dover Publications.

Baudrillard, Jean, 1983. "The Precession of Simulacra," *Simulations*, trans. Paul Foss, Paul Patton, and Philip Beitchman. New York: Semiotext(e).

Baudrillard, Jean, 1987. *The Evil Demon of Images*. Sydney: Power Institute Publications.

Baudrillard, Jean, 1988. *The Ecstacy of Communication*, ed. Sylvere Lotringer and trans. Bernard and Caroline Schutze. New York: Semiotext(e).

Baudrillard, Jean, 1990a. *Fatal Strategies*, ed. Jim Fleming, trans. Philip Beitchman and W. G. J. Niesluchowski. New York/London: Semiotext(e)/Pluto.

Baudrillard, Jean, 1990b. *La transparence du mal: Essai sur les phénomènes extrêmes*. Paris: Editions Galilée.

Baudrillard, Jean, 1993a. *The Transparency of Evil: Essays on Extreme Phenomena*, trans. James Benedict. London: Verso.

Baudrillard, Jean, 1993b. *Symbolic Exchange and Death*, trans. Iain Hamilton Grant. London: Sage.

Baudrillard, Jean, 2000. *The Vital Illusion*, ed. Julia Witwer. New York: Columbia University Press.

Berliner, Todd, 2001. "The Pleasures of Disappointment: Sequels and *The Godfather, Part II*." *Journal of Film and Video* 53 (2/3): 107–23.

Blackburn, Simon, 2005. *The Truth: A Guide*. Oxford: Oxford University Press.

Calhoun, Laurie, 2004. "Death and Contradiction: Errol Morris's Tragic View of Technokillers," *Jump Cut*, www.ejumpcut.org/archive/jc47.2005/teachnokillersMorris/text.html, accessed September 4, 2006.

Cavell, Stanley, 1979. *The World Viewed: Reflections on the Ontology of Film*, Expanded ed. Cambridge, Mass: Harvard University Press.

Cavell, Stanley, 1979. *The Claim of Reason: Wittgenstein, Skepticism, Morality, and Tragedy*. Oxford: Oxford University Press, 1979.

Cavell, Stanley, 2005. "What Becomes of Things on Film?" in *Cavell on Film*, ed. William Rothman. Albany: State University of New York Press, 1–10.

Cholodenko, Alan, 1987. The Films of Frederick Wiseman. Harvard University Ph.D. thesis.

Cholodenko, Alan, ed., 1991. *The Illusion of Life: Essays on Animation*. Sydney: Power Publications in association with the Australian Film Commission.

Cholodenko, Alan, 1997. " 'OBJECTS IN MIRROR ARE CLOSER THAN THEY APPEAR': The Virtual Reality of *Jurassic Park* and Jean Baudrillard," in *Jean Baudrillard, Art and Artefact*, ed. Nicholas Zurbrugg. London: Sage.

Cholodenko, Alan, 2000. "The Logic of Delirium, or the Fatal Strategies of Antonin Artaud and Jean Baudrillard," in *100 Years of Cruelty: Essays on Artaud*, ed. Edward Scheer. Sydney: Power Publications and Artspace.

Cholodenko, Alan, 2004a. "The Crypt, The Haunted House, of Cinema," *Cultural Studies Review*, 10, 2 (September): 99–113.

Cholodenko, Alan, 2004b. " 'The Borders of Our Lives': Frderick Wiseman, Jean Baudrillard, and the Question of the Documentary," *International Journal of Baudrillard Studies*, 1, 2 (July). http://www.ubishops.ca/baudrillard studies/vol1_2/cholodenko.htm, accessed July 1, 2008.

Cholodenko, Alan, 2005."Still Photography?," *Afterimage* 32 (March/April): 5–7.

Cholodenko, Alan, 2006. "The Nutty Universe of Animation, The 'Discipline' of All 'Disciplines,' And That's Not All, Folks!," *International Journal of Baudrillard Studies* 3, 1 (January), http:www.ubishops.ca/baudrillardstudies/vol 3_1/cholodenko.htm, accessed July 10, 2008.

Cholodenko, Alan, ed., 2007. *The Illusion of Life 2: More Essays on Animation*. Sydney: Power Publications.

Cockburn, Alexander, 2004. "The Fog of Cop-Out," *The Nation* 278 (February 9): xxxx.

Crapanzano, Vincent, 2004. *Imaginative Horizons: An Essay in Literary-Philosophical Anthropology*. Chicago: University of Chicago Press.

Cronin, Paul, 2004. "Interview: Errol Morris," *Sight and Sound*, 14 (April): 21.

Deleuze, Gilles, 1989. *Cinema 2: The Time-Image*, trans. Hugh Tomlinson and Robert Galeta. Minneapolis: University of Minnesota Press.

Derrida, Jacques, 1981. 'Dissemination,' *Dissemination*, trans. Barbara Johnson. Chicago: University of Chicago Press.

Derrida, Jacques, 1994. *Specters of Marx*, trans. Peggy Kamuf. New York: Routledge.

Eaton, Mick, ed., 1979. *Anthropology—Reality—Cinema. The Films of Jean Rouch*. London: British Film Institute.

Échard, Nicole, 1992. "Cults de possession et hangmen social: L'exemple du bori hausa de l'Ader et du Kurfey (Niger). *Archives des Sciences Sociales de Religion* 79 (2): 87–101.

Egan, Susana, 1999. *Mirror Talk: Genres of Crisis in Contemporary Autobiography*. Chapel Hill: University of North Carolina Press.

Eisenstein, Sergei, 1988. *Eisenstein on Disney*, ed. Jay Leyda, trans. Alan Upchurch. London: Methuen.

Eliot, T. S., 1964a. *Selected Essays*. New York: Harcourt Brace.

Eliot, T. S., 1964. *Selected Poems*. New York: Harcourt Brace.

Emerson, Ralph Waldo, 1983. *Emerson: Essays and Lectures*, ed. Joel Porte. New York: Library of America.

Faulkner, William, 1993. *Absalom, Absalom!* New York: Modern Library.

Feld, Steven, 2003. "Annotated Filmography." *Cine-Ethnography*, ed. Steven Feld. Minneapolis: University of Minnesota Press.

Foucault, Michel, 1983. *This is Not a Pipe*. Berkeley: University of California Press.

Freud, Sigmund, 2003. *The Uncanny*, trans. David McLintock. New York: Penguin Classics.

Frye, Northrop, 2006. *The Educated Imagination and Other Writings on Critical Theory 1933–1963*. Toronto: University of Toronto Press.

Fugelstad, Finn, 1975. "Les hauka: Une interprétation historique. *Cahiers d'etudes africaines* 58: 203–16.

Fugelstad, Finn, 1983. *A History of Niger (1850–1960)*. Cambridge: Cambridge University Press.

Gane, Mike, 2000. *Jean Baudrillard: In Radical Uncertainty*. London: Pluto Press.

Gardner, Robert, 2006. *The Impulse to Preserve: Reflections of a Filmmaker*. New York: Other Press.

Geertz, Clifford, 1983. *Local Knowledge*. New York: Basic Books.

Godard, Jean-Luc, 1986. *Godard on Godard*, ed. and trans. Tom Milne. New York: Da Capo Press.

Gourevitch, Philip, 1992. "Interviewing the Universe." *New York Times Magazine* (August 9): 618.

Gourevitch, Philip, 2004. "Swingtime," *New Yorker* (August 23): 34.

Grant, Barry Keith, and Jeannette Sloniowski, eds. 1998. *Documenting the Documentary*. Detroit: Wayne State University Press.

Griaule, Marcel, 1970. *Conversations with Ogotemmêli: An Introduction to Dogon Religious Ideas*. Oxford: Oxford University Press.

Grundmann, Roy, and Cynthia Rockwell. 2000. "Truth is Not Subjective: An Interview with Errol Morris." *Cineaste* 25 (3): 4–22.

Gunning, Tom, 1986. "The Cinema of Attraction: Early Film, Its Spectator and the Avant-Garde." *Wide Angle* 8 (3): 12–20.

Gunning, Tom, 1989. "An Aesthetic of Astonishment: Early Film and the (In)credulous Spectator." *Art & Text* 34 (Spring): 31–45.

Hansen, Miriam Brau, 2004. "Room-for-Play: Benjamin's Gamble with Cinema." *October* (Summer) 282: 3–46.

Henley, Paul, 2006. "Spirit Possession, Power, and the Absent Presence of Islam: Re-Viewing *Les Maîtres fous*." *Journal of the Royal Anthropological Institute* 12 (4): 731–63.

Hoberman, J., 2004. "Warmonger Blues," *Sight and Sound* 14 (April): 20–22.

Kerouac, Jack, 1976. *On the Road*. New York: Penguin.

Lacan, Jacques, 1979. *The Four Fundamental Concepts of Psycho-Analysis*, ed. Jacques-Alain Miller, trans. Alan Sheridan. Harmondsworth, Middlesex: Penguin Books.

Lawrence, D. H., 1972. "Surgery for the Novel—Or a Bomb," in *Phoenix: The Poshumous Papers of D. H. Lawrence*, ed. Edward D. McDonald. New York: Viking Press.

Leacock, Richard, 2000. "For an Uncontrolled Cinema" (1961), reprinted in *Film Culture Reader*, ed. P. Adams Sitney. New York: Cooper Square Press.

Leavis, F. R., ed., 1968. *A Selection from Scrutiny*. Cambridge: Cambridge University Press.

Morris, Errol, 2000. "Brash, Deep, and in Control." *Mother Jones* 25 (March/April): 82–83.

Morris, Errol, 2004. "*The Fog of War*: 13 Questions and Answers on the Filmmaking of Errol Morris by Errol Morris." *FLM Magazine* (Winter): 2–4.

Morris, Errol, 2005a. "The Anti-Post-Modern Post-Modernist." http://www.errolmorris.com/content/lecture/theantipost.html, accessed October 6, 2006.

Morris, Errol, 2005b. "There *Is* Such a Thing as Truth." Editorial for NPR, May 2, 2005. Text reprinted on http://www.errolmorris.com/content/editorial/npr505.html, accessed October 11, 2006.

Nichols, Bill, 1991. *Representing Reality*. Bloomington: Indiana University Press.

O'Brien, Tim, 1990. *The Things They Carried*. New York: Broadway Books.

Pasolini, Paolo, 1988. *Heretical Empiricism*, ed. Louise K. Barnett, trans. Ben Lawton and Louise K. Barnett. Bloomington: Indiana University Press.

Plantinga, Carl, 1999. "The Scene of Empathy and the Human Face on Film," in *Passionate Views: Film, Cognition, and* Emotion, ed. Carl Plantinga and Greg Smith. Baltimore: Johns Hopkins University Press.

Rank, Otto, 1989. *The Double: A Psychoanalytical Study*, trans. Harry Tucker, Jr. London: Karnac.

Rhu, Lawrence, 2004. "Home Movies and Personal Documentaries: An Interview with Ross McElwee." *Cineaste* 29 (3): 6–12.

Rothman, William, 1997. *Documentary Film Classics*. New York: Cambridge University Press.

Rothman, William, ed., 2007. *Jean Rouch: A Celebration of Life and Film*. Fasano, Italy: Schena Editore.

Rouch, Jean, 1978. "On the Vicissitudes of the Self: The Possessed Dancer, the Magician, the Sorcerer, the Filmmaker, and the Ethnographer." *Studies in the Anthropology of Visual Communication*, 5 (1): 2–8.

Rouch, Jean, 1979. "Le renard fou et le maître pale." In *Systèmes des signes: Textes reunites en homage à Germaine Dieterlen*. Paris: Hermann, 3–24.

Rouch, Jean, 1989. *La religion et la magie songhay*, 2nd Edition. Brussels: Editions de l'Université de Bruxelles.

Rouch, Jean, 1995. "Our Totemic Ancestors and Crazed Masters," in *Principles of Visual Anthropology*, 2nd ed., ed. Paul Hockings. New York: Mouton de Gruyter.

Rouch, Jean, 2003. *Cine-Ethnography*, ed. Steven Feld. Minneapolis: University of Minnesota Press.

Rourke, Constance, 1931. *American Humor: A Study of the National Character*. New York: Harcourt, Brace.

Scott, A. O., 2004. "Enter Narci-Cinema." New York: *New York Times Magazine*, December 12, 2004, 10.

Silverman, Kenneth, ed., 2003. *Benjamin Franklin: The Autobiography and Other Writings*. New York: Penguin.

Singer, Mark, 1989. "Predilections," *New Yorker*, 64 (51) (February 6): 38.

Singer, Mark, 1999. "The Friendly Executioner," *New Yorker* 74 (February 1): 33–40.

Sontag, Susan, 1966. *Against Interpretation*. New York: Dell Publishing.

Slattery, Damian, 1997. "Interview: Errol Morris," http://www.ifp.org/interviews/, accessed September 23, 1997.

Smith, Adam, 1984. *The Theory of Moral Sentiments*, eds. D. D. Raphael and A. L. MacFie. Indianapolis: Liberty Fund.

Stoller, Paul, 1989. *Fusion of the Worlds: An Ethnography of Possession among the Songhay of Niger*. Chicago: University of Chicago Press.

Stoller, Paul, 1992. *The Cinematic Griot: The Ethnography of Jean Rouch*. Chicago: University of Chicago Press.

Stoller, Paul, 1995. *Embodying Colonial Memories: Spirit Possession, Power and the Hauka in West Africa*. New York: Routledge.

Stoller, Paul, 1997. *Sensuous Scholarship*. Philadelphia: University of Pennsylvania Press.

Taussig, Michael, 1993. *Mimesis and Alterity, a Particular History of the Senses*. New York: Routledge.

Taylor, Lucien, ed., 1998. *Transcultural Cinema: David MacDougall*. Princeton, N.J.: Princeton University Press.

Thoreau, Henry David, 1985. *Walden; or, Life in the Woods*, ed. Robert F. Sayre. New York: Library of America.

Trechmann, E. J. (trans.), 1946. *The Essays of Montaigne*. New York: Modern Library.

Warren, Charles, ed., 1996. *Beyond Document: Essays on Nonfiction Film*. Hanover, N.H.: Wesleyan University Press/University Press of New England.

Wees, William C., 1992. *Light Moving in Time. Studies in the Visual Aesthetics of Avant-Garde Film*. Berkeley: University of California Press.

Whitman, Walt, 1926. *Leaves of Grass*. Garden City, N.Y.: Doubleday.

Williams, Alan, 1992. *Republic of Images: A History of French Filmmaking*. Cambridge, Mass.: Harvard University Press.

Williams, Linda, 1998. "Mirrors without Memories: Truth, History, and *The Thin Blue Line*," in Barry Keith Grant and Jeannette Slomiowski, eds., *Documenting the Documentary*. Detroit: Wayne State University Press.

Žižek, Slavoj, 1991. *Looking Awry: An Introduction to Jacques Lacan Through Popular Culture*. Cambridge, Mass.: M.I.T. Press.

Contributors

ALAN CHOLODENKO is Honorary Associate in the Department of Art History and Film Studies at the University of Sydney, where he was Senior Lecturer in Film and Animation Studies. He edited The *Illusion of Life: Essays on Animation* (Power, 1991) and *The Illusion of Life 2: More Essays on Animation* (Power, 2007). His Ph.D. thesis was on the films of Frederick Wiseman (Harvard, 1987), and he has published a number of essays on film and animation theory.

IRA JAFFE is Professor Emeritus and former Chair of the Department of Media Arts at the University of New Mexico. He is the author of *Hollywood Hybrids: Mixing Genres in Contemporary Films* (Bowman and Littlefield, 2007) and co-editor of *Redirecting the Gaze: Gender, Theory and Cinema in the Third World* (SUNY 1998).

MARIAN KEANE is co-author of *Reading Cavell's The World Viewed: A Philosophical Perspective on Film* (Wayne State, 2000) She has published essays on various aspects of film theory, criticism and history.

JIM LANE is the author of *The Autobiographical Documentary in America* (Wisconsin, 2002). He has also made several autobiographical films including *Long Time No See, East Meets West, I Am Not an Anthropologist*, and *Background Action*. He is the executive Director of the Emerson College Los Angeles Center.

MICHAEL LARAMEE is a Ph.D. candidate at the University of Miami School of Communication. He is writing his dissertation on African cinema.

DANIEL MORGAN is an Assistant Professor of Film Studies in the Department of English at the University of Pittsburgh. He has published articles on André Bazin and Jean-Luc Godard, and is working on a book about Godard's films and videos since the late 1980s.

GILBERTO PEREZ is Professor of Film Studies at Sarah Lawrence College and the author of *The Material Ghost: Films and Their Medium* (Johns Hopkins, 2000). His *Rhetoric of Film* will be published by the University of Minnesota Press.

CARL PLANTINGA is Professor of Film Studies at Calvin College in Grand Rapids, Michigan. He is the author of *Rhetoric and Representation in Nonfiction Film* (Cambridge, 1997) and *Moved and Affected: American Film and the Spectator's Experience* (forthcoming from California University Press) and co-editor of *Passionate Views* (Johns Hopkins, 1999) and the forthcoming *Routledge Companion to Philosophy and Film*. He is a current editorial board member of *Projections: The Journal for Movies and Mind*, a former editorial board member of *Cinema Journal*, and a member of the Board of Directors of the Society for the Cognitive Study of the Moving Image.

WILLIAM ROTHMAN is Professor of Motion Pictures and Director of the Graduate Program in Film Studies at the University of Miami and series editor for the Cambridge Studies in Film. Among his books are *Hitchcock—The Murderous Gaze* (Harvard, 1982), *The "I" of the Camera* (Cambridge, 1988), *Documentary Film Classics* (Cambridge, 1997), *Reading Cavell's The World Viewed: A Philosophical Perspective on Film* (with Marian Keane) (Wayne State, 2000), *Cavell on Film* (SUNY, 2004), and *Jean Rouch: A Celebration of Life and Film* (Schena Editore, 2007). He is currently working on a book tentatively titled "Emersonian Hollywood."

DIANE STEVENSON is a poet and scholar. She received an M.F.A. and Ph.D. from Columbia University, where she was Edward Said's research assistant when he was writing *Orientalism*. She wrote her dissertation under his direction. Her poems and essays have been published in *Boulevard*, *Pataphysics*, *Mississippi Review*, *The Nation*, *The Yale Review*, *Cineaste*, *Cinema Scope*, *Film International*, and other journals.

PAUL STOLLER is Professor of Anthropology at West Chester University. He has been conducting fieldwork among West Africans for more than thirty years. His books include *Gallery Bundu: A Story of an African Past* (Chicago, 2005), a novel, *Stanger in the Village of the Sick* (Beacon, 2004); a memoir; and *Money Has No Smell* (Chicago, 2002), which won the American Anthropological Association Robert B. Textor Prize for excellence in anticipatory anthropology. He is also the author of *The Cinematic Griot: The Ethnography of Jean Rouch* (Chicago, 1992). His latest book is *The Power of the Between: An Autobiographical Odyssey* (Chicago, 2008).

CHARLES WARREN is Adjunct Professor of Film, Boston University, and Associate of the Visual and Environmental Studies Department, Harvard University. He edited *Beyond Document: Essays on Nonfiction Film* (Wesleyan, 1996) and (with Maryel Locke) *Jean-Luc Godard's "Hail Mary": Women and the Sacred in Film* (Southern Illinois, 1993).

Index